OUT OF LINE

A literary and political biography of Nayantara Sahgal

Ritu Menon

FOURTH ESTATE • *New Delhi*

First published in hardback in India in 2014 by Fourth Estate
An imprint of HarperCollins *Publishers*
Building No 10, Tower A, 4th Floor, DLF Cyber, City Phase II,
Gurugram 122002
www.harpercollins.co.in

First published in paperback in India in 2018 by Fourth Estate
An imprint of HarperCollins *Publishers*

4 6 8 10 9 7 5 3

P-ISBN: 978-93-5302-405-5
E-ISBN: 978-93-5136-596-9

Typeset in 11.5/15.6 Sabon LT Std by
Jojy Philip, New Delhi 110 015

Printed and bound at
MicroPrints India, New Delhi

Contents

Literature is necessary to politics above all when it gives voice to whatever is without a voice, when it gives a name to what as yet has no name, especially to what the language of politics excludes or attempts to exclude.

– Italo Calvino

Preface & Acknowledgements

By the time she was thirty-five years old in 1962, Nayantara Sahgal had already published her autobiography, in two volumes. *Prison and Chocolate Cake* and *From Fear Set Free* set the tone for most of her subsequent writing – whether fiction, non-fiction, political commentary, essays or monographs – a tone that was uniquely personal, political and literary. These three strands were interwoven in everything she wrote, and just as it is impossible to separate a writer's life from her text, in Nayantara's case it would be remiss to read her without reference to the political life of the country. Her literary career spans at least five decades of India's contemporary history, from the 1950s to the present, a chronology that moves from the high idealism of the freedom movement to the disillusionment and cynicism that prevail today.

A biography of Nayantara Sahgal contends with two potentially overwhelming facts: that the subject is a member of one of the country's most high-profile political families, almost relentlessly in the public eye and the public domain; and that she herself has recorded or written about practically everything of significance in her life. What then remains for the biographer?

Gabriel García Márquez has said that each person's life is made up of the public, the private and the secret. I cannot presume to know, or even gesture towards, the secret in Nayantara Sahgal's life, but juxtaposing the public and private, counterpointing the literary with the personal and political, is like turning the kaleidoscope – the pieces remain the same but they fall differently each time, forming ever-changing patterns.

Nayantara Sahgal has described herself as 'a conventional woman whom circumstances drove to rebellion'. My biography tries to understand this apparent conundrum: a conservative among the Nehrus and Pandits, exposed to radical politics from her childhood? A young woman schooled in independence, in standing up for herself, persevering with a marriage that was clearly unequal? An astute chronicler of her times who, nevertheless, maintains that there is no direct link between her novels and her own life? A woman who was actually quite a homebody who felt compelled to publicly challenge a political heavyweight like her cousin, Indira Gandhi. A dutiful wife who walked out of her marriage at a time when divorced Indian women were a social embarrassment.

As with all things feminist, this book too tries to link literature and life, history and biography, the personal and the political, as it weaves in and out of its subject's personal life – childhood, family background, education, marriage, motherhood, divorce and remarriage; her literary life – writing, publishing and journalism; and her political life, so as to situate her, a woman in modern India, writing a modern India, at the centre of India's literary and political landscape.

None of this would have been possible without Nayantara Sahgal's support, unconditional access to all her material, and her always gracious and generous willingness to spend hours and hours in interviews and discussion with me. Every biographer should be so fortunate. As open, willing and informative were Nayantara's children, Nonika, Ranjit and Gita Sahgal, who shared letters, photographs, memories, facts and details, and most helpfully, insights into people and relationships. (Gossip too, but that's not in the book!) Nayantara's sister, Chandralekha Mehta, provided glimpses into their childhood and youth not only by reminiscing with me, but through her own book, *Freedom's Child: Growing Up During Satyagraha*. A real loss was being unable to meet and speak with Vijaya Lakshmi Pandit; with Nayantara's other sister, Rita Dar; and of course with Nirmal Mangat Rai, all of whom had passed away much before I began thinking of this biography. As had many of her Bombay, Delhi, Chandigarh and London friends and acquaintances. I realised in the course of conversations with others who might have known her, just how private a person she is, even for many in her extended family.

So many people responded so positively to the idea of a biography of Nayantara that it is difficult to name them all. But among those who read the first drafts of some chapters, I'm particularly grateful to Shashi Deshpande, Githa Hariharan, Aamer Hussein, Raghu Karnad and Laila Tyabji, for their comments on my unconventional approach to chronology, and to the narrative itself. And to Karthika at HarperCollins for her immediate and enthusiastic response to the first chapter – every author knows how important it is to receive this kind of affirmation, no matter how many books they may have written.

Closer home, Amita and Khalid Baig provided a home away from home in Dehradun, and I honestly don't know how to thank them for their always warm and welcoming hospitality. Transcribing tapes is usually quite tedious, but sitting on their veranda, with a pale view of the hills, surrounded by trees and birdsong, I hardly noticed the tedium.

Vanya Bhargava relieved me of hours of newspaper reading for the Emergency section in the book, and for skilfully summarising many of the columns Nayantara wrote during that time. Thank you, Vanya. And thank you, Ratna, for spotting those egregious errors that one always misses, and for suggestions to improve my syntax!

Finally, to Seema Sagar, who patiently, efficiently, tirelessly, keyed in and corrected draft after draft of every chapter, and without whom the manuscript might have been a very different-looking item – a big thank you. For, unlike Nayantara who types all her manuscripts herself, I still write by hand.

RITU MENON

New Delhi
April 2014

PART ONE

1927–1967

1

THE WEDDING: BEFORE AND AFTER

Prison and Chocolate Cake

From Fear Set Free

ON 2 JANUARY 1949, TARA PANDIT, TWENTY-ONE YEARS OLD and second daughter of Vijaya Lakshmi and Ranjit Sitaram Pandit, was married to Gautam Sahgal, then twenty-five, in her ancestral home, Anand Bhawan, Allahabad. The bride looked exquisite in a primrose yellow sari of fine khaddar, flower jewellery in her hair, her ears and around her neck. No gold-bedecked rich silks or family jewels for this child of the freedom movement, just Mahatma Gandhi's finely spun khadi, embellished with nothing more than a thin gold border. (Seven years earlier, her cousin, Indira, had worn a shell-pink khadi sari, hand-spun by her father, Jawaharlal, and trimmed with silver, at *her* wedding.) The groom was dashing and handsome, a child not so much of the freedom movement as of the partition of the country that followed in its wake. The Sahgals were a prominent Lahore family of professionals displaced to Delhi, like millions of Punjabis from across the border, having left behind agricultural land, urban property and other considerable assets, in the hope that they would return. As that possibility began to recede they set about re-establishing themselves in Delhi, determined to regain the social and economic status they had enjoyed in Punjab. But the bitter undertow of Partition, and of dislocation and loss, remained.

Tara Pandit could hardly have chosen a partner whose background and temperament were so completely at variance with her own, but their attraction to each other had been immediate and electric, and they made an extremely striking couple. Introduced to each other by Tara's aunt, Fori Nehru (who stayed with the Sahgals when she first came out to India from Hungary), they met at the Delhi Gymkhana Club on 9 December 1947, very soon after Tara's return from the US. She had just graduated in history from Wellesley College and was staying with her uncle, Jawaharlal Nehru, on York Road. Gautam was employed with the engineering company of Bird & Co. in Kanpur, finding his feet in a newly independent, but economically still colonial, business and corporate environment.

Delhi in 1947 was scarred and reeling from violence, with ragged and destituted refugees streaming into makeshift camps at Purana Qila and Kingsway, abandoned homes and havelis; a city stumbling to its feet as it came to grips with the dark side of freedom. Just a stone's throw away from the welter and confusion of the camp at Purana Qila, however, the shaded, high-ceilinged, pillared precincts of the Delhi Gymkhana Club still offered up an environment of gracious calm and abiding stability. As Gautam Sahgal led her on to the parquet dance floor of the ballroom, Tara's fantasies of history professors 'wavered like a reflection in water'. Everything in her upbringing inclined her towards the kind of person who was intellectually sophisticated and quietly reflective. Men like her father and her uncle who carried their erudition lightly, effortlessly combining cosmopolitanism with the common touch. Gautam couldn't have been more different, but he was nothing if not an assiduous suitor and he pursued her single-mindedly. They went out alone with each other for the first time on 14 January 1948 (Nayantara's father's death anniversary) and by 21 January they were engaged to be married. Phone calls and flowers, dancing till dawn, partying and picnicking, outings with his family – this was a whole new world for Tara, whose own family life had been marked by other kinds of arrivals and departures to and from an assortment of jails, and a home from which the absence of parents and elders was the norm.

Although Gautam belonged to a prominent West Punjab family and the Sahgals had considerable property in East Punjab as well as Lahore, the news of Tara's engagement to him was greeted with some concern. Letters flew between Mrs Pandit and her brother, between her and Fori Nehru, and between her and her brother-in-law in Bombay. The haste with which Tara announced her intention to marry Gautam, within forty-five days of meeting him, prompted even her beloved Mamu (as she called Nehru) into cautioning her. Nehru's misgivings about his young niece's whirlwind romance were expressed in characteristically mild tones: he thought she should do something with her education, work perhaps; there were so many ways in which she could make herself useful and there was time enough for marriage. She was only twenty, after all, and her education was just beginning. At the very least, she should take some time off to think it over, and so he suggested that she go to her mother in Moscow, where Mrs Pandit was India's first ambassador to the Soviet Union.

The Sahgals were cautious too. Although they were fond of Tara and approved of her gentle and accommodating nature, marrying into a high-profile nationalist family might not have been everyone's aspiration. Being in the public eye exacted its own price, not least being unkind gossip about social climbing. Tara herself was acutely aware of the mismatch. Because of Partition she had met a young man employed in a British firm, an Indian whose India was as different from hers as any man she could have met, whose home in Lahore had had the best of linen, glass and wine that his father's frequent trips to Europe could provide. This was in sharp contrast to hers, which in support of the Swadeshi movement had used only Indian-made goods. What was more, this was an Indian for whom Gandhi was just a name, and freedom for his country an event that had deprived him of his home and a part of his inheritance.

> I worried about the differences between us, and soon learned that hesitation was not a part of Gautam's make-up. He tackled problems with a figurative lawnmower. After a while they no longer existed. Everything eventually became smooth lawn. For me, life resembled a rock garden full of unaccountable small crevices and obstructions. How could I enter his world or he mine? We would make a new one, said Gautam. He envisaged no problems. He concentrated on the particular, and the particular issue soon became marriage.[1]

And so Gautam's elder brother, Narottam, went to meet Nehru to formally ask for Nayantara's hand in marriage, and it was given.

Anand Bhawan was dusted and swept, slip covers removed from furniture, the phone that had been silent for all the time that the house was unoccupied – Nehru in Delhi, Indira Gandhi in Lucknow, Vijaya Lakshmi Pandit in Moscow, the younger children dispersed across the world – started ringing again. Crockery, cutlery and linen were brought out, and wedding shopping commenced. On the day of the wedding, Nayantara's entire family gathered at Anand Bhawan, blue and white fairy lights twinkling in the trees and on the compound wall. The simple ceremony took place on the back veranda (where Indira and Feroze Gandhi had been married in 1942), with Nehru signing the marriage certificate. And so Tara Pandit left her known world 'of Gandhi caps and handspun cloth for that of European suits and ties ... from orange juice to cocktails ... from an atmosphere of political crusade to one of commerce'; a world where saying, 'So-and-so was in jail with me' was like saying, 'We were up at Oxford together'. For the first time in her life she would be participating in a pattern of life bequeathed to upper-class India by nearly two hundred years of British rule.

An unfamiliar domesticity together with the unaccustomed idleness of the upper-middle classes now encircled Nayantara. Days were spent in the shaded interiors of the double-storeyed hotel in Kanpur's cantonment where she and Gautam lived for the first two years of their married life. 'Going out' meant going for a walk or going to the ice-cream parlour, or to the one bookshop in town. Or visiting. But there was little conversation to be had with the other wives whom Nayantara met, and the men, as always, formed a closed male circle of office politics, local gossip, drinking and reminiscing.

Their first two children, Nonika and Ranjit, were born in 1950 and 1951 in New York and Allahabad, and by 1951, Gautam had left Bird & Co. and joined the Swiss pharmaceutical firm, Ciba, with whom he was to remain till his retirement in 1981. This meant moving to Bombay and

REGISTRAR'S CERTIFICATE.

I R.P. BHARGAVA certify that, on the Second day of January 192 1949,

appeared before me Nayantara and Gautam Sahgal each of whom in my presence and in the presence of three credible witnesses, whose names are signed hereunder, made the declarations required by Act III of 1872, and that a marriage under the said Act was solemnized between them in my presence

(Signed) Gautam Sahgal

R.P. Bhargava I.C.S.

Registrar of Marriages under Act III of 1872, (as amended by Act XXX of 1923) for the district of Allahabad.

(Signed) Nayantara Pandit

Jawaharlal Nehru
[illegible]
[illegible] (Three witnesses)

Dated the second day of January 192 1949.

Mis. 17P. B—017 Mis—1928.

finding a place to live, not an easy job even in 1951. For the many months that it took them to find a suitable place, Tara and the children stayed in Delhi or at the Cricket Club of India on Sir Dinshaw Vaccha Road in Bombay. They finally found a three-bedroom flat of their own in Dil Pazir in a lane off Warden Road. Although the flat itself was roomy and comfortable, street life teemed with the homeless and the hopefuls who came to Bombay seeking their fortune. From her balcony Nayantara watched it come to life as people made makeshift homes out of discarded crates, decorating them with flowers tossed out of florists' shops at the end of the day. Stray cats and dogs, children playing the mouth organ, disembodied voices floating up to her flat as she watched the moonlight suddenly strike silver on a piece of metal in the garbage.

'Bombay was a huge change for me,' she said,

> ... very cosmopolitan and westernised, a complete change from Allahabad. I had never been there except to visit Masi (her aunt, Krishna Hutheesing), during vacations. It was my first experience of what people call normal life, for which I had no preparation. I had no idea that people could go to the office from nine to five, come back, go to the Club ... the routine, the whole ambience, was foreign to me.[2]

Nevertheless, it was a routine that became hers as well, one that continued almost unvaryingly till she left Bombay in 1967. After the children left for school and Gautam for his office, she would sit down to write in her bedroom, notebook on her lap, at the edge of the bed or on a chair, and this was where she wrote her first novel, *A Time to*

Be Happy. It was only much later, when she was writing *From Fear Set Free*, that she graduated to a desk. Working steadily, she stopped only after the children returned in the late afternoon, and the rest of the day and the evenings were taken up with their activities, and her and Gautam's social life. 'When Mummy was working it was very clear that she couldn't be disturbed,' recalled her daughter, Nonika, 'we knew that if her door was shut, we couldn't barge in, we had to wait till she came out.' But when she did come out, her time and attention were made over to them completely.

Bombay's social life glittered with the city's corporate smart set and its old business elite, a circle in which Gautam felt completely at ease, and at home. Unlike Bird & Co., Ciba was Swiss and non-colonial, and was eager to enter the huge market for pharmaceuticals that India promised; the management trusted Gautam to do his best. He responded with characteristic vigour. The Sahgals entertained with gusto, and along with Gautam's business contacts, assorted diplomats and her mother's acquaintances, Nayantara frequently met Jeh and Thelly Tata; the painter Jehangir Sabavala and his wife, Shireen; Raj and Romesh Thapar; Peter Jayasinghe of Asia Publishing House and his wife, Lily; the journalist Frank Moraes and R. K. Laxman, the cartoonist. Through Premi Wagle, Santha Rama Rau's sister, she was introduced to a circle of lunchtime women friends who were much more varied than her evening company, but despite an extremely full and busy social and family life, she never really took to Bombay. She found its intellectual community tiresome, not real in any sense, with no 'real views'. She didn't, for example, join the local PEN Club because she thought the woman who ran it was a 'fraud, an absolute humbug ... with not half a brain in her head'.[3] Moreover, Bombay was still a 'Whites Only' city as far as some exclusive precincts were concerned, among them the Breach Candy Swimming Pool and Gardens, just a stone's throw away from Dil Pazir.

Yet Bombay in the 1950s was buzzing with creative energy. Despite Partition – or perhaps because of it – the city was alive with hope and possibility, with the promise of everything that freedom and independence could offer. A whole generation that had formed bohemian Lahore relocated to Bombay and Delhi, infusing both cities with an ebullience of spirit and unexpected drive. The film industry had the legendary Kapoors, the Brothers Anand, Dev and Chetan, Zohra and Kameshwar Segal, Balraj Sahni, K.L. Saigal, Ismat Chughtai and her scriptwriter husband, Shahid, all of whom would leave an indelible imprint on Hindi cinema. The then little-known building contractor, Shapoorji Pallonji, financed Dilip Kumar and director Asif to make *Mughal-e-Azam*; the very first screening of a film, *Pather Panchali,* by a then unknown director took place in Bombay; Roberto Rossellini was invited to make a documentary on India; and Zia Sarhadi made the classic *Footpath* with Romesh Thapar and Dilip Kumar in the two lead roles. The Indian Peoples' Theatre Association had Zohra Segal and her sister Uzra Butt, Ebrahim Alkazi was already experimenting in a far-reaching way, declaring that his was 'the only serious theatre' around; and Prithvi Theatres with its colossus, Prithviraj Kapoor, was making waves across the country with their hugely popular plays.

In the art world, modernists M. F. Husain, F. N. Souza, V. Gaitonde and Krishen Khanna were breaking free of the Bengal School; the Swiss architect, le Corbusier, had been commissioned by Nehru to design the new city of Chandigarh; and the Modern Architecture Research Group launched its new magazine, *MARG*, with Mulk Raj Anand and the Ceylonese, Anil de Silva, as its editors. There was a kind of headiness in the air, the exciting headiness of living in what Raj Thapar called 'building time in India'.[4]

It was a Bombay that passed Nayantara by. She was curiously, and more or less wholly, detached from it. Gautam, she said, was completely disinterested in the cultural and intellectual life of the city, and she was reluctant to venture out on her own. Breaks from the life of a high-flying corporate executive's wife came in the form of trips to Delhi where, enfolded by family and a way of life she was familiar with and comfortable in, she could put Bombay, housekeeping, wining, dining and entertaining behind her.

Christmas and New Year were spent in Chandigarh every year, in Anokha, a house designed for the Sahgals by Pierre Jeanneret who, with le Corbusier, was the architect for the new capital of Punjab. Given a choice between Delhi and Chandigarh as the place where he could claim compensation for property left behind in Lahore, Gautam chose Chandigarh at Nehru's suggestion. Here, amid half an acre of land in Sector V and within walking distance of Sukhna Lake, Nayantara spent her most peaceful and pleasurable days, sitting at her desk in her bedroom and writing, looking out onto a view of the low hills and then the lake in the distance. In the garden the roses would be ablaze with colour, and the rooms echoed with the children's laughter. Air and light streamed in through an expanse of glass, while a fountain splashed water in a pool separating the two wings of the house. It was just the place for writing, for regaining a sense of time and place; or, as she said in a letter to Nehru '... of peace and fruitful activity'.

Yet the urge to do something beyond the domestic, to partake actively in some way in the life of the country, made itself felt in Nayantara's life as early as two years after her marriage. In 1951 she wrote to Nehru, confiding in him her frustration at being just wife and mother, as well as her difficulties, and seeking his advice. Should she join the Congress? Engage in social work? Or, given her circumstances, just write? Nehru replied immediately and sympathetically, encouraging her to do something worthwhile outside the home. 'One cannot ignore the domestic sphere,' he said, 'but a wider activity gives more meaning to life.' He refrained from telling her what to do, however, remarking only that there were several ways of doing something socially useful. Should she decide to write, her writing should have some purpose. 'In the final analysis,' he wrote, 'one writes from one's experience of life. The richer the experience the better the writing.'[5]

But biology intervened; Nayantara's second child, her son Ranjit, was born nine months after she wrote to Nehru, and it was only a full year later that she had the time and leisure to pick up her pen.

Prison and Chocolate Cake became that work written from experience, her attempt at capturing the 'special magic' of growing up during India's struggle for freedom as part of a family whose men and women had committed their lives to it. 'I knew history would record the struggle,' she has said, but her purpose was altogether different. She wanted to present the 'texture of a time, the froth and bubble of a mood or a moment ...', the everyday reality of that struggle and what it meant as she experienced it, to offer a ringside view of history in the making.[6]

There may not be too many opening sentences in a memoir or autobiography as immediately arresting as the following:

> Some things will always remain a mystery to me. How did Mummie and Papu have the courage to send us to America in 1943? ... Few went as we did, at our age, from a peaceful country on a troop ship at the height of war.

'We' were Nayantara, then sixteen, and her older sister Chandralekha, nineteen, headed for the US and Wellesley College in Massachusetts, on an ocean journey that would take several weeks. The year was 1943 and India was part of Britain's war effort, while at the same time resisting British imperialism and demanding that they quit India. It would have taken an extraordinary set of circumstances for any parent to dispatch two teenaged girls, un-chaperoned, to a country several thousand miles away, while a war was in progress. And the circumstances were indeed extraordinary. On 8 August 1942, the All-India Congress Committee passed its Quit India Resolution in Bombay, and on 9 August, Gandhi, Azad, Patel, Nehru, Sarojini Naidu and other members of the Congress Working Committee were arrested and taken by a special train to Poona. The AICC office at Swaraj Bhawan was sealed yet again by the police, and because it was only a matter of time before she, Chandralekha, Indira and Feroze Gandhi were also arrested, Vijaya Lakshmi Pandit set about organising

Anand Bhawan (where the family now lived) in preparation for her absence. This included disposing of pamphlets and incriminating documents before the police got hold of them, sending valuables to friends' homes for safe keeping, and finding refuge for two young friends, fugitives from the police.

'If you courted arrest by breaking certain laws or defying a particular ban,' wrote Nayantara in *Prison and Chocolate Cake*,

> you did so by first sending a polite note to the district magistrate informing him of your intentions. He then promptly proceeded to arrest you, and you went to jail with the utmost simplicity, dignity and courtesy.

Arrests were often accompanied by the imposition of fines which the Nehrus refused to pay. Consequently, the arresting officers stripped Anand Bhawan of its carpets, select items of furniture, and whatever else they thought was of value, in lieu of money. 'People generally think we lived in great luxury,' Nayantara confided with a laugh, 'but really, the rooms were quite bare!'[7] And, as she recounts in *Prison and Chocolate Cake*:

> With the onset of the non-cooperation movement the two cuisines (western and Indian) were reduced to one and the cellar abolished altogether ... The vast retinue of servants was cut down, and Nanuji sold his horses and much of his treasured china and crystal.[8]

Lekha herself had been imprisoned for participating in the Quit India protests of 1942, and other family elders were liable to be picked up at any time. The political situation was likely to worsen very quickly, and so, at Mme Chiang Kai-Shek's suggestion, Nayantara and Lekha were sent to Wellesley, and in 1945 their younger sister, Rita, went to the Putney School in Vermont.

All this is recounted, sometimes humorously, at other times poignantly, in *Prison and Chocolate Cake,* interleaved with vignettes of family life at Anand Bhawan, with experiences of changing schools again and again as the uncertainty of their parents' presence at home grew, and the sisters learnt to come to terms with the fact that Vijaya Lakshmi and Ranjit Pandit were more likely to be in jail than out of it. The heartbreak of separation had to be borne without tears, with stoicism and a steely resolve to continue the fight. When Chandralekha at one point wistfully wondered whether life would ever be normal for them, Nehru responded with,

> 'Normal?' Mamu repeated, savouring the word as though it was as foreign to his vocabulary as it was to his life. 'The fact is that we live in an upside-down world, darling, and it's no use expecting life to be easy. It is not a simple matter adjusting to such a world, especially for those who are sensitive. It is not normal for most of us to spend our lives in prison cut off from our families and dear ones. It certainly should not be normal for intelligent human beings to spend all their time and energy killing each other off, as they are doing all over the world. It isn't normal either for some people to starve and others to get indigestion through overeating. All this is very abnormal and wrong, but it is happening.'[9]

The bleakness of those days in a sprawling house stripped of valuables, even carpets and furniture, would be temporarily banished whenever Padmaja Naidu, beloved friend of the family, alighted like an exotic bird to keep the children company. Brilliantly plumed in glowing silks and flowers in her hair, Padmasi (as she was called) dispelled the gloom with warmth and cheer and wit. Delicious tidbits like the girls being laughed at when they wore khadi frocks and little Gandhi topis when out for a walk; or a nervous Indira Nehru offering 'potato-Cripps' to Sir Stafford Cripps when he came to visit, are part of a happy recall of times when all the adults were in residence and Anand Bhawan buzzed with political activity, with streams of people, great and humble, passing through, staying, discussing and deciding strategy.

As a welcome counterpoint to that upside-down world was the excitement of New York, the pleasure of an uninterrupted four years in an invigorating academic environment at Wellesley opening up new intellectual vistas, and hugely enjoyable vacations on the east and west coasts of America or in Mexico.

After the first shock of arrival, that is. In September 1943, Nayantara wrote to her mother from Long Island to say:

> ... When we arrived in Los Angeles I felt so dreadfully homesick. I couldn't adjust myself to new surroundings, as you know I never can. I hated the way everybody rushed around day and night without a moment's rest, and I hated the way women seemed to be having a mad race to keep young looking, and I hated the way people demonstrated their affection on the streets ... I was thoroughly unhappy and made up my mind that I would never get used to the strange ways of this country...

> Gradually, however, I found underneath all the crudeness there was a really friendly and sympathetic spirit ... anxious that all newcomers should like their country. Little by little I began to be tolerant ...
>
> I'm sure that I shall hate to leave America. Like India it is the sort of country that grows on one ...
>
> Heaps of love,
> Taru

And it did, for New York dazzled and sparkled when Nayantara and Chandralekha arrived there on their way to Wellesley. They were swept up in a breathtaking round of parties, introductions to celebrities and high society as Nehru's nieces, and awash with all the openness and spontaneous warmth of America. It helped that American liberal opinion supported India's struggle for independence, and it also helped that their mother and uncle could ask their friends Pearl Buck, Paul Robeson, Margaret Sanger and Dorothy Norman to 'keep an eye on the girls'. Doors into drawing rooms and salons on the east and west coasts swung open for them, and the world of art, theatre and film in post-war New York offered up the most exciting fare to eager imbibers. They imbibed it with gusto.

The phone rang incessantly in John and Frances Gunther's apartment on 300 Central Park West where Lekha and Tara were staying, with well-wishers and the press eager for news about India and their imprisoned family members. Eleanor Roosevelt invited them to tea in her Gramercy Park apartment; Pearl Buck and her husband, Richard Walsh, were their surrogate parents in America, their house in Pennsylvania a vacation home for them; Agnes Smedley regaled them with stories about how she lost her toes to frostbite during the Long March in China; and Clare and Henry Luce's country home in New York was a window into the world of journalism and politics. Clare Luce had been to India and was close to Nehru, and both *Time* and *LIFE* were interested in the Indian freedom movement. In the house of Nancy Wilson Ross – who was married to Stanley Young, partner in the publishing house of Farrar, Straus & Young – they nearly met Orson Welles and his newly acquired wife, Rita Hayworth; only nearly, because Welles and Hayworth didn't emerge from their bedroom all weekend! And in Mexico, in 1947, while Nayantara and her younger sister Rita were staying with Rose and Miguel Covarrubias, they saw Eartha Kitt performing with the Katherine Dunham troupe, and met the avant-gardists, Diego Rivera and his wife, Frida Kahlo. As Nayantara disarmingly recalled, 'We were not meeting many ordinary people!'[10]

Among the ordinary people, however, was one who became quite special: Uma Shankar Bajpai, then a student in the US, became a close friend. He and Nayantara took classes in Russian together during the summer of 1944, and wrote to each other almost every day when they were apart. He understood her, she said, looked beyond her face, and she found in him a similar idealism and passion for reading. He wanted desperately that they get engaged, her mother approved, provided she finished her degree, but Nayantara demurred. Uma was much too possessive and she didn't want to be owned; and so she 'light-heartedly destroyed what was probably the sincerest attachment to me I've ever known'.[11]

The first taste of freedom, is how she recalled the impact

of being in the US; the experience of being in a free country, of knowing what it meant to live free, was exhilarating. At Wellesley, then, she revelled in indulging her passion for history, in discovering philosophy and art history, in being exposed to European art and haunting the museums and galleries of Boston. And there was the great happiness of learning new languages – Spanish, and Russian, which she learnt from no less a personage than Vladimir Nabokov. He was a most amazing teacher, she said, who brought a language and a whole world to life. Then just a professor at Wellesley, he was thrilled with Nayantara's keenness and her prior knowledge of the language. She blossomed in this verdant intellectual environment.

> I was very happy then. I don't think I've been so *full* inside myself, of discovery and enchantment, as I was at college. Everything was wonderful and exciting, even the leaves changing colour on campus, all the reading I did, the talks with friends. I loved my years there.[12]

Prison and Chocolate Cake, dedicated to Ranjit and Vijaya Lakshmi Pandit, was published in 1954 in New York. A network of friends and acquaintances in places that mattered enabled the smooth passage of the manuscript from Nayantara's typewriter to her editor, Herbert Weinstock, at the publishing house of Alfred A. Knopf. Her mother showed it to a friend, Govind Biharilal, who in turn showed it to *his* friend, the literary agent, Sarah Neumeyer, and she sold it to Knopf. The wonderful thing about writing then, Nayantara recalled, was that there was no one looking over her shoulder, no agent telling her how to write, how to package it, what to leave out, what put in. Weinstock did ask her to add an extra 10,000 words towards the end of the book and bring it up to date, which she did.

It was well-received and happily reviewed for a variety of reasons. The author was a young, well-connected writer, writing about a contemporary political situation in a country that had captured the world's imagination for its non-violent resistance to colonial rule. She presented an insider's view of India's freedom movement with all the freshness and idealism of a twenty-seven-year-old, and she wrote a limpid prose. Contrary to what might have been expected, hers was no picture of exotic India or of beleaguered womanhood, comforting to those who looked for conformity; rather, a warm and human account of an unusual family that lived in and shaped its country's fortunes at a historic moment. The book became a literary and commercial success, marking out a space for itself as a political memoir with a difference.

From Fear Set Free, the second volume of Nayantara Sahgal's autobiography, was written in Bombay and published in 1962 by W.W. Norton in the US, and by Victor Gollancz in the UK. Knopf, who had published *Prison and Chocolate Cake* declined *From Fear Set Free*, saying it didn't strike the right note for them, that they weren't confident about its marketability, even though they had met with considerable success with *Prison and Chocolate Cake*. Weinstock wrote to Nayantara to say that gross sales of the book in the US, not long after it was published, had been 7,000 copies in hardback. 'This is not a best-seller,' he said, 'but it is a very handsome sale in what has been a very poor publishing season.' Nevertheless, he wasn't confident about taking up its sequel. The left-wing British publisher, Victor Gollancz, who had published *PCC*, stepped in and was more than happy to take *From Fear Set Free*, and not only because he was a great supporter of Indian independence. At the time, Gollancz's stable of authors included the South African Nadine Gordimer, whose two collections of short stories, *The Soft Voice of the Serpent* and *Occasion for Loving* were published in the late 1950s; Kingsley Amis; A.J. Cronin; Daphne du Maurier; Dorothy Sayers; Ivy Compton-Burnett; Colin Wilson and a galaxy of other major writers. The only other Indian on his list, however, was the philosopher J. Krishnamurthi. Nayantara was one of his acquisitions from America, which Gollancz had begun visiting professionally during the 1950s. (Khushwant Singh thought Gollancz was 'a rogue and a rascal' who did nothing for his authors, but Nayantara differed: 'He always took me to lunch at the Savoy when I was in London and was always affectionate in dealings with me. And he was associated with every liberal cause from the early 1930s.')[13]

Beginning with her return to India from the US in 1947 after her graduation from Wellesley College, *From Fear Set Free* deals with the early years of Nayantara's marriage to Gautam Sahgal, the birth of their three children – Nonika and Ranjit were followed by Gita, born in 1956 – and the first few years of her life in Bombay. Interspersed with anecdotal accounts of family reunions and amusing but sharply observant comments on Bombay society, are glimpses of how the country was making its transition to independent governance. The first post-independence elections were held in 1952, but the five hundred princely states were still outside the political and administrative unity of India. Pandit Nehru undertook a nationwide tour to alert the electorate about the importance of voting, of exercising their franchise for the first time ever. Around the same time, Vinoba Bhave started out on the first leg of his Bhoodan Movement, spurred by his visit to Telangana in 1951 and his encounter with its desperately poor landless farmers. It was here that one man in the audience pledged one hundred of his two hundred acres to anyone in need; Vinoba's tour of Telangana that year netted 15,000 acres (mostly arid) for the landless peasantry; slowly other states followed suit.

The linguistic division of states in the 1950s was another change which began in the south, with Telugu speakers in the Madras Presidency demanding a state of their own – Andhra Pradesh. Bombay province was next, with the two dominant languages, Marathi and Gujarati, agitating for separate state status, with Bombay as their capital. The first of the language riots and stormy sloganeering erupted on the streets, but Bombay remained in Maharashtra, while a new capital was mooted for Gujarat.

In 1963, Nayantara embarked on a book tour of the US for *From Fear Set Free*, which consisted of eighteen speaking engagements at various public and educational institutions across the country, and though she enjoyed it, she said she didn't care to repeat the experience. (Writing in her *Chandigarh Diary* later that year, she remarked wryly, 'Lecture tour decidedly helpful in preparing one to face almost anything. Everybody ought to go on a lecture tour which, if it doesn't drive one mad, has character-building possibilities. Grateful my tour over and character built.') The book itself received mixed reviews, some decidedly tepid; one in fact called it 'a glamourised version of a housewife's diary,' an assessment with which Nayantara herself agreed reluctantly. In a letter to her friend, E.N. (Bunchi) Mangat Rai, dated 7 September 1964, she wrote:

> *From Fear Set Free* has irritated me profoundly, the fact that I allowed it to be published at all without a struggle. Originally, it was very political and the publisher—Knopf—said no one would be interested in that kind of book from me. They wanted something lighter, more 'readable'. They are very fond of using words like 'heart-warming' and 'charming'—both of which make me a little ill. Anyway, the whole thing was rehashed in a lighter vein and it became all about nothing in particular.

Left to herself, she would have dwelt on India's prickly relationship with the US and its hawkish Secretary of State, John Foster Dulles; she would have introduced much more of the political context in the country, the business and social environment they lived in. But, of course, the times had changed too. By 1962, when *From Fear Set Free* came out, the political climate was decidedly different to what it had been in the mid-1950s. Neither the US nor Britain approved of Nehru's – and India's – unwavering commitment to non-alignment and disarmament; US foreign policy demanded that the 'non-aligned' take sides. It was not surprising that Knopf dissuaded Nayantara from portraying a political India that might have alienated its readers or risked censure for being open to Soviet influence. The irony was that, despite the rehashing at its request,

Knopf declined to publish the book and they ceased to be Nayantara's publishers after this experience.

The book's reception in London was decidedly warmer, with *The London Times* and *Birmingham Post* complimenting the author on being 'brilliantly vivid and entertainingly sophisticated', yet simple and compassionate; and Vera Brittain remarked that Sahgal's style 'sparkled like a spring torrent'. It was left to Mrs Robert Henry to deliver the final encomium in *Books and Bookmen,* declaring this 'major work more capable than a thousand political speeches of making modern India understood ... Nayantara Sahgal steps into the front rank of contemporary women writers.'

In April 1948, a little over three months after she met Gautam Sahgal, Nayantara wrote to Isamu Noguchi, the Japanese-American sculptor, telling him about her decision to get married.

> You know I had believed very strongly in my background and in India as a necessary part of me ... I have a sense of belonging to my country for better or worse – and it may often be for the worse – I don't know. At any rate, I feel after I got home I must give my fullest to be an Indian, live like one, think like one ... I have decided to get married, and I want you to know why. Perhaps I shouldn't get married. There's you – and your outlook and opinions which I value above all others as far as my personal life is concerned, but you are always drawing me away from my sense of duty, and my feeling of believing to fulfil myself as an Indian. You cannot help that, and I feel close

> to you as you do. That's why I have always felt that our relationship had nothing to do with time, age or country, or conventions. That's why it meant so much. But life isn't like that – not as I've seen it after I got home – it demands a great deal that one has no right to refuse.[14]

Isamu Noguchi met Tara Pandit in New York in 1943, at a party thrown by J.J. Singh, chairman of the India League of America, an organisation that supported the cause of Indian independence. It was a small party, only ten guests or so, for Tara and Chandralekha. Tara, a teenager at the time, was nevertheless strikingly beautiful in a sombre, even demure, way and Noguchi was immediately captivated. Always drawn to India, Noguchi had been attending meetings of the India League during the War years and had acquired a deep respect for Nehru. Moreover, his father, Yone Noguchi's friendship with Rabindranath Tagore had already predisposed him to India and a yearning to visit it.

New York in the 1940s was the hub of European émigré creativity, and Noguchi was at its heart. 'His studio in MacDougal Alley is one of the loveliest places in New York,' wrote the French writer Anaïs Nin in her diary, during a brief affair with him. Clustered around Greenwich Village in assorted studios and lofts were the refugee artists of Nazi-occupied Europe – Max Ernst, Marcel Duchamp, Jean Arp, Salvador Dali, Yves Tanguy and others of the European avant-garde. The exiled writer Arshile Gorky was a special friend of Isamu's, as was the modern dancer and choreographer, Martha Graham, with whom he shared a close personal and professional bond. It was Noguchi who designed the sets for all of Graham's iconoclastic, later classic, masterpieces, among them *Frontier Appalachian*

Spring, with music by Aaron Copeland, and *Cave of the Heart.*

Noguchi introduced the young Nayantara to museums and galleries, to an eclectic, bohemian group of artists, to the creative ferment of New York – but he also became for her a listening ear, a mature, sensitive artist, thoughtful and charming who, as she said to Noguchi's biographer, 'swept me off my feet'. He was forty years old to Nayantara's seventeen, and in a way, almost a father figure: a fount of knowledge, guiding her in art appreciation, in literary discovery and, one could almost say, self-discovery, too. In 1927, the year Nayantara was born, Noguchi made his first trip to Paris, then the Mecca of the art world, inspired by Brancusi and determined to absorb as much as he could of the energy and excitement of post-war Paris. By the time they met in 1944, Noguchi was a much experienced man of the world with a series of romantic involvements behind him. Ruth Page, a modern dancer in Chicago, Dorothy Hale, an aspiring actress, the painter Frida Kahlo, and the writer Anaïs Nin had all been the objects of his passionate attentions at one time or another. Beauty and intelligence in women were irresistible to Noguchi, and young Tara Pandit had plenty of both. In addition, she was Indian, and Isamu had a deep and abiding interest in the country and its art. It was almost as if everything had come together in Tara.

Through Noguchi, Nayantara met Duchamp and Dali, but also Frida Kahlo on a memorable visit to Mexico in 1947, after she graduated from Wellesley. She wrote to Isamu every day from Miguel Covarrubias's idyllic home in Mexico City, imploring him to come to Mexico and personally show her all the sights and architectural buildings that he had told her about. Their affair, tender, wondrous and exciting for Nayantara, was never destined for marriage, although Isamu proposed to her again and again. Inspired by her feelings for him, he began and completed work on his most ambitious sculpture to date, *Kouros*, a beautifully modelled and sculpted figure of ideal youth, dedicated to Tara. She posed for him in his studio and he tried to 'capture her sadness and distress' in clay. In a way, this was his parting gift to her for she had decided to return to India, to leave Isamu and America. But in the end his actual present to her was a small nude plaster statue entitled *Primavera* that he had sculpted while Tara was in Mexico. Her gift was a sweater she had knitted for him, with a note to say, 'The thought of you is the only sane wholesome thing that I have to hold on to in all this confusion.'

Back in the turmoil of post-Partition Delhi, in Nehru's ceaselessly active household, she wrote to Noguchi to say,

> I think of you a great deal in one connection or another and realise more and more what an important part of my life and particularly my growing up process you have been ... Whatever the future holds, your value to me will never grow less. I can't appreciate art or poetry or fairy tales without thinking of you ... All my notions of happiness have been altered by you – and you have shown me that a human being can be considerate, courteous and civilized in closer contact. I appreciate you for this and much more – our talks and silences and love ... Please don't ever forget this. You can only mean more and more to me.[15]

Decades later, when I asked her in Dehradun about the happiest time in her life, Nayantara replied, 'I'm not a happy person, you know... but – New York. Full of discovery and excitement.'[16] She felt in New York what she could never feel in Bombay – stretched, in the company of creative people, in a city that was always and enormously exciting. What could be further removed than WASPish, exceedingly proper Wellesley?

Although Nayantara thought of herself as Isamu's 'creation' and told him that he 'would always be the love of her life', there is no mention of Noguchi anywhere, either in *Prison and Chocolate Cake* or in *From Fear Set Free*. A brief, light-hearted account of their trip to Mexico in 1947 appears towards the end of *Prison and Chocolate Cake*, and it is peppered throughout with several references to the many celebrities and public personages the Pandit sisters met in New York and across the country, especially when their mother was India's ambassador to the US and India's delegate to the UN. It is unlikely that Mrs Pandit was aware of Tara's relationship with Noguchi, although he offered to make a portrait bust of her, and he is completely absent in her own memoir, *The Scope of Happiness*, in which she speaks at length about her daughters' sojourn in the US.

In an exceptionally candid letter to Bunchi in May 1965, Nayantara wrote to say that 'going to America was a wrong and harmful thing for me in two ways':

1. It valorised 'self-expression' and 'youth' and both are a deadly combination.
2. In the realm of sex, starting with the image of the sort of man I was attracted to, America ... appealed to my grossest instincts, developed them, gave me the capacity to admire and be greatly attracted to physical

> strength. Whenever there was a choice between two men, one gentle, the other tough, I took the tough one ... It added to one's credentials and one's popularity to be seen with that kind of man ... I became very sex-sought-after, so that much older men made their attentions and intentions evident.[17]

Yet Noguchi was hardly 'that kind of tough man'; on the contrary, in a conversation with Noguchi's biographer, Masayo Duus, Nayantara compared him to her kind and caring Papu, 'as much a surrogate father as a lover'. She told Duus that she had seldom met anyone as gentle or considerate, and that she found in him a personality as complexly layered as her own. She was moved by his fascination with India, in its way nearly as intense as her own, but marriage was never in the picture for her. 'The chief reason I think I became involved with (him),' she told Bunchi years later, 'was because he was a sculptor and had an interest in and understanding of ideas and attitudes that my friends of my own age did not.'[18] But she could not have married him because basically, she was married to India in some peculiar, passionate and unalterable way, and nothing could change that. She couldn't conceive of living anywhere but in India, with an Indian; as she told Noguchi in a letter written after Gandhi's funeral in January 1948, 'I feel I will not be happy unless I serve India as fully and uncompromisingly as I am capable of doing.'[19]

When Noguchi finally visited India in 1949 he came and went without meeting Tara, for she had earlier written to say, 'I am glad that it (the trip) seems to be working out, but I don't think I will have the strength to see you there. The strength, perhaps, not the heart.'[20] They remained in touch, however, even met a couple of times in London when both happened to be there at the same time; and in 1986, when Noguchi was in his eighties, he wrote her to say:

> Dear Tara,
>
> Your letter filled me with the most conflicting emotions. I was in Japan, where it was forwarded, deep in the perplexities of my work and not knowing what to write, kept thinking instead of when we knew each other so briefly in New York and of the years since.
>
> I was so happy to get your telephone call and know then that this memory lives with you as it has with me. It will never fade, more real than the real, whatever life we lead – a factor of our imagination.
>
> With my love,
> Isamu

He died three years later, in 1989.

Gautam Sahgal could neither forget that there had been an Isamu Noguchi in her past, nor forgive Nayantara for her teenage love. Early on in their courtship she had told him about Noguchi and he replied, 'I wouldn't care if you had fifty affairs and sixty children.'[21] But his jealousy drove her to throw away all Noguchi's letters as well as the ring and necklace he had made for her, and all the books he had given her. As she moved further and further away from Gautam emotionally, his love for her grew more desperate and his possessiveness impossible to deal with. He resented her male acquaintances, was never comfortable with them around her unless he was in close proximity, and he was always, always, haunted by Noguchi. And Nicky. Nicolas Wyrouboff, a young Russian aristocrat whom Nayantara had met in Paris in 1948. When she and her sister, Lekha, had accompanied their mother to a UN General Assembly meeting. Nicky was smitten and Nayantara enormously attracted to him, enough to think seriously of ending her engagement to Gautam. Like Noguchi, however, Nicky too was a foreigner.

Very soon after their wedding, barely beyond the honeymoon stage, Nayantara had made up her mind *not* to let her heart be broken, and so reversed a whole process of growth and maturity. She did it in self-defence, for one night, very early in their marriage – it was still January 1949 – the inquisition began, reducing her almost to pulp.[22]

> 'Day and night,' Nayantara recounted, 'I was a prisoner on trial. The questions never stopped. Why? Where? How? And above all, why, why? I could feel G's torment through them and I tried to atone by giving him everything I could, assuring him that nothing like it could ever happen again, that I had been young and unthinking, had never realized there might be consequences for the future. But he couldn't stop torturing himself or me. There were days on end when he could not speak to me, when the sight of me repelled him, and the deathly stillness was terrible.[23]

By the mid-1950s, the 'electricity' that had sparked between Nayantara and Gautam had lost its powerful charge, and suppressed strains in the marriage were beginning to surface. Nayantara felt confined and dissatisfied in her role as corporate wife, had few close friends in Bombay, and missed the deep and direct engagement with the country's political life that had been bread and butter for all her growing years. She cut herself off from old contacts, isolated herself from everything she had known and thought. People who knew her before her marriage were aghast at the change in her, so devoid of joy and gaiety had she become. Gautam didn't see it happening because he was happiest when she was docile and obedient, when her life revolved around him. Things went on in this fashion for ten years, ten years of inquisition with intervals of normalcy, of a slow divorce from herself. But ten years was perhaps as much as she could take in this respect for that was when she rebelled, when the explosion came.

In 1959, Gautam's fears regarding Nayantara's male friends came to the fore in the person of Kjeld Packness, the Danish trade commissioner in Bombay, in whom Nayantara found the possibility of friendship. The Sahgals and Packnesses met as couples, often at the same Bombay parties, then gradually at each others' homes as well. There would be film or theatre shows with the children, a picnic every now and again, the kind of cordial exchanges that threatened no one.

But when Nayantara wanted to lunch alone with Kjeld or meet him on her own, Gautam was beside himself with suspicion. Why did she want to meet him alone? What could she possibly have to say to him that couldn't be said in his, Gautam's, presence? Stunned by the sharpness of his response she would give in, but she persuaded him to continue a social relationship with the couple and invited them to a dinner they were hosting for their tenth wedding anniversary. It was a disaster. Kjeld stayed back after the other guests left to talk to Nayantara, but both he and Gautam had been drinking steadily, and what followed was a most unholy row between them.

Nayantara was shaken to the core by this episode. How could she continue with a marriage that was floundering so badly? How would she pull herself together? As always, when beset by doubt and confusion, she turned to her uncle for advice. Nehru suggested that she and Gautam go to Nagpur where he was attending the AICC session, and discuss the problem in as open and accommodating a way as possible. He did offer one piece of advice though, which Nayantara didn't ultimately take. 'Whatever you decide,' he said, 'don't be like Indu, neither married nor divorced.' At Nagpur, Nehru talked to them singly and together. He listened patiently and Gautam, whose admiration and affection for him were enormous, heard him respectfully. The contentious issue of Nayantara's friendship with Kjeld was the immediate cause of the crisis as it had provoked all Gautam's insecurities and suspicions about Nayantara's attractiveness to men; he had already called her mother in London to tell her how her daughter's behaviour had outraged him. When he mentioned that he had also told Mrs Pandit that he was divorcing Nayantara, Nehru said, 'We are not afraid of divorce in our family,' but there were children to consider and Tara's unhappiness to deal with. Why didn't Tara spend some time with him, Mamu, in Delhi, then go to her mother in London and take time to think matters through? Separately, with Gautam, he confided the hurts and disappointments in his own marriage, which helped Gautam get a perspective on a relationship that both he and Nayantara valued. At Nehru's urging, Tara did go to Delhi and returned to Bombay after a month, 'nearly whole'. She and Gautam, two wounded birds, tried hard to make a fresh start, but they had been badly shaken by what had happened to their relationship.

There followed an uneasy and fragile truce. For a brief while Gautam was distracted by the planning and building of Anokha in Chandigarh, but before long storm clouds began gathering again over the summer of 1959 in Simla. Nayantara told Gautam that she had written a letter to Kjeld explaining the reasons for her abrupt and complete silence; Gautam's reaction was volcanic. Afraid and increasingly vulnerable in the face of his fury, Nayantara decided to take Nehru's suggestion and visit her mother in London and give herself a chance to think about her marriage, away from her own home.

London decided Nayantara. In several letters to Gautam she sought some kind of response from him to her genuine misgivings about their relationship, some acknowledgement or reassurance that he understood her unhappiness with the life they were leading. He evaded the issue and she returned to Bombay with her mind made up – she and Gautam would have to part.

Not a ripple disturbs the smooth surface of *From Fear Set Free*, written *after* Nayantara's return from London and dedicated to Gautam. The month she spent in Delhi is recalled only towards the very end of the book and only obliquely, with a telling reference to a conversation with her uncle: what quality, she asked him, did he consider most important for a successful marriage? 'It is important always to leave the way open to talk,' he replied, 'as long as two people can talk there is a way back to understanding.'[24]

When she came back from London, Gautam was unexpectedly gentle and considerate, promising to give her the space she required for herself, to doubt her less, trust her more. He wanted to give the marriage another chance, he said. And so Nayantara left neither her home nor her marriage.

Things seemed to get better for a while with Gautam busier and more successful at work, drumming up business contacts and lucrative contracts for Ciba-Geigy. He was lionised in Basel, C-G headquarters, his abilities recognised and rewarded. The directors warmed, too, to his easy charm, his way with people and, not least, his beautiful and intelligent wife. Gautam at parties was witty and engaging, a great raconteur, and the Sahgals could be guaranteed to keep a fine table. And then there was Chandigarh, where he felt completely and confidently at home, back in Punjab. At Anokha, built for Nayantara as a testament of his love, he relaxed visibly.

But for Nayantara there began now a long period of emotional freeze, of vacillation and uncertainty, and on Gautam's part, alarming mood swings as he ricocheted between adoration and uncontrolled jealously, vile temper and deep depression. As he became more and more mercurial, Nayantara crept further and further into her shell.

> I wanted to be left alone in my privacy. I didn't want to explore myself at all ... my own life, as always, continued hidden. I never talked about my feelings. I couldn't ...

> For myself I decided to fill my life with work, write more, do whatever I could to make a life for myself ...[25]

Increasingly solitary, she was unable to confide in anyone, not even her sisters. 'I longed to have a proper conversation with somebody, just someone to talk to,' she told me in 2008, but couldn't. Didn't dare, is how she put it. The one person she might have confided in, whom she would have wanted as a friend, was Frank Moraes, but he was absolutely clear that this was not possible. He was greatly attracted to her, he told her, so simple friendship would be difficult for him.

Writing became her refuge, a daily discipline; what sustained her were her children and her writing: 'I write the way some women go into the kitchen and cook,' she told me. 'If I wrote something I liked or was working satisfactorily on a book, I felt I'd eaten and slept. It was nourishment.' But her life was lived on two different planes: the conventional one of domesticity in her role as mother and as the wife of a successful corporate husband, within the norms of acceptable behaviour; and an inner world of feeling, thinking and growing discontent which remained a closely guarded secret.

> 'Why didn't I write what I'm telling you?' she said, when discussing her dissatisfaction with *From Fear Set Free* with me, then continued, 'It never said a word about anything that was really happening in my life then, nothing about the difficulties, emotional and otherwise, that I was up against at the time. The diaries that I kept, the letters that I had from before my marriage, I tore them all up because I was so afraid ... My husband was

> a very jealous man and I needed to destroy everything. I didn't want him to be reminded of anything even though he knew everything about me. Nothing was hidden, but I couldn't take a risk.' [26]

Gautam Sahgal was a giant of a man, a man who could make the sunshine come into your life in a second, but could also make you cry the next minute. Strikingly good-looking, with a wonderful sense of humour, he is remembered by family and friends as a person who couldn't be ignored. He was a conventional Punjabi male, his daughter Nonika said, used to giving orders and to being obeyed, yet capable of setting everything aside to help out in times of need, to put himself out for you. A person of extremes, in love and hate, quick-witted and quick-tempered, both. With a flash of insight she identified the fundamental difference between her parents as being her mother's 'westernised thinking', too liberal and independent for her autocratic, patriarchal father to accept. Too reserved and quiet, as well, unable to reach out and counter her husband's larger-than-life presence.[27]

Gautam took it for granted that he could manage his household the way he ran Ciba-Geigy, by the sheer force of his personality. The children were to be punished if they didn't do well at school; their mother treated to bouts of simmering rage and silence if he disapproved; friends banished from their home if they transgressed. But he was brilliantly successful at work, able to cultivate bureaucrats and politicians and anticipate changes in government policy to his advantage. (During the Emergency of 1975–77, for instance, he made sure he remained on Indira Gandhi's right side, but kept all lines of communication open with Morarji Desai as well. When the 1977 elections saw the Janata Party in power at the Centre, Ciba, almost alone among the large business houses, had nothing to fear from the new government. Nor, because of his enlightened labour management, did his company experience the widespread strikes that others did once the Emergency clampdown was lifted.) His relationship with his mother-in-law was one of love and admiration, deferential yet comradely, and with Jawaharlal, frankly – almost unabashedly – worshipful. Tara's sister Lekha recalled that Nehru enjoyed Gautam's company enormously, and that their cousin Indira kept up her contact with him even after he and Nayantara had separated.[28]

In his younger daughter Gita's assessment, both facets marked him out as a personality driven to prove himself in the world of business, to achieve social recognition and status through all the means available to him; yet never quite overcoming his feeling of inferiority as a younger son who had been denied his inheritance and remained in the shadow of an elder brother who was his parents' golden boy, academically and otherwise. The mismatch between her parents, she believes, couldn't have been more glaring.[29] Yet Ranjit, her brother, recalled, 'They were beautiful together, a fairy tale couple, I can't tell you how beautiful they were. The quality of their combined presence, their dialogue… it was extraordinary.'[30]

When she met Gautam in 1947, Nayantara asked him whether he was interested in the three things that mattered most to her: accuracy, metaphysics and art. He replied in the affirmative, but obviously not in the way she meant it, and the gap remained. And when, at the height of their troubles, Gautam asked her if she would marry him again, she quite unequivocally said, 'No.' She also told him that she no longer believed in marriage as an institution, and that conventional considerations like 'security' had no meaning for her.

And yet she stayed on.

> I am one of those strange creatures (she told Bunchi) whose single ambition was a home. I wanted the permanence and security of the kind I'd not had, the solidity of no-change, of parents in the home with their children, of knowing exactly what would happen ... Writing and all that was there, too, but it was in the background.[31]

She yearned, she said, for continuity, she had a craving for permanence, and so she encased herself in a hard, protective layer and a resolute determination to make her marriage work. Self-discipline became a cultivated habit, a strategy she used in order to cope with the stresses of her relationship with Gautam. Her epitaph, she said, could be, 'She was only half-alive while she lived, but at least she was disciplined' and for the times she wasn't, she made up by being twice as disciplined afterwards.

> I believe, once again, what has always been true for me and of my attitudes, that there is very little in life more contemptible than people who do not buckle down and do the task in hand whatever it might be, to the best of their ability.[32]

Perhaps it was only Pearl Buck who most accurately and presciently understood Nayantara's personality, for as early as July 1947 she had written to Vijaya Lakshmi Pandit to say that 'Tara must marry a brilliant and complex man, they will probably fight, but she cannot be happy with simplicity.' Comparing the two sisters, Rita and Tara, she noted how both had grown during their stay in the US, but that Tara had developed inwardly. 'Outwardly she is much the same, although prettier than ever. You know she was chosen the most beautiful girl in her class …' but, said Buck, she was also emotional and susceptible, and this would 'make her life a troubled one insofar as men are concerned … Men follow her, whether she knows it or not.' Uncannily, she predicted that while Rita would marry, be happy and lead a normal married life, Tara 'will be complex and questioning and never quite happy, but always fascinating. Her own happiness will depend on her ability to integrate herself.' While advising her friend to hasten Tara's marriage should she fall in love with someone suitable, she nevertheless warned her that 'she will need more than marriage, anyway. No one thing or person will satisfy her complexity.'[33]

The Nehrus and Pandits were not simply a family of rebels against empire, but a family of rebels against empire who also wrote – and wrote autobiographies. Nehru, Vijaya Lakshmi Pandit, Krishna Hutheesing; 'It is odd,' wrote Jawaharlal to Mrs Pandit in 1943, 'that the whole family should feel an inner urge for autobiography – I set a catching example.' But it was also a family that, in a subtle way, wrote back. Nayantara has said,

> There was no such thing as an Indian point of view, we were always being interpreted by others ... as people under occupation one of the main ways you were suppressed is that you were not allowed to express yourself politically ... even the fiction and non-fiction written at the time was through the lens of the Raj. It became a way for me to have my say about what really happened. A political way of writing was for me a very fundamental thing because one had been denied freedom of speech. There was very real censorship then ... a degrading and humiliating experience to have one's mouth shut ... To write politically was the only way for me to proceed.[34]

Nayantara's foray into writing, then, was not so much an exercise in self-expression or a young woman's dabbling in the realm of the literary. Rather, it was the medium she chose in order to fulfil a clear purpose: communicating an idea of India in an idiom inflected with an Indian accent, presenting a perspective that was a counter to prevailing and received wisdoms; presenting moreover, an account of an alternative politics.

Although she has written that, 'The process leading to freedom had so closely affected my family and my upbringing that it seemed to me an event almost of personal significance,'[35] the difference in tone and texture between *Prison and Chocolate Cake* and *From Fear Set Free* is marked; it marked, as well, a shift, albeit temporary, in her preoccupations. *Prison and Chocolate Cake* was focused almost exclusively on the struggle for freedom, in which the intertwined histories of the nationalist movement and family involvement came together seamlessly in a narrative that was, at once, charming autobiography and incipient national biography. This was what made it unusual and interesting as the maiden venture of a twenty-seven-year-old.

The two memoirs, then, cannot be read in the same register. Where *Prison and Chocolate Cake* is wholeheartedly about the tumult and exhilaration of political action and an intense personal commitment to it, *From Fear Set Free* is about concealment, with the tension of uncertainty replaced by the mundane detail of daily, or what Nayantara called 'normal', life. It was written in 1959, after she had made a conscious decision to bury her past so that her marriage could continue peacefully. The writing became a 'polite exercise', reflecting nothing of what was going on, it became part of her attempt to bring the curtain down on everything that had happened earlier. Superficially, it was a continuation of her life as it had ended in *Prison and Chocolate Cake*, but of course, it was a very different life. 'Before marriage and after marriage, a woman's life changes,' she said, by way of explanation, 'a woman's life is very different from a man's.'[36]

Although this provides a clue to the differing tone and temper of both books, it tells only part of the story. In *Prison and Chocolate Cake* the author's personal and political selves are a harmonious whole, there is no disjunction between the life she and her family led, the politics they believed in and practised, and her recounting of it. Although she might later have described it as 'naïve', and wondered how it could have 'come out sounding like this (i.e., upbeat) when it was about emotional strain and tragedy, about financial pressures, the repeated hardships of jail sentences'[37] and the uncertainty about how they would affect the family, she never doubted the integrity of the endeavour or of her own place in it.

From Fear Set Free, on the other hand, sees a split in this personal/political persona, where both personal *and* political are concealed; the former as a conscious, deliberately exercised choice, the latter, because she was no longer connected to the historic and heroic in the same way. Was far removed from it, in fact. Tara Pandit had become Nayantara Sahgal. Although her family connections obviously exposed her to the political life of the country – her mother was a diplomat, she contested elections, became governor of Maharashtra while Nayantara was living in Bombay, and so on – her own circumstances at the time militated against anything more than a superficial involvement in it.

Yet, all this notwithstanding, one could hardly expect such writing by a woman in her late twenties and early thirties to be a 'complete' or even substantial account of her life. Nor, really, should one wonder about whether or how much Nayantara Sahgal revealed or concealed in her two texts, how 'true' she was to her experiences, how 'authentic' her representation, or how 'reliable' her recall. The self is seldom represented as unvarying, stable and consistent over time; representations of it will change as the autobiographer or memoirist's contingent reality and circumstances change – indeed, as her life is lived. There is no serious contradiction between the self that Nayantara foregrounded in her autobiographies and what she revealed to me in her interviews close to fifty years later. Concealment, or what is also called self-censorship, is a spontaneous and understandable reflex when the issue is as intimate as marriage or when relationships are being negotiated. (By the same token her 'concealment' of her association with Noguchi in *Prison and Chocolate Cake* proceeded from the same impulse, but also perhaps from not wanting to attach too much importance to a teenage romance.)

Nayantara Sahgal's married life began to fall apart when she tried to deviate from a male-designed social and gender script for women, and very specifically, from her husband's script for her – and for them as a couple. Ostensibly, and certainly as far as Gautam was concerned, she had everything a woman could want – a husband who idolised her, the comfort and security of his success, a future of assured privilege. What could be ailing her? But as we know, by her mid-twenties she had begun to want to create another script for her life, perhaps even to create another self. In the eight years that elapsed between *Prison and Chocolate Cake* and *From Fear Set Free* she simultaneously found and suppressed an emerging self, an alter ego who held the promise of freedom but who also threatened to rock the marital boat. The terrible poignancy of her decision, in 1959, to reconcile herself to an arid marriage, to bring the curtain down, as she said, on everything that might provoke another violent outbreak of jealousy, signified a deliberate and willed silencing. *From Fear Set Free* reads like a 'polite exercise' because, at a superficial level, it is a monument to a buried self; as an autobiographical text, therefore, it could go no further. But we must read it as a testament to Nayantara's determination to continue writing, and through her writing to create 'another possibility of female destiny' both for herself and for her female characters. It is in her fiction, in the novels she wrote after *From Fear Set*

Free, that we see a more composite self articulated; it is in them, written through what has been called 'a curtained autobiographical practice', that we see a less troubled reconciliation than what she had been able to achieve in her own life, till then.

Endnotes

1 Nayantara Sahgal, *From Fear Set Free* (New York: W.W. Norton & Company, Inc., 1962), pp. 34–35.

2 Personal interview, Dehradun, May 2008.

3 Nayantara Sahgal to E.N. (Bunchi) Mangat Rai, letter dated 8 June 1965 (unpublished).

4 Raj Thapar, *All These Years* (New Delhi: Seminar Publications, 1991).

5 Jawaharlal Nehru to Nayantara Sahgal, letter dated 2 February 1951.

6 Nayantara Sahgal, *Prison and Chocolate Cake* (New Delhi: Harper Perennial, rpt. 2007) P.S., p. 6.

7 Personal interview, Dehradun, May 2008.

8 Nayantara Sahgal, *Prison and Chocolate Cake,* p. 48.

9 Nayantara Sahgal, *Prison and Chocolate Cake*, p. 139.

10 Personal interview, Delhi, August 2010.

11 Nayantara Sahgal to E.N. Mangat Rai, letter dated 21 August 1966 (unpublished).

12 Nayantara Sahgal to E.N. Mangat Rai, letter dated 5 September 1966 (unpublished).

13 Personal interview, Delhi, March 2009.

14 Masayo Duus, *The Life of Isamu Noguchi: Journey Without Borders*, tr. Peter Duus (Princeton University Press, 2004), p. 197.

15 Ibid., p. 196.

16 Personal interview, Dehradun, May 2008.

17 Nayantara Sahgal to E.N. Mangat Rai, letter dated 11 May 1965 (unpublished).

18 Nayantara Sahgal to E.N. Mangat Rai, letter dated 24 February 1965 (unpublished).

19 Masayo Duus, *Isamu Noguchi*, p. 197.

20 Ibid., pp. 198–99.

[21] Nayantara Sahgal and E.N. Mangat Rai, letter dated 14 September 1964 in *Relationship: Extracts from a Correspondence* (New Delhi: Kali for Women, 1994), p. 32.

[22] Nayantara Sahgal to E.N. Mangat Rai, letter dated 16 April 1967 (unpublished).

[23] Nayantara Sahgal and E.N. Mangat Rai, letter dated 14 September 1964 in *Relationship*, p. 33.

[24] Nayantara Sahgal, *From Fear Set Free*, p. 237.

[25] Nayantara Sahgal and E.N. Mangat Rai, letter dated 14 September 1964 in *Relationship*, p. 39.

[26] Personal interview, Dehradun, May 2008.

[27] Personal interview, Delhi, July 2009.

[28] Personal interview, Dehradun, May 2008.

[29] Personal interview, London, April 2008.

[30] Personal interview, Chandigarh, November 2008.

[31] Nayantara Sahgal to E.N. Mangat Rai, letter dated 25 April 1967 (unpublished).

[32] Nayantara Sahgal to E.N. Mangat Rai, letter dated 25 August 1965 (unpublished).

[33] Pearl Buck to Vijaya Lakshmi Pandit, letter dated 7 July 1947.

[34] Personal interview, Dehradun, May 2008.

[35] Nayantara Sahgal, *From Fear Set Free*, p. 9.

[36] Personal interview, Dehradun, May 2008.

[37] Nayantara Sahgal, *Prison and Chocolate Cake*, P.S., p. 13.

2
LIVING WITH MARRIAGE

A Time to Be Happy
This Time of Morning

NAYANTARA DEDICATED HER FIRST NOVEL, *A TIME TO BE HAPPY* (published by Alfred Knopf in the US and Gollancz in the UK in 1958) to her uncle, Jawaharlal, acknowledging both her love and admiration of him, as well as his encouragement of her writing. 'You love to write,' he had said to her, 'so continue', then went on to remark that if *he* wanted to write another book, he would have to go back to jail in order to do so! Her own childhood and experience of growing up in the 1930s and '40s were the material she drew on for the novel which served, she said, to 'clear the decks' for her later work.

The story revolves around two families, the Shivpals and Sahais, in an industrial town, Sharanpur, an obvious clone of Kanpur, the city in which the newly-wed Nayantara lived for a couple of years with her husband. The narrator, a nameless man, is a friend of both families, and the story unfolds through his recounting the life and career of the Shivpals' son, Sanad, against the backdrop of the simultaneously unfolding story of independent India and her transition from colonial subject to sovereign nation. Sanad is a young employee of an old British firm, Selkirk and Lowe, and his experiences there are drawn largely from Gautam Sahgal's employment with Bird & Co. Gautam's decision to leave their employ is, in fact, the opening line of *A Time to Be Happy*. 'We were walking past the Sharanpur

Club one morning when Sanad said he wanted to give up his job with Selkirk and Lowe.' The last days of the Raj, but also the beginning of the end of zamindari and feudalism, are presented while tracing the fortunes of the Shivpals and Sahais in an intermittent backward and forward movement of reminiscence, recapitulation and recollection by the narrator. He is clearly a nationalist in the mould of many young men of the time, who turned their backs on a life of security and privilege and joined the freedom movement.

> When I adopted khadi (he says) I made, I felt, the first major decision of my life, for mill-made cloth was my family's source of income and my own future inheritance. In choosing to wear khadi I surrendered forever my rightful claim to my inheritance and, in doing so, severed all contact with my father's business.[1]

Sanad's father, Govind Narayan, is a Lucknavi landowner in the classical mould: refined, unhurried, detached from the distressing crassness of the world around him, a connoisseur of the good things of life that are his entitlement. His brother, Harish, his exact opposite, is a brown sahib anxious for assimilation into the modern world via an assiduous emulation of the erstwhile ruler. His caricatured counterpart is Sir Harilal Mathur, a businessman, knighted for his service to the Empire in the form of a donation of Rs 6 lakhs to the Imperial War Fund. Sir Harilal has a 'private' wife who seldom leaves the house, and a 'public' wife who is presentable and graces his social occasions. Sanad's own brother, Girish, an upwardly mobile boxwallah, is impatient with his younger sibling's chafing at the (British) bit, and recommends a stiff drink to set him right whenever he sees him slipping. A relatively minor but remarkably memorable cast of women characters – Harish's wife, Maya; Govind Narayan's Lakshmi; Harilal Mathur's wholly, and wholesomely, grounded (private) Prabha; and Sanad's future bride, Kusum; but more than Kusum, her extraordinary mother, Savitri, and the no-nonsense Kunti Behen – are the foil to the ambitions, the prevarications, even the posturings, of their menfolk, caught in the cleft stick of history.

A reader may be forgiven for thinking that the narrator is modelled on the author's father, Ranjit Pandit, even though Nayantara herself demurs. Nevertheless, the choice of a nameless first-person narrator for her first novel was unusual. 'I thought it an easy way to write a story, as if it were coming from me, as it were,' she told me.

> I could write unselfconsciously, without having to feel I had to create a character. It came easily ... I'd read a lot of Somerset Maugham and there's this ease that comes out of his writing, *The Razor's Edge*, for instance ... it just seemed to come naturally. And it also came off the top of my mind – well, a first novel always does, you don't burrow and you don't plan, it comes out of your experience of life. So it was my experience of childhood and growing up, I didn't really have to think of a plot ...[2]

As the novel proceeds, however, the narrator does actually become a 'character', and though not her father, is clearly inspired by Ranjit Pandit. The likeness was a consequence of her 'only knowing that kind of man, that kind of work'. Congress-man, passionate advocate of rural development, Gandhian, of course, and dedicated to the idea of free and egalitarian India, the narrator becomes the vehicle for inscribing the first chapter of independent India's story, but pentimento-like, the story of India's first family hovers just beneath the surface. Never literally, certainly not naively or sentimentally, but as a kind of hidden referent in an account of that moment in time; 'it was absolutely inextricable from what was going on', says Nayantara, 'tied in a tight knot'.[3]

The family – that is her own natal family – as emotional anchor, political lodestar and moral touchstone was critical in Nayantara's personal, political and literary life. She relied on her 'three parents': Vijaya Lakshmi and Ranjit Pandit, and Jawaharlal Nehru, for advice and action-by-example, and derived enormous sustenance from her grandparents and other elders while growing up in Anand Bhawan. By any measure, it was a larger-than-life family; it is hardly surprising that it should have been such a major influence to the extent that, as she readily acknowledges, she had little need of other intimate, confidence-sharing relationships. In itself this may not have been very unusual, but it was accompanied by great admiration for what they represented, the values they stood for and the causes they took up. 'Family', 'politics', 'jail', 'arrests', none of these carried the normal meaning for her as they swirled about her childhood and adolescence; much later, she was to say of them:

> I feel my life has been empty and somewhat worthless by comparison, just incidents and no patterns, no real meaning. That is why I have lived in the past, the long ago past of my childhood, cherishing it and its values

> perhaps too much, clinging to the memory of it far more than was healthy or wise.[4]

Nayantara was heir to both the liberal, westernised education of the Nehrus, as well as to its reasonably conservative social and family conventions. Widowed women like her Bibima (Motilal Nehru's teenaged sister-in-law) were expected to observe all the prohibitions of widowhood; in extreme cases, like that of her paternal great-grandmother, even a self-immolation on her husband's funeral pyre seemed to be in order. The world outside the home was negotiated by the men in the family, for which a certain adjustment to Western manners and modes of behaviour was permissible, but there was no good reason for this to invade the private, domestic space; and so kitchens for vegetarian and non-vegetarian cooking were scrupulously segregated and the inner courtyards remained screened from public view. Vijaya Lakshmi Pandit's mother may have emerged in response to Gandhi's call for satyagraha, but this was an exceptional crossing over the threshold onto the streets. Nayantara's own mother was educated at home by governesses (albeit in a modern idiom), a mark of privilege no doubt, but also of a generational and social norm. Riding and swimming were also allowed her, but she was told quite firmly that she couldn't pursue her love for dance, and when it came to marriages, well, these were still arranged; Jawaharlal's to Kamala Kaul (of Sitaram Bazaar, Old Delhi) was not significantly different from his father's – or, for that matter, his sister's. Both acquiesced with the custom.

While still in her teens, Vijaya Lakshmi Pandit had become romantically involved with a young man, Syed

Hossain, from a prominent then-nationalist Muslim family, who had been made editor of a newspaper just started by Motilal Nehru, *The Independent*. Their relationship developed far enough for them to consider 'eloping', but they were apprehended and their plans nipped in the bud. Gandhi's intervention in preventing this potentially unacceptable interfaith marriage has been noted by several commentators, but he did more than just express his disapproval: he suggested that Vijaya Lakshmi Pandit spend some time with him in Sabarmati Ashram where the rigours of a 'simple life' and a disciplinary denial of all indulgences, physical as well as emotional, would be an effective antidote to any fanciful romantic tendencies. Vijaya Lakshmi's subsequent engagement to Ranjit Pandit, eleven years older than her, within three days of their meeting, had the blessings of all concerned. In many ways, Ranjit's family was similar to the Nehrus, though not Kashmiri. His father, like Motilal, had trained as a lawyer at the Bar in England, and had migrated from Maharashtra to Rajkot where they were landowners. And Ranjit, like Jawaharlal, followed in his father's footsteps; he was educated at the Sorbonne, the University of Heidelberg and the Middle Temple. After returning to India, he joined the legal firm of Sir B.L. Mitter in Calcutta, and this is where he and Vijaya Lakshmi lived after their wedding.

After marriage, Sarup Nehru became Vijaya Lakshmi, conforming to yet another norm, that of relinquishing both maiden names and taking on what was assigned to her by her in-laws: the conquering goddess, Lakshmi, to match her husband's Ranjit – victory. Had it not been for her brother's and husband's encouragement, she may never have entered politics; once she did, however, she achieved considerable political, diplomatic and public success in her own right. Syed Hossain apparently never recovered from his love for Sarup Nehru; he remained single, opted for India after Partition and was the country's ambassador to Egypt before his sudden death in 1949. Nayantara and her sister, Lekha, were received by him in Cairo in 1948 on their return from Paris to India.

As a role model, Vijaya Lakshmi Pandit would have been formidable. Westernised, yet completely Indian in her gregarious open-heartedness, plunging into the turmoil of the freedom movement and all the dislocation of family it entailed, yet never failing to keep the children within her warm and loving embrace. Her political activity was almost as frenetic and sustained as her brother's and husband's, but she combined it with housekeeping when in Allahabad, attending to the demands made on a household that, in fact, was open house not only to friends and relatives but to vast numbers of Congress workers and people in general.

Though idealised by their daughters, their parents' marriage of twenty-three years was marked by long absences as each of them was imprisoned by turn, or at the same time but in separate jails. Ranjit Pandit was already a Congress volunteer, and party work would have claimed him almost totally during the times he was out of jail. By the early 1930s, Vijaya Lakshmi Pandit herself was fully active, referring to herself as the 'dictator' of the Allahabad City Congress Committee; she presided over the meeting in January 1932 when the Independence Pledge was reiterated. Naturally, they were all arrested and dispatched to the Allahabad District Jail. Vijaya Lakshmi was sentenced to one year's rigorous imprisonment and a fine of fifteen hundred rupees. This, her first prison term, was to be served in Lucknow – a pattern that would be repeated again and again, with prison an almost indivisible part of her marriage.

In 1944, when Vijaya Lakshmi was forty-four years old, Ranjit Pandit died soon after his release from custody, as a direct consequence of medical neglect and bureaucratic dereliction; one might even say, deliberate callousness on the part of jail authorities. In December 1943, while in Bengal on relief work for the Bengal Famine, she received a telegram from the superintendent of Bareilly Central Jail to say that Ranjit had suffered a 'mild heart attack' a week earlier. Her initial request for an interview was denied, but a letter to the governor gained her permission and she left immediately for Bareilly. Ranjit Pandit was in very bad shape. After a series of frantic moves and interventions by the civil surgeon, she succeeded in having him moved to the Civil Hospital in Lucknow, where he appeared to be improving. A month later, however, on 14 January 1944, he passed away – his release from prison had come too late.

Vijaya Lakshmi Pandit was bereft and completely alone. Nehru was in Ahmadnagar Fort Jail, her daughters were in the US, the few relatives they had in Lucknow were in the service of the British government and couldn't help. Stunned with grief after her husband's last rites were performed, she found she was in for another shock: because Ranjit had died without writing his will, all his assets, moveable and immoveable, were inherited by his brother; his widow could make no claim on them. Sir Tej Bahadur Sapru, a friend and colleague of Motilal Nehru's, was appalled by the swift and decisive action taken by Ranjit's brother, Pratap, who froze all Ranjit's bank accounts in Allahabad. Sir Tej decided to file a suit on Vijaya Lakshmi's behalf. 'You can't win,' he told her, 'but I want to make this an example and will appear in court myself.' They lost, of course, but newspaper editorials on the injustice of existing Hindu law appeared across the country. In despair, and hoping that he could intercede with Pratap, she turned to Gandhi, who was then in Juhu after his release from prison. He wrote back to say: 'You are the daughter, sister, wife of great men. I will not condole with you. Come to me as soon as you can.' Gandhi tried to intervene with Ranjit's brother, Pratap, but with little success; the latter claimed that the law was on his side, which in fact, it was. He agreed only to transfer the small amount of money that was in his joint account with his brother, that which represented Ranjit's own earnings. Gandhi advised Vijaya Lakshmi to return to Bengal, to never look back. In March that year, Nehru, writing from jail, said he regretted Ranjit's lack of foresight in not leaving a will, but reminded Nan (as she was known in the family) that, as far as he was concerned, his sisters were co-owners with him of Anand Bhawan, and of any other property their father might have left.[5]

Somewhat comforted but still bewildered, Vijaya Lakshmi Pandit left Allahabad to continue her relief work in Bengal. Over four decades later, when she was India's high commissioner in England, Winston Churchill said to her, 'We killed your husband, didn't we?' 'No,' she responded, 'every man lives to his appointed hour.'[6]

The death of her father dealt a huge emotional blow to Nayantara. Her last meeting with him had been in 1943 at Naini Central Prison in Allahabad, where she visited him with Lekha before the two of them set sail for the US. Less than six months later, on a bitterly cold, snowy day in January in the home of Elly and H. H. Razzack, an Indian engineer in New York, they received the news of his passing away. This untimely death, more tragic because it could so easily have been prevented, deprived his daughters of an adored and idealised father. Their adolescent and teenage years in the US would most probably have seen a lively correspondence between them as new vistas and experiences, both intellectual and emotional, opened up before them. But letters to and from prison were never easy, always censored and delayed; and Nayantara remembers receiving just one from her father between August 1943 and January 1944. Although both she and Lekha bravely rallied round their mother from afar, the feeling of being orphaned was acute:

> Never again would I see him walking on the dew-wet grass of early morning, as he had loved to do, a brown Kashmir shawl thrown over his white, khadi-clad figure. Never again would I be able to talk to him of books and music, of stars and trees and people, of the thousand things he had taught me to understand. Never again would I be with him in the pine-scented air of Khali, watching the sunsets on the snow-topped mountain peaks or hearing him sing as he worked in the garden.
>
> It was ironic that he had had to go, my gallant, laughter-loving father to whom life was adventure, a day-to-day challenge accepted with zest and enthusiasm. His was not the dreary world of politics and prisons to which he had chosen to be confined. He had called

> himself a 'proud pagan'. He should have been free and untrammelled, left to think and write creatively, to fulfil his vast talent for living. An independent India could deservedly have flaunted his scholarly genius, hailed him as an ambassador of her culture to foreign lands. But a subject India had chosen him to serve among her martyrs, and a prison, the grey symbol of all that was opposed to his nature, had claimed him in the end. For me, India would be empty without him, every familiar place echoing his gay voice, mirroring his smile. I wanted to run back through time into the security of his presence and his wisdom, cancelling the years that had taken him from me, but I had to go forward. Lekha had already gone back to India, and Rita had been there at the time of Papu's death and after. For me, the lonely ordeal still remained.
>
> Bitterness filled me that he had to die, till I remembered that bitterness had been his most scorned enemy. He had sent us away so that we would grow up free from it, strong and proud, 'children of the light', as he had said. To bow before it now would be to deny all that he had lived for and the purpose for which he had died.[7]

Ranjit Pandit was a polymath. Lawyer and linguist, he was fluent in French and German in addition to other European and Indian languages. He was also a Sanskrit scholar and his translation of the Kashmiri classic, *Rajatarangini* (which he did during one of his jail terms and dedicated to his father-in-law, Motilal Nehru), was highly regarded. He was a crack rider, sportsman and shot, had studied Western and Indian classical music, and played the tabla and violin with considerable talent. During their brief courtship, Vijaya Lakshmi Pandit recounts how he 'recited beautiful Sanskrit verses' and gifted her a tiny silk-bound Gita that had been his father's treasured possession with the words, 'It is the most precious thing I possess'.[8]

The Pandit house in Rajkot was nearly as grand as Anand Bhawan, a sprawling estate with tennis courts and stables, and Ranjit's parents kept an open house that was visited by all the local luminaries, among them the young lawyer from South Africa, Mohandas Karamchand Gandhi. It was Gandhi who drew Ranjit Pandit into the nationalist struggle, much against his family's wishes, and through whom he was introduced to the Allahabad Nehrus. He was a reluctant recruit. Not only because he would have to give up a promising legal career with Sir B.L. Mitter in Calcutta, but because he had reservations about Gandhi's creed of non-violence. What was more, he 'loathed the masses', according to his wife, and he did not want her, especially, to be rubbing shoulders with them. Having married the young Sarup Nehru, however, and become a son-in-law of the freedom movement's leading family, it was only a matter of time before his induction was total.

Nayantara doubted that her father would have continued in politics had he lived in independent India, recalling how, on his deathbed, he laughingly told a friend who had come to visit, 'My wife is a very foolish woman, her only interest is politics.' His own interests were far more wide-ranging and eclectic; he would most probably have indulged his passion for translation, collaborated perhaps with Edward Thompson (the historian E.P. Thompson's father) on a history of the River Ganga; and pursued and developed his love of horticulture on his estate in Khali, in the Kumaon foothills. Here, in this idyllic spot, he planted fruit trees – apricot, peach, apple, cherry, orange and pear; tended a flower garden in which fuschia, geraniums and primulas were resplendent, raised chickens and kept cows for milk; and grew wheat and vegetables. Everything that was consumed in Khali was home-grown, with days set aside for baking bread and biscuits, and making jams whenever the fruit ripened. From Khali too, he wrote charming, funny, serious letters to Lekha and Tara at Woodstock in Mussoorie, news about the poultry farm ('Khali now has a hundred chickens: here a chick, there a chick, everywhere a chick-chick'), experiments with Lysenko's method of vernalisation, and the health of the wheat crop, interspersed with political news and views:

> The Viceroy in India appealed to everyone to pray for the British Empire and victory against Hitler ... I was rather far from the Viceroy and was pretty sure he would not notice if I did not pray. In fact I did not.[9]

At Khali, moreover, Ranjit Pandit hosted writers like Rabindranath Tagore, who urged him to translate Kalidas's *Ritusamhara* into English, which he did during his prison term in Naini Central Jail. It was published posthumously, with a frontispiece by Nandalal Bose and a salutation by Sarojini Naidu.

Nothing really happens in *A Time to Be Happy*, no dramatic unfoldings, no unexpected denouement. Its tone is measured and unhurried, almost leisurely, but it contains many of the seeds that germinate in Nayantara's subsequent novels. Here is a newly independent nation, its citizens caught in a kind of suspended animation while the country tries to arrive at a self-definition that is in consonance with its political ideals. Our nameless narrator becomes the bridge between pre- and post-independence India, an interlocutor as it were, carrying forward Gandhi's call for village upliftment, reviving handicrafts and handloom, offering an alternative both to British trading and British manufacturing. Sanad gives up his comfortable life and job in an Anglicised Indian society to work with the poor; and Maya, Harish's unhappily married wife, does likewise.

All the marriages in *A Time to Be Happy* are dysfunctional – except one, Govind Narayan and Lakshmi's – and this was to remain a preoccupation in Nayantara's future novels, a leitmotif in a way; ('marriages go wrong in all my novels,' she says) and the narrator and Maya's painfully realised but unfulfilled love for each other is a precursor to later unhappy realisations and relationships. It is not difficult to see why this is so; in *A Time to Be Happy* all the women are more fully developed as characters, with a depth and weight that their male counterparts lack. Savitri and Prabha, especially, demonstrate the kind of maturity that comes of inner poise and a wise understanding of people and circumstances. Savitri's response to the choices made by her beloved son, Sahdev, and to his accidental and terrible death after a student demonstration, is extraordinary. When asked whether he has her permission to take part in the fight, she replies:

> He has my prayers, since I cannot stop him, but there is one great consolation. Though they must fight, they will fight peacefully. There will be no bloodshed. The Mahatma when he preached non-violence understood many things,

> but the greatest of these was his understanding of a mother's heart.[10]

When she receives the news of Sahdev's death, she says quietly:

> It was so needless. I cannot believe his Bharat Mata expected such a sacrifice of him … I could not understand why I had not been taken in his place …
>
> God himself, all powerful though he is, is omnipotent only in the realm of goodness. Who knows, perhaps he himself weeps for all who suffer, realising his own helplessness before evil.[11]

One cannot say that Savitri or Prabha are new India's 'modern' women, but one can see in them that moral fibre and compassion – and what Nayantara calls 'an immense quiet strength' – that enables them to, metaphorically speaking, leave their husbands behind. They were the extraordinary, ordinary women of the freedom movement for whom Nayantara had no obvious model (as she did for her narrator or Sanad or Sahdev) but who were all around at the time, and were on the cusp of huge change. Maya, shadowy and insubstantial in this first novel, will appear later as a more evolved and sentient character, an actor in her own right.

But Nayantara's continuing character is India, or as she herself puts it, 'a glittering aspiration called India', as translated through people's experiences, through the political and social scene, and the implications of politics on character. Starting out as a passive observer of what seemed to be a benign national environment where things could only get better, she 'watched the landscape darken and become beset by every kind of evil'. Her early novels follow a kind of chronological sequence, right upto the Emergency of 1975, and each one after *A Time to Be Happy* has one central concern, usually of national importance.

Pearl Buck, in India at the time to film *The Guide,* told Nayantara that she thought *A Time to Be Happy* was a very good *first* novel, but John Masters, who reviewed it in London, was impatient with the fact that 'things could have happened but nothing did'. He was particularly annoyed by what he thought was a completely 'unreal' situation, that Maya and the narrator did not have an affair. Indeed, Maya's disappearance from the narrative is somewhat inexplicable, but in Nayantara's view, the whole novel is 'an ongoing scene' with no real ending in the conventional sense. And yet, she said, she would have written it differently had she been writing it now, developed the narrator more fully instead of using him as a device, and reworked the last part of the novel, the one dealing with the immediate post-independence period.[12] Yet, despite its absence of plot, the novel was warmly received both in the US and UK, partly because it was one of the earliest novels in English about independent India to come out of India, and also because India herself was of considerable interest as an emerging nation.

It was also markedly different from the novels of her contemporaries writing in English about India, writers like R.K. Narayan, Raja Rao, Kamala Markandaya, Mulk Raj Anand; albeit loosely structured, its realism was refreshing and her obvious empathy with her protagonists infused her writing with the kind of warmth that endeared them to her readers, even though there might sometimes have been a hint of caricature about them.

This Time of Morning, Nayantara's second novel, dedicated to her sisters, Chandralekha and Rita, was published in 1965 after a gap of seven years, and by this time she had reached a turning point in her life. Despite the hiatus in her marriage, her personal life had continued more or less predictably in its settled groove of Bombay-Delhi-Chandigarh, divided up according to the children's school vacations, and short breaks with her mother and sisters wherever in the world they happened to be. But in 1964, an encounter with Nirmal Mangat Rai, an ICS officer in the Punjab cadre, during their winter holiday in Chandigarh affected her with what she would later call 'fatality and finality', though at the time it was merely an irritant.

Chandigarh was India's first post-independence city, not only because it was planned but because its very existence was a consequence of independence – and of Partition. Having lost Lahore to West Punjab and Pakistan, East Punjab was left without a capital, and the problem was compounded by the fact that much of what was now Punjab was actually part of Patiala state. From 1947 till 1953–54, when Chandigarh was officially inaugurated, the state capital shifted from Ambala to Jalandhar to Simla, the government always in transit and with no fixed address. The question of where to build the new capital was beset by all kinds of thorny issues, ranging from local political pressure to financial considerations. One thing, however, was clear: none of the existing cities could be converted into the capital. Amritsar was too close to the border and a hostile Pakistan; Ambala was a cantonment town and didn't have the infrastructure for future growth; Jalandhar and Ludhiana couldn't accommodate the flood of refugees or provide good enough communication facilities. Three things were considered essential for the new capital: strategic and military security; adequate space for the government machinery, for refugees and for future expansion; and the potential to replace the material and psychological loss of Lahore, the cultural and commercial hub of Punjab.

Chandigarh, chosen after much to-ing and fro-ing between the prime minister, the premier of East Punjab, Gopichand Bhargava, and its governor, Chandulal Trivedi, was selected by airplane reconnaissance. Located approximately 390 kms. north of Delhi, it is situated at the bottom of the picturesque Shivalik range of the Himalayas, bounded on the east and west by two seasonal rivers, the Sukhna and Patiala Rao. Eight thousand five hundred acres of fertile land, dotted with mango groves, covered the first phase of ten square miles of capital-building. The total area to be acquired for the two phases of development consisted of 28,000 acres in fifty-eight villages, in the Kharar tehsil. Nehru, on his first visit to the site, declared happily, 'The site chosen is free from the existing encumbrances of old towns and old traditions. Let it be the first large expression of our creative genius flowering on our newly-earned freedom.'[13]

The best possible talent was engaged to plan the new capital. An initial idea to hold an international competition for its design was abandoned, not only because it might have been too expensive but also because a planner from the West was unlikely to know the social context of the country. A new city, a planned city for a modern India, would clearly need to break with some aspects of the past, but it would surely have an Indian character. Two Western town planners, Albert Mayer and Otto Koenigsberger, were already in India at the time, the former having served as a lieutenant-colonel in India during World War II, and the latter, a German Jew, who had fled Nazi Germany and arrived in India at the invitation of the diwan of Mysore. He had been involved as a consultant in planning Orissa's new capital, Bhubaneswar, as well as Faridabad in Haryana and Gandhidham in Gujarat. Mayer was similarly familiar with social development projects, most actively with Franklin D. Roosevelt's New Deal programme on housing policies. In India as a US Army civil engineer, he built airfields in Bengal, was adviser to the city of Kanpur, and had worked on preliminary studies for the master plan of Greater Bombay.[14]

Both men welcomed the opportunity to prepare a plan for Chandigarh, but ultimately Mayer was selected. A master plan was drawn up by him, but fate and circumstances intervened to prevent him from designing the housing and government complex. In the event, and after visits to various European capitals, the English architects, Maxwell Fry and Jane Drew, and the Swiss-French architect, le Corbusier (who famously said, 'Your capital can be built right here, at 35 rue de Sèvres,' when told he would have to spend at least three years in Chandigarh) were hired to implement Mayer's plan.[15] Together they embarked on a design project that was not only bold and experimental in architectural terms, but also sought to 'redesign' social relations by reconfiguring the relationship of private and public space, between the government and those governed. This experiment was not, and has not been, without its detractors and naysayers, professional and lay, and planned Chandigarh has come in for its fair share of criticism. But as Nehru, in many ways the original inspiration and 'architect-planner' for Chandigarh, said in 1959:

> I have welcomed very greatly one experiment in India, Chandigarh. Many people argue about it, some like it, and some dislike it. It is the biggest example in India of experimental architecture. It hits you on the head and makes you think. You may squirm at the impact but it has made you think and imbibe new ideas, and the one thing which India requires in many fields is being hit on the head so that it may think. I do not like every building in Chandigarh. I like some of them very much. I like the general conception of the township very much but, above all, I like the creative approach, not being tied down to what has been done by our forefathers, but thinking in new terms, of light and air and ground and water and human beings. Therefore, Chandigarh is of enormous importance.[16]

He could not, in 1959, have known just how important it would become in his niece's life.

Gautam Sahgal bought his piece of land measuring 4,550 sq. yds. in Chandigarh in August 1953 for the sum of Rs 22,218, and was directed to complete the construction of a residential unit on it within five years. His choice of Pierre Jeanneret as its architect was unsurprising, as much of Chandigarh's domestic architecture fell to him and the Fry-Drew team. The only private homes he designed, however, in addition to the Sahgals', were the residences of prominent Chandigarh citizens Nirlep Kaur and Mrs I. D. Oberoi (of the Patiala royal family and Oberoi chain of hotels, respectively) and of P. L. Varma, chief engineer of Chandigarh's Capital Project. All four homes were located along Uttar Marg, the avenue defining the north-east edge of Chandigarh's residential area, and all the plots were roughly one acre each. Zoning regulations required that boundary walls along this avenue be kept low in order to afford an uninterrupted view of the hills beyond, and this became a major asset and common design determinant for all four homes.

The Sahgal home, situated on a corner plot, sits on about a fourth of the entire plot. It was designed as a duplex unit with public spaces and service areas on the ground floor, and bedrooms on the upper floor. These were arranged in a single row, each oriented towards a view of Sukhna lake and the hills in the distance. The most dramatic feature of the house was a ramp connecting the ground to the first floor, a bold design statement, setting off the black terrazzo floors and white painted walls. A shallow pool (built against Gautam Sahgal's wishes) separated the two wings of the house, and was regularly used by him to cool his bottles of beer!

Anokha (so named by Nehru) was built with Nayantara in mind, but she was far from happy with its design. She disliked the ramp intensely, said it made her feel as if she were in an airport, and complained about the 'sheer impracticality' of the whole house: 'What possessed anyone to design or approve it? Obviously both people responsible were men: Jeanneret and Gautam. More and more am of the opinion that men least practical creatures on God's earth.'[17] She listed the house's 'absurdities': it assumed its owners' great wealth, the presence of a retinue of servants, and high maintenance – miles of black floors and glass doors and windows. She decided to beard the lion in his den and speak to Jeanneret about a compromise solution to The Ramp. Her account of their exchange in her *Chandigarh Diary* is hilarious.

> Jeanneret arrives – small, bald, with fringe of longish white hair at base of skull. Bow tie, bell-bottom trousers. 'You and me combat?' he asks. I assure him no combat. 'Then why this here?' 'This' is Ranjit's chest-expander lying on stool, which I assure Jeanneret is not preparation for combat.
>
> We study ramp. Gautam gives alternative solution which he had propounded two nights earlier when he, I, and Shiv returned from Bill Mathula's dinner. Solution: Wall to break up hall. Lower half of ramp to be replaced by staircase. Solution presented by Gautam as mine. Jeanneret aghast. Pronounces it architectural imbecility. 'Le ramp est le ramp! Cannot be half stair, half ramp!' Adds: 'Le ramp est signature of house!' Adds: 'This no bourgeois conception like every other house of staircase.' Says Gautam: 'My wife thinks entrance dominated by ramp resembles airport.' Jeanneret burst out: 'But airport one very modern building!'
>
> I venture to say airport inside house rather inconvenient. Feel I am culprit as Gautam declares he loves ramp. Argument back where we started. We repair to drawing room to resume drink, then again to corridor to study ramp.
>
> 'Le ramp majestique! One beautiful view of whole corridor upon entrance,' says Jeanneret.

> Much discussion, at end of which Jeanneret says, 'Only for you will think of systême. But very difficile. Must keep la vérite.' I agree. So grateful that Jeanneret will think of 'systême' that I invite him to soup and salad on 9th.[18]

The ramp stayed. But Anokha had its pluses too: the children loved it, the garden was a pure pleasure, and the views were spectacular.

The excitement of living in a brand new city with a designer stamp isn't hard to imagine, but it wasn't only its physical aspect that was newly minted. Everything started from scratch – offices, schools and colleges, marketplaces, hospitals, businesses, the government, fledgling cultural groups. Chandigarh, as its historian Ravi Kalia notes, represents the '... individual and collective account of its citizens, striving for self-determination, self-knowledge and self-actualisation...'[19]

Who were they, the new citizens of Chandigarh, who inhabited the city and defined its post-Partition personality? Just as much of pre-Partition Lahore's cultural community – painters, writers, film-makers – gravitated to Bombay, its professionals and bureaucrats moved to Delhi – and to Chandigarh, if they happened to belong to the Punjab cadre of the ICS and IAS. College teachers and university professors, doctors and lawyers, government servants who had first relocated to Simla, then moved to Chandigarh, made up its social circle. And among them were members of Lahore's bohemian set, free-thinking, liberal, either in the arts or in education and government service. Khushwant and Kaval Singh, Bunchi and his wife Champa Mangat Rai, Jaya (Kikook, who also happened

Dec. 1962 Jan. 1963

Jan. 6, 1963

Pen to paper again. What a relief, though not as satisfactory as typewriter, particularly since subject also full of endless annoyances, eg. sheer impracticality of entire house. What possessed anyone to design or approve it? Obviously both people responsible were men: Jeanneret & Gautam. More and more am of opinion that men least practical creatures on God's earth. The ramp. It must go. Gives one feeling upon entering house that it's airport – up ramp with luggage, alongside with passport & health papers. Aside from this, aesthetically wrong. No proportion. Too large & space-eating, quite hideous.

to be Bunchi's cousin) and Jivat Thadani, Sarla and Balbir Grewal, both with the government; the playwright Balwant Gargi, Arthur and Sheila Lall (Bunchi's sister). Prem Kirpal, then a journalist, and the Tony Fletchers (the same A. L. Fletcher who, as officer on special duty, Capital Project, had opposed holding an international competition to select a planner for Chandigarh). The *Hindustan Times* had its correspondent, Krishan Bhatia, *The Statesman* sent Pran Chopra, and *The Indian Express* had its local reporters. Dr Kaka Swift, in charge of government hospitals, and his wife Prem; Guddo and Navin Thakur, who did a great deal for Hindi theatre in Chandigarh, the architect Jugal Chowdhury and his wife, Eulie, and many others formed a close-knit social circle that remained constant for many years. It was a highly westernised, cosmopolitan group; most of the men had been educated at Oxford or Cambridge and all the women had university degrees. More than this, however, was their completely open and somewhat unusual attitude to marriage and extramarital relationships. At one time or another, some of them had had romantic and sexual liaisons with each others' husbands or wives, which were neither clandestine nor considered reprehensible. Such had been their way of life in Lahore, and so it continued in Chandigarh – intellectually vibrant, socially gregarious, sexually and romantically freewheeling.

Nayantara loved being in Chandigarh but was a complete misfit in this circle. Her winters at Anokha saw hectic socialising and constant comings and goings between the families and their children – and of course, visits by her sisters and their children – but deep down, she remained aloof from it all. The best times of the day for her were afternoons and after dinner, when she could read in bed. These were simply not to be 'jeopardised by aimless chatter and drinking', a complete waste of time in her view. She was aware that she was considered a curiosity in Chandigarh because: '1) live in slacks; 2) like privacy and only too happy to be alone; 3) have tendency to make remarks like: "Indians don't hold their liquor well". Have a feeling am not too popular on this score.'[20] In an unguarded moment at one of the Chandigarh parties, Bunchi Mangat Rai confronted her with her reserve: 'You have been coming here for four years,' he said, 'and we still don't know you.' She could not deny the truth of his observation. 'I am essentially a secret person,' she responded, 'reserve is natural to me even with those I know best.'[21]

And so, although she knew – could not but know – of Bunchi's affair with Kaval Khushwant Singh, of his own wife Champa's liaison with his brother-in-law, Arthur Lall; of Prem Kirpal's undying devotion to Kaval; and the dalliances of the Fletchers and Thadanis and Chowdhurys, she kept herself to herself. She admitted that she had never lived in a society that demanded more of her 'than I, in my reticence was prepared to give', but that she could not share herself indiscriminately, that her rewards derived from solitariness. That chance remark, Bunchi's astute observation, however, would catapult her into a relationship that eventually changed the course of her life and, in some ways, of her writing too.

Edward Nirmal Mangat Rai or Bunchi (as a baby his cheeks were like a bunch of roses) belonged to a family of prominent Punjabi Christians in Punjab, all of whom were in education, government service or the professions. The Mangat Rais were a Multan family settled in Abbottabad. At the age of eighteen, Bunchi's father formally and openly abandoned Hinduism and became a Christian, out of choice and conviction. This made for a more or less permanent break with his family, compounded by the fact that his parents filed a civil suit against him because he refused to relinquish his surname after his conversion. Lala Lajpat Rai argued on behalf of Bunchi's grandparents, but the court ruled in his father's favour.

Bunchi's maternal grandfather, Kali Charan Chatterji, had similarly turned his back on his Kulin Brahmin heritage and converted to Christianity in 1854. He too renounced his home and family, left Bengal for Jalandhar, and in 1862 married the second daughter of Reverend Golak Nath, at whose invitation he had moved to this city. Subsequently, he joined the Forman Christian College in Lahore as junior professor of mathematics, but his heart was in missionary work and he was ordained to the priesthood in 1868. Through his maternal grandmother Bunchi was related by marriage to the Kapurthala clan, as one of his grand-aunts married Raja Harnam Singh who gave up his claim to the Kapurthala *gaddi* because he had converted. This side of his family, Bunchi said, represented 'the leadership of the Christian community in Punjab's Doaba' and included Rajkumari Amrit Kaur (India's first health minister), Raja Sir Maharaj Singh and Kanwar Dalip Singh, a prominent judge.[22]

Bunchi and his siblings – Priobala Nina, Charles Rajinder, and Lena Susheila – grew up on a five-acre homestead just outside the town of Abbottabad, and it was here that he received his early education. This was followed by St Stephen's College in Delhi, from where he did his BA and MA with history as his subject, and thence to Oxford, to Keble College, to prepare for the Indian Civil Service. Two years later he returned as a civil servant to Lahore, in the Punjab cadre. Although affected by the fervour of the freedom movement Bunchi remained a passive nationalist as a student; indeed, his choice of the ICS as a career, though difficult, was nevertheless without conflict. Of his other siblings, Priobala stayed on in Lahore after Partition when the rest of the family moved to India, and retired as principal of Kinnaird College. His brother, Raj, was in the army, and a second sister, Sheila, married Arthur Lall, also a Punjabi Christian, who worked for the UN in New York.

In 1944 Bunchi married Champa Singha, daughter of S.P. Singha, also Christian, and living and working in Lahore as a teacher. The Singhas, Rudras, Lalls, Mangat Rais and Chatterjis were part of Lahore's progressive Christian community, with a lively interest in the arts, theatre, music and literature. Uma Chatterji, who later married the film-maker Chetan Anand, was a theatre enthusiast and produced plays in which Champa, Ram Advani (the legendary bookshop owner in Lucknow), and the painter Krishen Khanna took part at various times. The Singhas were a large family and Champa's young niece, a very beautiful woman, married Chetan Anand's younger brother, Dev. Champa herself, an ardent thespian, was senior lecturer in English at the Women's College.

When Punjab was partitioned in 1947 and Lahore assigned to Pakistan, Bunchi opted for India and moved to

Simla where the East Punjab government had established itself in the interim, pending the decision regarding a capital for the new state. In the early 1960s, he moved to Chandigarh as finance commissioner, where he met Gautam Sahgal and assisted him with permissions for the building of Anokha.

Bunchi himself was not a Lahori, was not part of the claret-blazer-silver-grey-trousers set from Government College, nor of that other great Lahore institution, Forman Christian College, or even Punjab University. But he took to the city like a duck to water and his six years there, from 1941 to 1947, were where he 'lived, moved and had his being' as he was to say later. His closest friendships were made in Lahore, and that was where he met and married Champa. Prem Kirpal was teaching at Dayal Singh College; Khushwant Singh had set up his legal practice in the city; Bunchi's sister, Priobala, was vice principal of Kinnaird College; and their reading group included G.D. Khosla, Agha Abdul Hamid, also of the ICS, and Mahmud and Satnam Kaur, son and daughter-in-law of Nawab Muzaffar Khan of Wah. Here too were Wilburn and Usha Lall, who were not just close friends but relatives by marriage, for Bunchi's sister, Sheila, was married to Wilburn's brother, Arthur. And of course, there was Faiz Ahmed Faiz, a great friend of Champa's, along with W.H. Morris-Jones, later employed by Lord Mountbatten in the Viceroy's Secretariat. Pre-Partition Lahore was a city like no other, 'home and hearth, memory and striving, flesh and blood to most of its citizens'. It was catholic in its mix of religions and communities, a seat of learning, culturally vibrant and diverse. Confident in its attraction both for business and the professions, it benefitted from being favoured by the British as well, and was next only to Calcutta as a destination for festive occasions.

Chandigarh could never be Lahore, but to this small group that found itself there post-Partition, it offered the possibility of recreating some of the more congenial aspects of life in Lahore, if not its style or vitality. What it lacked in these, it made up for in warmth and friendliness.

In 1964 Nayantara was thirty-eight years old, a successful writer with three published books, a fourth in progress, and the very real potential for a sustained literary career. Materially, her circumstances reflected both her husband's continuing success and their privileged social and family status. Beautiful, accomplished, adored, popular – to all outward appearances, she led a charmed existence. Yet she was beset with a growing, gnawing unhappiness. The years between her return from London in 1959 and the writing of *This Time of Morning* had been marked by something like a charade of socialising and public activity, a superficial 'reconciliation' with Gautam, accompanied by an intense and increasing solitariness. Never an extrovert, she found herself withdrawing more and more from their varied friends and acquaintances, experiencing a kind of 'deadly detachment' despite having plenty to do.[23] Close and emotionally fulfilling relationships with her parents, sisters and uncle meant she had never made an effort to look beyond them or seek other deep friendships. In any case, she was not given to exchanging confidences, not even with those closest to her – her mother and sisters.

Impossible for her, then, to share with them the depth of her despair over her marriage and her relationship with Gautam. For Nayantara, the two levels at which she lived her life were becoming an unbearable strain, yet she could no more abandon her commitments – what she called her 'sacred duties'[24] – than she could betray a trust. Contrarily and contradictorily, she also acknowledged that she had always kept herself to herself most assiduously, never allowed anyone to come a fraction closer to her than necessary, never reached out a fraction 'more than the exact and measured need of the moment',[25] and if that wasn't selfish, what else could one call it? She was aware too that 'there is a side of me I could never share or involve with any human being, and this side is free and amoral, and perhaps deceitful, if that is what I must call the pursuit of many hungers'.[26]

At the heart of Nayantara's despair about her marriage was the knowledge that not only was it a mismatch, it was fundamentally incompatible; she and Gautam were temperamentally at opposite ends of the pole, disagreeing on relatively minor matters of style as well as on major ones of substance. The values she lived by, he might have acknowledged but couldn't subscribe to himself, and he was unyielding in what he demanded of her – loyalty, total fidelity and complete and utter silence about their marriage. Gautam insisted on nothing less than unconditional obedience to his moral codes, for his part smothering her with unconditional, possessive love.

But Nayantara wanted a companion with whom she could share her interests, not a husband whose adoration would become a cross to bear. She wanted conversation, not social chit-chat, she wanted the space, the freedom to find herself – and be herself, not just a social asset. The more she withdrew from Gautam, the more desperate he became in his ardour; and the more he realised that she was moving away, the greater his attempts to constrain her. Gautam knew, absolutely and intuitively, that Nayantara was hugely attractive to men and that they sought her out avidly. It drove him to distraction and into a state of extreme insecurity. Each time she began to develop an independent friendship or cultivate a relationship based on mutual interests, he reacted violently. Her affair with Noguchi and her attraction to Nicky and Kjeld Packness were dredged up again and again as proof of her unreliability, her waywardness and untrustworthiness. When Nicky visited Bombay in the early 1950s and arranged to meet Nayantara, Gautam locked her into their room at the Cricket Club – and Nicky would have left without seeing her, had a friend (Lily Guzder) not unlocked her room and driven her to the Taj Mahal Hotel to apologise to Nicky. But Gautam continued to subject her to the kind of punishment that would become a habit – refuse to talk, drink recklessly for days, succumb to mood swings of ferocious anger and explosive accusation: How could she have had that affair with Noguchi? What had Nicky meant to her? Who else was there? What was *wrong* with her? Sullen and suspicious he raged against his own helplessness, thrust her from him even as he demanded, and yearned for, her love. He simply couldn't accept that anything was amiss. When she said that there was no meeting of minds between them, that they shared less and less, he said that was nonsense.

> He didn't realise something was wrong and he continued to take refuge in our physical relationship. What was wrong was that I had known another man before him. That was the poison in our marriage.[27]

'You would not lie to me, would you?' Gautam beseeched her. 'If only I could feel I trusted you I could let you have the freedom you want.' But, as she said in a letter to Bunchi in August 1964,

> I found out very early in my marriage that Gautam must be protected from the truth if the truth concerns me. I must enter his world and stay there with him. Then I am free intellectually. Any other kind of freedom he is not prepared to tolerate or discuss.[28]

She longed for something different, for a life of calmness, a life without hysteria, for the 'great unimaginable luxury of being myself'.

In May 1964 Jawaharlal Nehru passed away, and his death created the kind of emotional void in her life that Nayantara had been dreading ever since his health had begun to fail earlier that year. She had wanted to spend a few days with him in Delhi in April but was up to her ears in children, household, school and pointless comings and goings, all of which came in the way of her leaving Bombay. Early on the morning of 27 May, her mother was woken up by a call from Indira Gandhi to say that her father was not at all well and that Vijaya Lakshmi Pandit should rush to Delhi. Nayantara, Mrs Pandit, Nehru's other sister, Krishna Hutheesing and her husband left immediately for Delhi on a special plane sent for them by the president, Dr S. Radhakrishnan. Half an hour short of the capital, the pilot announced that Pandit Nehru had passed away. When they reached Teen Murti House, the crowd that had collected was so thick that their car couldn't get through – they got down and fought their way into the house. Nayantara's sisters – Lekha, who had come from Cairo, and Rita from Europe – Padmaja Naidu and Indira were already there, of course, in a house filled to the brim with people and overflowing with sadness. The whole city was a sea of mourning, with wave upon wave of mourners flowing into the house, ebbing temporarily, then breaking into grief again. Another river of people accompanied the cortège to the samadhi at Rajghat, the family walking beside it as they had last walked with Gandhi's in 1948. This time too it was the last time they would walk with Nehru. After the funeral, when all the mourners and her immediate family had left, Nayantara stayed back at Teen Murti for a few days walking in the gardens with Indira, both weeping silently, struggling to come to terms with their terrible loss.

On 7 June, they took Nehru's ashes to Allahabad. Crowds lined the roads as their motorcade made its way slowly through the streets, and at Anand Bhawan were gathered friends and relatives and staff and servants in sombre mourning. That house which Nayantara remembered as an abode permeated with the joy of living, where the sound of laughter rippled through every room, was now wreathed in silence. She left the others and made her way up to the library where Munshi Kanhaiyalal, the family's general secretary, had laid out a collection of newspaper clippings and magazine articles, photographs and news reports on Nehru from youth to maturity, from handsome young man to care-worn premier. Nayantara scanned them through a mist of tears, then turned and left the room for the last time.

With Nehru's death, Nayantara felt as if the bottom had fallen out of her world – he had been succour and solace, someone she could turn to with all her confusions and contradictions, and get from him comfort and sane counsel. The loss of her father when she was in her teens had been a terrible blow, but at least she still had Mamu; preoccupied and beleaguered though he was as PM, he was always available to her, and in him she found the refuge she needed in her turbulent marriage. He was gone now, at a time when her relationship with Gautam was at its lowest ebb. Her sorrow was unbearable.

Back in Bombay, although her normal routine resumed and there was more than enough to keep her busy, she was strangely disconnected from everything around her. Occasional weekends with her mother, now governor of Maharashtra, at Raj Bhawan and at the beach near the governor's cottage allowed her to escape the flat for brief spells. In August she and Gautam went to Srinagar for the weekend, stopping in Chandigarh on the way to plant a magnolia sapling that Gautam had brought back from Switzerland. The garden at Anokha was ablaze with roses in full bloom; Nayantara picked them by the dozen, stowed them in the car that took them back to Delhi, then drove straight to Rajghat and laid them at Nehru's samadhi.

She remembered 1964 as a year of grieving.[29]

Gautam's frequent trips to the Ciba head office in Basel and to Delhi, where his skills in networking and entertaining were shown to great advantage, afforded Nayantara some temporary respite from the non-stop socialising that Gautam relished in Bombay, but which she found dreadfully boring. She might then go across to meet Frank Moraes – then editor of *The Indian Express* – for whom she wrote the occasional political column and whose company she liked; or drop in to see Noshu Banerjee, her mother's neighbour at E 8 Mafatlal Park, with whom the writer Attia Hosain would stay on her visits from London. On the rare evenings that she and Gautam spent at home she enjoyed a quiet drink with him, her feet up, and the hope of some companionable conversation. She would have liked to talk to him about her writing, even though Gautam never read what she wrote, or her worries about Ranjit, sensitive by nature, and how he was faring at the Doon School where he had been sent much against her wishes. But Gautam was usually unresponsive.

That September, she went with the girls to her mother in Poona, a wonderful break from the incessant rain in Bombay. The garden at Raj Bhavan was a riot of colour, it was cool and light in the evenings, and at night the scent of jasmine filled the air and wafted into the veranda where Nayantara slept. She relaxed, wrote easily and felt somewhat restored, as if she 'had had half a glass of wine at eleven o'clock in the morning of a medium-warm day'.[30] She was close to finishing *This Time of Morning*, needing only to tie up a few untidy ends and put the final touches on her minister, Kalyan Sinha.

This Time of Morning is not only a more assured and confident novel than *A Time to Be Happy*, it has a much more clearly developed storyline with stronger characterisation and delineation of relationships. Once again, the time is the early post-independence years but the scene has shifted to Delhi, capital of the new bureaucracy and of power politics. Its protagonist, Rakesh, a young foreign service officer, grows up in Allahabad at a time when young men are ardent nationalists. Like them, he flirted with student politics; when the time to opt for a career came up, he chose to serve the country rather than enter corporate life much to the disappointment of his father, who had sent him to America, not England, for further education.

Rakesh returns after a long stint abroad to find subtle but unmistakable shifts in the power dynamics of the foreign office. The controversial but charismatic Kalyan Sinha (whom Rakesh had first encountered as a student in Boston) has the prime minister's ear and has managed to upstage both Sir Arjun Mitra, the Secretary General, and Kailas Vrind in the ministry of external affairs. Maverick and arrogant, accustomed to leading from the front, Kalyan Sinha has little use for protocol or social niceties. His personal history is a question mark; he has come up from his bootstraps, single-handedly and tirelessly raised funds, fought for India's freedom in the US – and left behind a trail of broken hearts. Back in India he becomes the fulcrum around which a new kind of rough and compromised politics comes into play, accompanied by a moral corruption which old stalwarts like Sir Arjun and Kailas Vrind are unable to either accept or withstand.

At the centre of the novel is the revered PM and his idea of independent India – progressive, democratic, a non-aligned alternative to the great games of the superpowers. A nation ready to take its place in the modern world, ready moreover, to experiment boldly with socialism and secularism. With him in government are fellow-travellers from the freedom movement but also, now, impatient go-getters like Kalyan Sinha and opportunists like Hari Mohan, a one-time halwai of Allahabad, now made good, and his political beneficiaries in UP. Their idea of India is somewhat different from that of the PM's and of officers like Sir Arjun and Kailas, as well as young hopefuls like Rakesh.

The PM's dream of his country becoming a beacon across Asia is symbolised by the Peace Institute, a project dear to his heart. As the novel progresses, however, it begins to attract the kind of adventurers and shysters who are drawn towards Hari Mohan and Kalyan Sinha like moths to a flame. Slowly, the dream project is contaminated by corrupt practice, and even though old-guard values eventually triumph and Kalyan is worsted, the canker of destruction has taken hold.

A secondary set of characters coalesces around this core and, through them, another institution begins to unravel: marriage. The thread that had come loose in *A Time to Be Happy* now unwinds rapidly. Rashmi – Kailas and Mira's young daughter and Rakesh's childhood sweetheart – has left her husband and come back to her parents' home; Sir Arjun's wife, Uma, has long made a mockery of their marriage, scorning both her husband's bed and his dignity; Neil Berenson, the Danish architect of the Peace Institute to be built in Buddha Jayanti Park, is divorced and enters into an extramarital relationship with Rashmi; Kalyan, the quintessential bachelor, would never allow himself to be contained by marriage anyway. And Nita, the nubile and impressionable young daughter of a minor couple in the book, the Narangs, acquiesces to a marriage that she knows will be bleak and loveless. In a desperate yet supremely self-aware gesture, she allows Kalyan to take her to his bed before she gives herself up to her future husband and to a game of pretence for the rest of her life.

As with *A Time to Be Happy*, the characters in *This Time of Morning* mirror many familiar personalities. Kalyan Sinha is clearly the magnetic Krishna Menon, who aroused strong feelings in all those he came into contact with, but enjoyed the trust and confidence of Nehru – the PM in the novel. Kailas is Nayantara's mother, Vijaya Lakshmi Pandit, whose differences with Krishna Menon at the United Nations were well known and documented. So close was the resemblance that Dr S. Radhakrishnan, writing to Mrs Pandit after the publication of the novel, began his letter with, 'Dear Kailas!' And Rashmi is the author herself, just prior to the break-up of her marriage. Sir Arjun Mitra is based on Sir Girja Shankar Bajpai, India's first Secretary General in the Ministry of External Affairs (and her New York friend, Uma Shankar's father) – but there the resemblance ends.

The central and most compelling character in the novel is Kalyan Sinha, a man driven by a burning zeal to get things done, to forge change, to bulldoze his way through obstacles. He suffers neither fools nor the favoured, but he pauses to take note of knaves – if they serve his purpose. In a startlingly eloquent passage the reader is made privy to perhaps the only moment of self-reflection that he allows himself:

> Kalyan stood at the long window of his office, overlooking the courtyard where cars were parked. A tall, bearded,

scarlet-clad sentry stood at the wrought-iron gates leading to Rashtrapati Bhavan. All around him lay the planned precision of New Delhi and beyond it, the layer upon layer of the old city. Dilli! The cry of plunderers from the north, the seat of great vanished empires, and now the heart of this young republic. Kalyan was amused by the conjectures about himself. Everyone seemed so concerned with what he wanted because so much was now within his reach. He had, without seeking it, acquired a following and it was more than the garlands at airports and neat receptions arranged for other ministers. It was more than the coterie of admirers collected in his drawing-room several evenings a week, because every minister had those. His hold was subtle, intellectual. He had loyalty to command. He was aware that he was as intensely disliked as he was admired, but he also knew he could not be ignored. And so the conjecture continued. He wanted, he thought, what any man wanted, to leave his mark. There were two great motivating forces, it was said, love and hate. But he knew a third, the hunger for identity, and in his search for it he had never been able to tolerate one that challenged his own. Now no one did, and it no longer mattered so much who he was or where he had come from, for he stood at the heart of Delhi.

Paradoxically, the knowledge brought little satisfaction. He had arrived where he wanted to be but he was bedeviled by a sense of urgency. He felt it during the dark hours when he could not sleep, and he had never been a sound sleeper. He felt it most of all at this hour every day, the haunting twilit prelude to night when anguish closed in on the spirit, reminding it not only of past emptiness but of all the tortures of loneliness to come, and somewhere beyond it, death that would erase identity for all time. He

> struggled to remind himself at this time of the place he had carved for himself in a society indifferent to chronic poverty and despair. Every hand and foothold he had grasped in the slippery granite of that indifference was a triumph. Where he stood was a triumph. What he had become was a triumph – and yet not complete, for time was the great tormentor. No nation with this plethora of problems had time to spare. To arrive and find that there was so little time to do what you had planned was a mockery of your entire effort. He thought of the PM down the corridor whom he had come to respect more than any man he had known. Yet even he did not understand the meaning of haste. Even he was deluded into the miasma of patience, a dangerous and doubtful virtue in this time-bound existence.[31]

Although Kalyan has been invested with such dynamism and been drawn so skilfully, the author makes him strangely vulnerable, a loner deep in the very core of his being. Kalyan is central to the story because he is the focus of two kinds of betrayal: of the political and ideological significance of non-violence in a world permanently under a war cloud; and of the moral force of satyagraha, by allowing corruption to compromise the cherished ideals of the nationalist endeavour.

The parallels with Krishna Menon are unmistakeable. Menon had made England his home ever since he was sent there by Annie Besant as one of her scholars who would later join the theosophist movement. He did nothing of the kind. He joined the London School of Economics where he was greatly influenced by Sir Harold Laski, and soon became actively associated with left-wing politics. Brilliant and versatile, he started the India League in the early 1930s, raising funds and raising awareness about India's fight for freedom, but he was controversial even then.

The face-off between Vijaya Lakshmi Pandit (Kailas) and Krishna Menon (Kalyan) began in the United Nations during Mrs Pandit's first presentation to the General Assembly in 1946. She noted his tendency to ignore India's permanent representative to the UN, Sir B.N. Rau, and to routinely flout the united decisions of the official delegation, claiming he was answerable only to the prime minister.[32] Universally disliked, arrogant and discourteous, and a disaster in the UN, Menon was Nehru's 'blind spot' according to Y.D. Gundevia, who was foreign secretary when Nehru was the minister for external affairs in the early 1960s. In 1955, Vijaya Lakshmi Pandit succeeded Krishna Menon as India's high commissioner in London, and it fell to her to sort out the mess left behind by him, soothe ruffled feathers and restore a level of diplomacy and goodwill in India's relations with Britain. Lord Hume, secretary of state for Commonwealth relations, told Gundevia (then India's deputy high commissioner in London) that he was 'right glad Krishna Menon was out of London'. Out of London, perhaps, but not out of commission, for he returned as part of official Indian delegations to the Commonwealth Prime Ministers' Conferences, always as Nehru's trusted advisor.

Frustrated and annoyed, Mrs Pandit wrote to her brother about Menon's concerted attempts to discredit her in London. His reply was characteristic both of his temperament as well as of his particular relationship with Krishna Menon.

> I have known Krishna now for a long time and have a fairly good appreciation of his abilities, virtues, and failings. All these are considerable. I do not know if it is possible by straight approach to lessen these failings. I have tried to do so and I shall continue to try. This is a psychological problem of some difficulty and has to be dealt with, if at all successfully, by rather indirect methods. I propose to deal with it both directly and indirectly.
>
> I hope I have the capacity to judge people and events more or less objectively. I am not swept away by Krishna; nor would I like my affection for you to influence my judgement to any large extent, though to some extent, of course, affection does make a difference and indeed should. Krishna has often embarrassed me and put me in considerable difficulties. If I speak to him, he has an emotional breakdown. He is always on the verge of some such nervous collapse. The only thing that keeps him going is hard work. There is hardly a person of any importance against whom he has not complained to me at some time or other. Later, he has found out that his opinion was wrong and he has changed it.[33]

Nayantara, who met him often at Teen Murti House, the PM's residence, felt there was a meeting of minds between him and Nehru, whom he accompanied when the latter went to Spain during the Spanish Civil War. He was able to influence the prime minister's decisions on vital issues, often with rather alarming consequences. Gundevia hints at corruption in the purchase of defence equipment when Menon was defence minister in the early 1960s – a tendency he had noted earlier, when Menon tried to scuttle the deal between India and Britain for the supply of Gnats and Canberras in the mid-1950s. Ultimately, of course, he was fired as defence minister in October 1962 for his complete failure to anticipate the Chinese attack in the North East Frontier Agency, for in fact, dangling the red herring of Pakistani military action on the western front when no such activity was taking place. His innings in government finally came to an end in November 1962, when he was relieved of his charge as minister for defence production.[34]

Kalyan Sinha comes to a similar end in Nayantara's novel. Although his misdeeds and the scandals that attend him are of a lesser magnitude than those that surrounded Krishna Menon, he exits the scene as abruptly and conclusively. But he lingers in the reader's consciousness as a dangerously romantic rebel, a male version of a femme fatale.

The Peace Institute, a cherished project of the PM's, becomes the symbol of Kalyan's double betrayal. Hari Mohan has made good his humble beginnings by making his money work for him in the UP legislature. Slowly, but unerringly, he has singled out those in key ministries who are susceptible to material and financial considerations; in time, he infiltrates the inner circles of the Congress in UP, wielding power and influence across the state, moving bureaucrats and ministers around like so many pawns on a chessboard. Inevitably, he sets his sights on Kalyan Sinha in Delhi, recognising in him a man who understands the worth of intermediaries like himself, and has little time for the Kailas Vrinds of the world. Through him, Hari can simultaneously settle old scores with Kailas, place a man of his choice as director of the Peace Institute, and award its building contract to his son's firm. Kailas's humiliation at Kalyan's hands is sweet revenge, made sweeter for knowing how easily it was accomplished.

That something so dear to the PM should have been tainted by his closest aide only proved what those around Kalyan had feared – that he believed in 'rapid accomplishment' at any cost, and that 'faith and compassion' had no place in governance 'as long as there were starving, ignorant men'. Kalyan believed that Gandhi had 'emasculated' two generations of Indians; but for him

> there would have been a revolution like any other ... and there would not have been these anomalies to contend with today, this oil-and-water regime that could command no singleness or unity of purpose.

When Prakash, the die-hard Gandhian, exposes Kalyan's collusion with Hari Mohan he is forced to resign, lampooned now in newspaper editorials as the 'Minister without Responsibility'. Kailas has been vindicated, and Point Ten in Gandhi's strategy of civil disobedience – avoiding abuse and violence – has been reaffirmed.

'Peace,' wrote Nayantara, 'was Nehru's prime objective, as a fundamental human need, and as the condition for lifting India out of colonial stagnation.' When he learnt of America's atomic test on the Bikini Atoll in 1946, for instance, he wrote an editorial in *The National Herald*:

> This is not the way to lay the foundations of peace ... Peace seems far distant now, a dream that has faded, and mankind apparently marches ahead to its doom ... Have words lost all their meaning and have men's minds lost all anchorage? For this is surely the way to madness ...[35]

Why then does Kalyan, so discredited, seem to have the last word in the novel? Nita comes to him, possibly the last time she will be able to, as he sits alone in the house he will shortly walk out of, and Rakesh drops in after she has left, to participate in one of Kalyan's discussion evenings, a continuation of those he had attended in Boston, years ago. Kalyan demands roughly whether Rakesh has come to see how he is taking his dismissal. Partly, replies Rakesh, but really he has come for the discussion.

> 'Then you are interested, and you think this discussion group serves a purpose?'
>
> 'Discussion always serves a purpose,' said the young man gravely.
>
> 'In that case we ought to continue it – you and I, that is – since no one else has considered it worthwhile to come.' Kalyan indicated a chair. 'What were the points you had in mind?'
>
> Rakesh sat down, collected his thoughts, and began to talk.

Kalyan is a man who believes in discussing an issue threadbare, believes moreover, that talking things through is the only way. It is not surprising then, that Rakesh, who has put his faith in democracy, in the importance of rational thinking, should seek him out in order to clarify his own thinking, for nothing seems to have been resolved satisfactorily either in his career or in his personal life.

This irresolution is deliberate because in Nayantara's view, there are no clear answers in life and a novelist cannot invent them artificially. Things don't end tidily. And so Kalyan re-enters the narrative just when one thought he had been written off, and is back in focus. His power of attraction for the two young people, Nita and Rakesh, endures; for her, at an emotional and physical level, and for Rakesh at an intellectual one.

Looking back, Nayantara said she thought the novel was much too preoccupied with issues and ideas, not enough with feelings. 'Had I been a whole person then, the intellectual part would have been there, but so would the emotional. The book would have been a whole book too.' But her personal inhibitions meant she hung back, and hung back over a long period of time, so that the women in her novels, she believed,

> ... had a terrible time coming forth. If I were writing about Rashmi today I would use very different language, wouldn't be guarded. I would let her be more open ... but I was surrounded by constraints and I was afraid of expressing myself to the hilt on anything related to sexuality. Everything was alright if it was within boundaries.[36]

Endnotes

1 Nayantara Sahgal, *A Time to Be Happy* (New York: Alfred A. Knopf, 1958), p. 9.

2 Personal interview, Dehradun, August 2008.

3 Ibid.

4 Nayantara Sahgal to E.N. Mangat Rai, letter dated 26 October 1964.

5 Nayantara Sahgal (ed.), *Before Freedom: Nehru's Letters to His Sister 1909–1947* (New Delhi: Roli Books, 2004).

6 Vijaya Lakshmi Pandit, *The Scope of Happiness: A Personal Memoir* (New York: Crown Publishers, Inc., 1979), p. 177.

7 Nayantara Sahgal, *Prison and Chocolate Cake* (New Delhi: HarperCollins, 2007, reprint, pp. 192–93.

8 Vijaya Lakshmi Pandit, *The Scope of Happiness*, p. 71.

9 Ranjit Pandit to Nayantara Pandit, 24 May 1940.

10 Nayantara Sahgal, *A Time to Be Happy*, p. 188.

11 Ibid., p. 193.

12 Personal interview, Dehradun, August 2010.

13 Encapsulated history of the making of Chandigarh is taken from Ravi Kalia, *Chandigarh: The Making of an Indian City* (New Delhi: Oxford University Press, 1990), p. 12.

14 Ibid., pp. 25, 31–32.

15 Ibid., pp. 40–41.

16 Ibid., p. 29.

17 Nayantara Sahgal, *Chandigarh Diary*, MS.

18 Ibid.

19 Ravi Kalia, *Chandigarh: The Making of a City*, p. xi.

20 Nayantara Sahgal, *Chandigarh Diary*, MS.

21 Nayantara Sahgal and E.N. Mangat Rai, *Relationship: Extracts from a Correspondence* (New Delhi: Kali for Women, 1994), p. 1.

22 See E.N. Mangat Rai, *Commitment My Style: Career in the*

Indian Civil Service (New Delhi: Vikas Publishing House, 1973) for details.

23 Nayantara Sahgal to E.N. Mangat Rai, letter dated 23 July 1964, in *Relationship*, p. 5.

24 Ibid., letter dated 15 August 1964, p. 7.

25 Nayantara Sahgal to E.N. Mangat Rai, letter dated 23 September 1965 (unpublished).

26 Nayantara Sahgal to E.N. Mangat Rai, letter dated 15 August 1964 in *Relationship*, p. 7.

27 Ibid.

28 Ibid.

29 Personal interview, Dehradun, August 2011.

30 Nayantara Sahgal to E.N. Mangat Rai, letter dated 7 September 1964, in *Relationship*, p. 20.

31 Nayantara Sahgal, *This Time of Morning* (New Delhi: Kali for Women, reprint, 2000), pp. 137–38.

32 Vijaya Lakshmi Pandit, *The Scope of Happiness*, p. 212.

33 Ibid., p. 287.

34 Y.D. Gundevia, *Outside the Archive* (Hyderabad: Sangam Books, 1984), pp. 167–69.

35 Nayantara Sahgal, *Jawaharlal Nehru: Civilising a Savage World* (New Delhi: Penguin Viking, 2010) pp. *x*, 20.

36 Personal interview, Delhi, August 2008.

3
BREAKING UP

The *Relationship* Years

THE STRAY REMARK BY BUNCHI MANGAT RAI EARLY IN 1964 in Chandigarh set in motion a chain of events that would prove to be cataclysmic. The first time he and Nayantara met was in Simla at its fabled club, the Green Room, in the very early 1950s when the Sahgals visited Gautam's elder brother, Narottam, in the summer. Nayantara was tangentially involved in the Gaiety Theatre's productions, one of them being J.B. Priestley's *There Lay the City* produced by Uma Anand, in which Bunchi's wife, Champa, had a role. Bunchi himself was an active member of the East Punjab Club, opened to supplement the Green Room's modest offerings and to cater to the influx of government servants and professionals from Lahore in 1948. But it was in Chandigarh, where Bunchi was posted when it became the new capital, that their meetings became more frequent.

Stung into responding to Bunchi's implied criticism of what he thought was her snobbish distaste for Chandigarh society, Nayantara wrote him a letter when she returned to Bombay after their Christmas break, and there began a correspondence between Nayantara and him that would define their relationship for the next couple of years. Bunchi was now in Kashmir, posted to Srinagar as its chief secretary; meanwhile though, a major upheaval had taken place in his life, one that would have a significant impact on how their friendship evolved. While in Lahore, Bunchi had become a close friend of Kaval Khushwant Singh, and in time their friendship grew into a full-blown affair which continued for more than twenty years. By 1964, both Bunchi and Kaval had decided to leave their respective marriages and set up house as a couple. Khushwant and Champa may not have known about this eventuality but both were certainly aware of the relationship, as indeed was all of Chandigarh. On 27 July 1964 Kaval informed Bunchi that she would not, after all, be able to leave her marriage, and that it would be best for all concerned if they agreed to a clean break. The shock of her announcement hit Bunchi like a thunderbolt. Engulfed by despair, puzzled and wounded and in an agony of doubt about his own worth, he took to drinking heavily, desperate to relieve the intensity of the pain he felt. Why, if Kaval had not reciprocated his love, had she agreed to commit herself to their relationship? There had been nothing forced or precipitate about their decision to live together, it was slow and deliberate, had matured over months, even years. Could it be that she wanted the best of both worlds, the convenience of marriage and the romance of an affair? But no. 'I somehow do not think she is that kind of person,' he confided to Nayantara, 'nor is she a wholly instinctive creature, acting on the spur; she is, in fact, very practical and careful and weighs things with clarity.'[1] Nor was she capricious or uncaring. What then? The fault must lie in him. He was inadequate and that was why he had failed to keep Kaval; he repelled compassion and tenderness, no one approached him 'because of some inability, some dryness, something in me. Of that I have no comprehension ... but of the fact I have little doubt.'[2]

> Both the women who have loved me never could give these (tenderness and compassion) to me, not because they were lacking but because it did not occur to them as something possible for me. Champa has known of my predicament for twenty years but never thought of it except as an immorality, an infatuation, a good man (perhaps) attracted by a bad woman – it has never occurred to her once that I may need freedom ... And Kaval could not have done this to me now, after years, if she had not thought me quite human, it would have revolted her soul.[3]

Bereft, unable either to reconcile himself to Kaval's decision to end their relationship of long standing or to reach out to those closest to him, Bunchi poured his heart out to Nayantara in letter after letter, written almost every day, from wherever he happened to be – Srinagar, Chandigarh, Delhi. In her he found a person whose humanity he could accept, from whom a kind gesture reassured him that he could belong again, could feel and be himself.

In Srinagar he was alone with his estrangement – Champa was still in Chandigarh, teaching – but there were the pressures of work to distract him, and then, in his leisure time, trekking up to Shankaracharya temple, which he did often, or walking in Chashma Shahi, overlooking water, valley and fields, that helped to ease his troubled mind. He wrote to Champa at length about Kaval, asking for time and solitude to recoup. Although he regretted the hurt he had caused her he was not asking for forgiveness because he was not penitent, and he had to live his truth, however it might emerge. He said he was now abandoning the past, daily and determinedly, and looking to the future.[4] Later in September that year he visited Delhi, staying with his friend Prem Kirpal at Sujan Singh Park, where naturally enough, he met Kaval as well – the Khushwant Singhs lived opposite Prem, at 51 E. It was a harrowing experience and he returned to Srinagar, sore and bruised, somewhat limp. To Nayantara he wrote:

> Kaval seemed in a bad way altogether – completely numb, as if the light and confidence had gone out of her ... no spark at all.
>
> ... I have now a tremendous bitterness of the way I have been dealt with, not, queerly enough, a bitterness with Kaval, for even though I must *judge* that she has dealt with me without decency or consideration, I do not *feel* this against her, as I can see how she is a victim as much as I. No, the bitterness is against God, if he exists, against Man, definitely, for the orders and untruths and conventions he accepts ... We are victims of the system, stronger than us, and I am terribly, terribly bitter about that.
>
> With you, it is very different, and I come near you with a need to love – a need to give and take emotionally ... It is as if something filled this being, almost to bursting, and needed to be touched, and to give.
>
> I am lucky that you accept, and will share with me and take from a maimed person like me.[5]

On 7 August 1964, Nayantara and Gautam had travelled to Srinagar for a short break, a day that would become what Bunchi later referred to as 'the birthday of my heart'. The heartbreak caused by Kaval notwithstanding, he was already predisposed towards Nayantara, had always wanted to get to know her better. Earlier, he would have sought her out from a place of confidence and affirmation, could have taken and given at that level; now, with a personal catastrophe that had robbed him of both, he found in her the promise of solace, of the kind of sympathy that perhaps could only come from someone similarly affected. A steady exchange of letters before they met in Srinagar had already established a close communication between them, but now they talked and talked and talked as they walked in his garden or spent an afternoon in Dachigam – where Bunchi presciently told her, 'At thirty-seven you can still learn to live, at fifty it may be too late' – or simply lingered after dinner, when everyone else had left. For Nayantara too, this opening up to another was new. She, who kept herself to herself, could now discuss matters close to her heart with someone who simply refused to leave her alone in her shell. In Bunchi, moreover, she found a man who was not afraid of admitting vulnerability, who readily confessed to hurt, to doubt and confusion, yet was her intellectual equal, discussing issues with the kind of serious engagement she had seldom encountered in Gautam.

On her return from Srinagar she wrote to him saying she had been thinking of the kind of relationship she would like to invest in with him.[6] She was acutely aware of the risks and difficulties entailed in pursuing their friendship, cautious and realistic in accepting that what she wanted personally was probably far more than she could expect to have. 'I know how delicate and uncertain the ground is beneath this relationship – not between you and me but because of the other people concerned,' she wrote. There were lots of untidy ends in her life, unfinished things, things that she herself felt were 'wrong'.

> There is a destructive element in me, I know, and a callousness ... Very little actually touches me, almost nothing moves me. The only person who had a hold on me – and it has lasted all my life and will till I die – was my uncle. It is an empty world without him.[7]

In 1964 Bunchi was fifty to Nayantara's thirty-eight years, mature, secure in his career and a highly regarded civil servant. Like Gautam, he was a Punjabi, at home in Punjab and deeply committed to its welfare and development. Unlike Gautam, he was even-tempered, cerebral, but able to relate easily to people on equal terms and with a genuine interest in their well-being. Patient and tolerant, he had time for everyone and was respected and loved by his junior colleagues. He drank heavily, of course, but then so did Gautam. Nayantara responded to all of this, but his most attractive attribute for her was his 'goodness and gentleness', and the fact that they were on the same wavelength. Kaval Khushwant Singh had once remarked that Bunchi was 'like Panditji', and Nayantara immediately agreed.[8] Very early in their correspondence they were discussing religion and the place it occupied in their lives, and in the moral codes they subscribed to. Bunchi spoke about his Christianity, but also recognised the Hindu in himself,[9] more even than her perhaps, who was emancipated from the backlog of its cultural and religious traditions. She, in turn, wrote about her ideas on spirituality, immorality and amorality. They discussed politics, the situation in Kashmir, the trouble brewing on the western border with Pakistan, and her early political writing.

Both Bunchi and Nayantara were aware of the repercussions that would almost certainly follow if they allowed this fledgling friendship to develop into something more serious, but obviously, the consequences for Nayantara would be far greater. There were the children, for one, there was the likelihood of a scandal, partly because of who she was, there was Gautam's extreme (but understandable) anger that she would have to face, and there were her own deep uncertainties about how she ought to proceed.

The rapidity with which Bunchi was drawn to Nayantara and in a sense pursued her (the word she used was 'bombarded') could have been because he was on the rebound from Kaval, but even so, it was remarkable. Within one month of Kaval's repudiation of their commitment he was in regular and meaningful correspondence with Nayantara, baring his mind, his heart, possibly even his soul, and demanding the same of her. He set the tone of the correspondence, writing two or even three times a day, every day, in the kind of detail that was quite unusual for a very busy senior civil servant. Up at six or six-thirty in the morning to pen a letter to her before leaving for his office or meetings, and then after dinner again on most days, it was as if he was consumed by the need to know her. On her part, finding someone she could communicate with, feel comfortable communicating with, moreover, was a powerful impulse. She knew only too well that there would have been no such communication had Kaval still been part of his life; they might perhaps have corresponded but

> ... You would have been happy and fulfilled in your paradise and letters would have been an extra. Strange, isn't it ... I am unselfish enough – for the first time in my life – to want for you what you want for yourself ... All this would mean my disappearance from the scene but I

> wouldn't mind if you had what you wanted. Is this what love means? I don't know, I have never known. You, with your experience, are better qualified to judge.[10]

Much later she confided to him that she thought she had fallen in love with his love for Kaval, with an unflinching devotion that she had encountered in men for a cause, never for a woman.

Thousands of miles separated Srinagar and Bombay, however, allowing them to spend time with each other only on paper, via pen and ink; and through that daily exchange of letters, fraught as it was with tension and the apprehension of discovery, there developed a kind of sharing that was quite at odds with Nayantara's reflexive habit of reticence about herself. She was also painfully aware that Bunchi's relationship of twenty-two years with Kaval had defined him for so long, made him what he was, that he would be unable to find a comparable equation with anyone else.[11] Yet she missed him, felt simultaneously liberated and confused by their relationship, so that when he suggested that she spend a little time in Srinagar in order to complete the novel she was working on, she decided that she would.

The proverbial storm broke over her head.

Gautam was dead set against her going, refused to agree to her staying with Bunchi, un-chaperoned, demanding to know why it was necessary for her to go at all. As it turned out, he was more than justified in his apprehensions, for that fortnight in Srinagar would be the turning point, not just in his marriage but in all their lives.

In Bunchi's house on 1 Church Road, Srinagar, Nayantara's tensions fell away like so much dross. In her room on the first floor, she sat at the typewriter he had hired for her and worked quietly and steadily through the day, freed from all domestic and parenting claims on her time. The evenings were infused with a different kind of sociability, the warm and easy comradeship of a small group in a small state, already politically fragile following Sheikh Abdullah's imprisonment and release, and an uneasy truce with the Union. The group, all leftists, formed a relaxed and friendly circle into which Bunchi had been admitted rather easily, and with him Nayantara informally met G.M. Sadiq (then chief minister of Jammu and Kashmir), D.P. Dhar (home minister), Mir Qasim (revenue minister), and others. And then, Srinagar in October was glorious, the chinars turning red-gold, the gardens, Shalimar and Nishat, suffused with colour in the dying light. Walking along the Bund with Bunchi every evening, Nayantara experienced a feeling of such calm as she hadn't known for a long time – she felt as if she had come home.

Returning to her own home in Bombay was like a child returning to school, to curbs and constraints, to pretence, to the many obligations she had to fulfil. Still, she felt a window was now open which had been shut before, and knew without doubt that her feelings were reciprocated. Bunchi and Nayantara's letters are not explicit, but it is almost certain that there was between them now a physical intimacy that reinforced their emotional and intellectual bonds. Writing to Nayantara a day after she left Srinagar on 24 October, Bunchi said:

> Whatever we did or said was homecoming, without pretence or effort. And now you have confirmed the

> fatality and finality for me, as if this between us was of the ages, not of the fury and passion of feeling only but of the substance of being, the substance of life and friendship ... It had none of the flare-up of an affair, none of the high fever merely of sexual attraction, but has been the fullest sharing.[12]

After Nehru's death, his parliamentary constituency, Phulpur (UP) fell vacant, and according to the rules a fresh by-election to it had to be held within six months. The two most obvious candidates to replace him were Nehru's daughter, Indira Gandhi, then minister for information and broadcasting; and his sister, Vijaya Lakshmi Pandit, then governor of Maharashtra. Lal Bahadur Shastri, the then prime minister, left it to the Congress high command to decide who the candidate should be, after a field visit by senior Congress leader, Uma Shankar Dikshit, established that both women were acceptable to voters. The party high command in turn diplomatically left it to aunt and niece to choose; after some delay, Indira Gandhi informed Mrs Pandit that she would like her to accept – she herself wasn't ready for an election just then, and so it was that Vijaya Lakshmi resigned her governorship and left for Allahabad early in November 1964 to campaign. (There was speculation in political circles in Delhi that Mrs Gandhi withdrew because Ram Manohar Lohia and the Socialist Party had threatened a dirty campaign should she contest.)

Nayantara joined her mother and her sister, Lekha, in mid-November to help with electioneering, and soon after,

Bunchi arrived for a brief visit. He stayed with the Shervanis, close family friends of the Nehrus, while Mrs Pandit and her daughters were at Anand Bhawan – Nayantara told Bunchi that she could enter it without returning to the past for the first time, because he entered it with her.[13]

Campaigning was hectic, with election meetings and speeches in dusty villages, travelling many miles in order to canvass support, with both Indira Gandhi and Lal Bahadur Shastri campaigning for Mrs Pandit. Nayantara accompanied her mother to Phulpur every day, where Mrs Pandit would address small groups of villagers in different locations; she was heard respectfully, as one would listen to a family elder who was familiar and well regarded. As the final campaigning days approached, election tempo picked up with enthusiastic reports of support for Mrs Pandit pouring in. On 17 November Nayantara prepared a press release for her mother but left Allahabad before the results came in on 23 November – her mother won by a thumping majority, only slightly smaller than that recorded by Jawaharlal Nehru in the previous round.[14]

Nayantara's Allahabad sojourn was personally momentous in other ways as well, cementing the bond between Bunchi and her, confirming for both of them their growing need for each other. She wrote to him from Allahabad to say that for the first time in her life she felt a wholeheartedness and a belief in a relationship. 'I want to burst with it and don't want to admit a single note of restraint or caution ... Something is happening, Bunchi, and every chord in me is alive and responsive to it.' A week after her return to Bombay she wrote again to say that she had had enough of marriage, and did not believe that it was possible for people to grow in freedom through it. 'Mentally, I've shed it,' she said, 'spiritually it was never mine.'[15]

Although she had never kept her meetings with Bunchi a secret from Gautam, he understood immediately that this time it was different. Nayantara told him that she was committed to keeping their marriage going but that she could not agree to giving up her friendship with Bunchi; she needed her independence, needed some space and 'freedom' to relate to people of her choice. Gautam responded sharply and predictably, saying he would never share her with anyone, that if she persisted in her relationship with Bunchi he would be consulting his lawyer in order to draw up the papers for a divorce.[16] He was shocked by her gross immodesty and what he called her immorality, by being and doing what no 'decent' woman should be or do. Because she herself felt no sense of shame or 'sin' he accused her of being 'corrupt', of publicly and inexcusably besmirching his honour. She could – or, as she told me later, she should – have denied what her friendship with Bunchi meant to her, could have belittled its significance, but she believed strongly that honesty between Gautam and her was absolutely necessary if any dignity was to be maintained in their relationship.

Back in Jammu, Bunchi wrote to say he was quite certain that, for him, she was the good, the true and the beautiful:

> 'Picture me in the DITCH OF DEVASTATION – and you are, by some strange miracle, at the edge of this ditch, and by some further miracle, you stretch both hands out to me and ask me to climb out of it ... It is not that you have me out of your own strength alone, but that I also

> can combine my strength with yours, and the footholds to the top are partly mine, and the pull upwards and outwards is partly yours.'[17]

By December that year Nayantara realised that Bunchi mattered very much to her, more than anything else, realised too that she had recognised that this would happen much earlier. 'Do not be afraid,' she had said in November, 'for it does not involve you. I feel very happy in the thought of you, very unhappy to be so far from you, somewhat uncertain of you too – and very certain that I love you.'[18] As her preoccupation with Bunchi and corresponding emotional distance from Gautam grew, so too did her feelings of guilt towards him. For the first time she admitted to a kind of dishonesty and discomfort in her relationship with him, felt that what she was doing now was a betrayal that would destroy him. She recognised in Gautam a kind of desperate need, both physical and emotional, for her, and while she could still respond to the first she herself was now emotionally committed elsewhere. She was remarkably unsentimental and frank about her ability to effect a separation of the sexual from the emotional.

> The fact of sex for me (she wrote in a letter to Bunchi) is not bound up with moral principles and scruples ... I have never had either a sense of guilt or a sense of involvement from sex. I've had enjoyment, it has filled a need, but never made me feel either regret or remorse. Nor has it been an emotional dose I could not cope with ... All this does not mean I am, or have been, promiscuous. I would consider that as disgusting as stuffing at each meal or drinking too much.[19]

Nothing could have been more of an anathema than this to Gautam, for whom physical fidelity was the one absolute non-negotiable in marriage. Alarmed and angry, he declared he would not allow Nayantara to meet Bunchi alone ever again; he retreated into stormy silences and threatened to complain about her to her mother. How in the midst of this turmoil was she to find the mental space in which to write? How assemble the peace of mind to start another book? How to get it going and how 'to protect its conception and growth from being shaken and damaged'?[20] Yet, not to have a focus, a job to do, made her restless and was contrary to the intellectual discipline she tried to maintain, despite everything. Fortunately, it was now December and time for their annual holiday in Chandigarh with family, hers and her sisters', something she looked forward to with happy anticipation. Walks, winter sunshine, relaxed days – and the fact that she would meet Bunchi again during his and Champa's Christmas break at home.

The visit was a nightmare. Gautam was in a ferocious mood, often not eating for days together, occasionally staying away all night, making it clear to everyone they met that he was suffering and that Nayantara was responsible. He told her that he had decided to sell Anokha and was in the process of negotiating a deal. Meeting Bunchi on her own was out of the question and Nayantara's only solace was the brief notes they exchanged furtively. On 1 January 1965, at a New Year's Day party at Anokha, Gautam chanced upon one such note that she had carelessly left on her desk in their bedroom, and the morning erupted in the kind of violence that Gautam, blind with fury, was driven to. He crashed into the drawing room, confronted

Bunchi, delivered a couple of stinging blows to his face, then rounded on Nayantara and dealt her a few as well. There was a shocked silence in the room. Nayantara stumbled out of the house and half-running, half-falling, made her way to the lakeside. Gautam followed her out, caught up with her and began hitting her again till she fell. And there she stayed, the sun beating down on her, an object of curiosity for passers-by. After a while she got to her feet and made her way slowly along the path to her usual lake walk. She found a kind of niche in the hillside where she sat, a mild breeze playing in her hair, till she felt somewhat restored. Reluctant to return but with no choice really, as the children had invited friends to tea and her mother awaited her, she began the walk home. Coming up the path she ran into Gautam and Bunchi, and the sight of her provoked Gautam into another towering rage.

Mrs Pandit had arrived in Chandigarh the same day, tired from parliamentary responsibilities and hoping for some restful time with her daughter and grandchildren. But Gautam was determined to have it out with Nayantara and Bunchi, and the next day, post-lunch, launched into an accusatory tirade against them to Mrs Pandit. Used though she was to some of the upheavals in her daughter's marriage, this outburst was particularly upsetting. Gautam seemed set on a separation and divorce, and on 3 January, insisted that Nayantara leave Anokha and move into a hotel. She refused, said she would do nothing to disturb the children, but decided that the following morning she would somehow find a way to go to Delhi.[21]

Gautam's violent outburst in Chandigarh made public what had hitherto remained a private and domestic unhappiness. A slow but unmistakeable disapproval began to make itself felt, from strangers and mutual friends, from Bunchi's wife, Champa, his cousin, Kikook, and even from Bunchi's mother-in-law, Mrs Singha, who remarked obliquely, 'Men who know better should not run after strange women and build temples to them.'[22] Others, among them those whose affection and regard for both Bunchi and Nayantara as individuals was undiminished, withheld judgement, but Gautam's vocal and visible assault on them made Nayantara feel that she had been judged and declared guilty in the marketplace. In a rare first, soon after she left Chandigarh, Mrs Pandit wrote to her daughter, cautioning her that the divorce option couldn't be considered for several reasons, among them the fact that Bunchi was a senior government official 'and our moral government might view the matter in a different light, specially when your name is involved'. More importantly, however, she offered advice born of personal experience. She wrote:

> Throughout my life I have constantly met and been drawn towards men for various reasons, most of them on planes other than the physical – but there is always an underlying physical attraction which at some moment carries one away. Very often it isn't worth the emotion and idealism one has put into it and it leaves a sordid memory ... So I would suggest you should not drive this thing too hard, however great the provocation. Breaking up of homes, even in this age of advanced thinking, is a delicate and dangerous thing.[23]

Nothing could have been further from Nayantara's intentions than divorce – indeed, it was Gautam who threw the gauntlet down repeatedly. For herself, she would have settled for a measure of freedom and a negotiated marriage partnership, naively believing that such an arrangement would be acceptable to a man like Gautam; believing also that leaving him would be a sort of dereliction of duty, a violation of contract, something she would not do voluntarily.[24] Nonetheless, that winter of 1964 in Chandigarh was tense and fraught, lurching between a forced normality and an ever-present apprehension of another blow-up. There was a kind of menace in the air surrounding the house, and Nayantara slept fitfully, one ear open for Gautam's footsteps as they echoed up and down the ramp. He drank every night, hid in the bushes in the garden, couldn't bear to hear the sound of her voice. Often she would wake at night to see him standing at the foot of the bed, staring fixedly at her, wordless and motionless. Every nerve in her body screaming, but in as normal a voice as possible, she would ask him to go to sleep as it was late, then wait for dawn to break and dispel the darkness.[25]

On 16 January 1965, the Sahgals left Chandigarh for Delhi, where Gautam was receiving the chairman of Ciba, Dr Keppeli, his daughter, and Mr and Mrs Rohner, senior colleagues from Basel. There followed three or four days of hectic hospitality, sightseeing and socialising in the company of their Swiss guests, whom Nayantara found stodgy and conservative, and whose wives had no preoccupations other than housewifery. There was little she could share with them, and the men's endless business talks were exhausting. But Dr Keppeli was clearly impressed with Gautam and had complete confidence in him; almost reciprocally, it seemed to Nayantara that Gautam was beginning to confide in

Dr Keppeli, occasionally letting fall a comment about her or their marriage that provoked the good doctor into remarking that docile women were preferable to stubborn ones. The Keppelis and Rohners left with the Sahgals for Chandigarh, from where they departed on 22 January. The Sahgals returned, soon after, to Bombay. The Ciba interlude offered something of a respite from their marital troubles, but hardly had they entered their new flat in White House on Gamadia Road, than Gautam ordered Nayantara to either move to her mother's place in Mafatlal Park or go to Delhi.

Writing to Bunchi soon after this ultimatum was delivered, Nayantara said a watershed had been reached in their marriage, she felt she had aged suddenly, as if one phase of life and feeling had come to an end.

> I have believed in compromise, endless compromise, in making more and more room for the other person, in giving in again and again and again. I have never felt this was defeat in any sense, only that it was life. But it seems Gautam's behaviour in Chandigarh has dried up this capacity in me.[26]

Bunchi felt appalled, bewildered and helpless in the face of Gautam's black fury and Nayantara's bruised vulnerability. His restlessness and dissatisfaction with his own emotional and marital situation paled into insubstantiality by comparison, for Champa, fully aware of his feelings for Nayantara, was coolly sardonic, simply creating what he called a 'running sore of non-acceptance'.[27] Moreover they had both lived with each other's infidelities for some time, lived apart for long periods while working in different cities, so that the kind of personal space and freedom that Nayantara craved and Gautam would not countenance was already a settled fact in their marriage. Bunchi's restlessness was a respone to the absence of any emotional involvement with Champa, to the lack of both love and friendship. Although the same may not have been true for Champa – indeed his cousin Kikook maintained that Champa's dalliances were simply a reaction to Bunchi's extramarital relationships – their marriage survived because neither of them sought to change the status quo.

This left Bunchi free to worry, almost on a daily basis and almost exclusively, about Nayantara's immediate and urgent marital crisis, not least because it became the subject of much of their correspondence. She and her situation interrupted his thoughts during cabinet meetings, while writing briefings, preparing drafts of speeches, or simply dealing with administrative details and matters of state. A strange and sudden intimacy was forged between them, a consequence, in part, of daily exchanges regarding the domestic see-saw that Nayantara's life had become. One day she would be told to leave the flat immediately, with the children, the next day that the children could stay but that she should move to Mafatlal Park. One day she would be instructed (via Gautam's secretary) to plan a dinner for forty, the next evening it would be cancelled or the venue changed abruptly, with the terse comment that she need not be present. In the morning he would inform Mrs Pandit that his mind was made up, that a separation was the only solution to Nayantara's waywardness, to which her response was that in that case there was nothing more to be said! His bluff called, the rest of the day would pass pleasantly.

Bunchi found he was a father figure, confidant, avuncular hand-holder – and friend and lover; he performed each role with uncommon commitment, finding in the process that his own involvement with Nayantara was rapidly becoming irrevocable. Enmeshed with this realisation was the admission that it was he who had brought her face-to-face with this new crisis in her marriage, he who was the immediate cause of Gautam's uncontrolled violence towards her. In a peculiar reversal, the turmoil and torment and the awfulness of their experience of this violence 'wiped the slate clean', as he said to Nayantara in a letter written early in January 1965. His love for her took on a sharp and clear outline, strong and certain of its rightness. He was, he said, filled with joy and happiness, despite everything.

His statement found an echo in Nayantara, for whom the friendship with Bunchi was a lifeline she could no more give up than breathing itself. Her stubbornness, as Gautam saw it, was born of conviction not obstinacy, of real need, the need to be free to choose. Despite her declaration to Bunchi that she could not, would not, give him up, her whole being became a battleground between conflicting emotions. Love for Bunchi collided with a sense of loyalty to Gautam and their marriage; despair at her situation was coupled with guilt at what she was putting Gautam through '... dragging him into corners where he doesn't want to go, tearing off covers he wanted left undisturbed'.[28] By February of 1965 she could say quite clearly that she wanted a clean break from what had become a hideous burden, and in the same breath admit that she was beginning to treat Gautam like an invalid needing care, a wounded creature whose wounds she was responsible for.[29]

> What have I done to an honourable man ... a man of integrity, a hard and harsh man but one who acts with integrity in his black-and-white world ... I have made it impossible for his pride to yield.[30]

The strain of keeping to a normal but volatile routine, hurtling between calm and storm, was getting to her. She was exhausted, felt arid and hopeless, so hopeless that she thought it might be best to kill her relationship with Bunchi altogether, rather than maim it in this way.

> To what purpose is this relationship, can you tell me? How does it help or serve us? ... I cannot reconcile myself to this starvation diet. I feel the harm it does me, the terrible punishment and penalty it imposes of silence ... it is worse than a prison sentence, it is solitary confinement.[31]

Added to this was the strict regimen of letter-writing that she and Bunchi had imposed on themselves – only one personal letter a week from Bunchi to Nayantara in order to avoid a confrontation with Gautam, should he suspect that a regular correspondence was taking place. The anxious waiting for his letter and an equal anxiety about not being around when the post arrived became quite unbearable, especially when her spirits were low. At such times she would send him a terse telegram to say: 'Difficult survive austerity. Please write.' Letters from him became her emotional bank balance, to be drawn upon after the second and fourth Monday of the month when Bunchi would write 'personally', while she would reply (personally or otherwise) on first and third Mondays. In addition, Bunchi would post her a personal letter, addressed to Mrs

Yeats and sent to Thomas Cook (the travel agent) every Saturday, from where she would collect it personally. Again and again she implored him to destroy her letters, and each time he resisted, asked her to reconsider. They would never be able to recapture the mood and sentiments expressed in the letters, he said, but also that they were much more than a record of events, of news and views. They would always continue to write, but not with the same intensity, the same sense of discovery. He would get rid of them if she insisted, but in his view, that would be 'tantamount to MURDER'. And so another elaborate ruse was devised for their safe keeping – Nayantara would return all his letters to her to him, after responding to them, and he would lock them up, together with hers to him, in a safe in his office.

In February Nayantara had been invited by the minister of state for tourism to be part of the Tourist Advisory Committee of the Jammu and Kashmir government. A meeting had been scheduled for April in Jammu, which she attended in the face of Gautam's cold fury at her decision to do so. Difficult though it had been, she felt she owed it to herself to live and act in keeping with her resolve, just as, in the past, she had felt she owed it to her marriage and to Gautam to accept the compromises that both demanded of her, and live by them. The ten days she spent with Bunchi in Jammu, 17–26 April, marked the second milestone in their journey, after the unintended and unasked for first in Chandigarh in January. In the violence of Gautam's response lay the foundation of their commitment to each other, the day that Bunchi said he had 'married' Nayantara, recognising a 'complete and devastating commitment of myself'. Now, in Jammu, that commitment was cemented.

In Jammu was the calm – and rare – luxury of getting to know each other without the tension of being 'discovered', and of doing so in an expansiveness of time and space that enabled a flowering, the creation of 'something nearly flawless between us.'[32] As in Srinagar the previous October, they walked and talked, sharing and discussing in love and in anxiety, their individual and common problems. Bunchi confided that his relationship with Champa, though far from turbulent, was nevertheless, distant. Theirs should have been a vibrant, compatible marriage with reciprocal interest in each other's development; but, he maintained, she seemed indifferent to his essential being, was impatient with (though respectful of) the values he lived by, thought his ideas on freedom and love and honesty, self-indulgent. To the extent that they gave each other enough room to cultivate serious relationships outside marriage, they were on equal terms; in this, their marriage was fundamentally different from hers and Gautam's – although he thought that the latter's inability to share Nayantara's values was akin to Champa's. And unsatisfactory though both marriages might be, they agreed that ending them was also beset with problems. Round and round they went, devising ways and means of meeting, coming up with and rejecting strategies for coping with Nayantara's precarious, 'normal' life, yet sustained and regenerated by their unshakeable belief in their love, its absolute certainty.

By March, Nayantara seemed to have turned the corner in her marriage, had resolved what she called the conflict of loyalty to Gautam with allowing herself her relationship with Bunchi. Yet, like many women in her circumstances, she vacillated, and the pendulum swung between resolution and hesitation, between conviction and despair. In March her mind was made up, but in April she worried about behaving rashly, going on a public, unconventional visit to Bunchi in Jammu. In May she might be buoyant, but by June be plunged again into what she called 'The Crisis'. And so it continued, as did their heartbreaking, back-and-forth discussions on giving each other up, holding on, letting go, making a final break, never breaking up. For it seemed to them that being together could never happen in the normal course, never be easy, never anything other than a struggle attended by violence. What, asked Nayantara in April 1965, could 'be simpler than that I should come to you, wherever you are, and we should both make a clean break and start afresh. Only how complicated and nearly impossible that would be.'[33]

Gautam vacillated too. Faced with his own ultimatum to Nayantara he retracted quickly, realising that she needed to live her life, within limits. She could continue living in the flat, he declared, but if she 'let him down' he would kill her, and Bunchi too. His predicament and frustration were acutely painful, for here were two human beings who responded non-violently, even sympathetically, to his verbal and physical assaults, admitting that they had flouted conventional norms, yet refusing to surrender to them. Where, and how, on earth was he to find release for his excess of love and possessiveness?

On 29 April 1965 after her return from Jammu, Gautam informed Nayantara that at most he could concede one visit by her to Bunchi, for one week, once a year; anything more than that would be monstrous and unpalatable. But this was less than crumbs for Nayantara. She informed

Gautam that this being so, she was willing to be discarded by him; she was prepared to compromise but not to back down, that she could no longer toe his line just to keep the peace. Having brought herself to the brink, having been brazen enough to demand her freedom she could not now step back. By June of the same year, she had decided that there was no turning back for her, that her relationship with Bunchi was her priority; she also believed that any success she might achieve in her life would be because of Bunchi, that as she said to him, 'I simply don't see myself as capable of achieving anything without the assurance of you in my life.'[34]

Gautam returned from his business trip to Switzerland, saying it was the best trip he had ever had, but that everyone had remarked on his appearance and that Dr Kapelli had said, 'When a man marries well, either he ruins his wife or is ruined by her.' But to Gautam's pointed question about who, in their marriage, Kapelli thought had been ruined, he replied that neither Gautam nor Nayantara seemed to be. He did, however, advise a medical check-up and holiday for Gautam, and so it was that the Sahgals arranged a visit to Kashmir in July. They stayed at the Palace Hotel, overlooking Dal Lake, and Gautam seemed to unwind a little although he was drinking heavily. He had told a common friend, the journalist Prem Kirpal in Delhi, that he had lived a good life, had everything a man could want, but now wanted to die; the very next month in Srinagar, Bunchi told Gautam about his love for Nayantara, spoke at length about their friendship, about her need for some personal space. But, he said, he could not live with the realisation that he was causing an 'unjustified and unsought break' between Nayantara and Gautam, and so he would withdraw. To which Gautam replied, 'But I am getting out – not you. My mind is made up.'

Bunchi's decision to speak openly and honestly to Gautam was neither unilateral nor impulsive; he and Nayantara had gone back and forth on it, discussed the pros and cons, and agreed to go ahead because both believed that concealment was repugnant, and both hoped that a genuinely sincere and well-intentioned conversation between them might make for an acceptable resolution for all concerned. Both were aware of the risks, afraid that their decision might backfire; both wondered whether anything would be gained by it. Indeed, after he met Gautam in Srinagar, Bunchi wrote to Nayantara to say:

> Should I abandon the pursuit of living love forever and proceed to live alone, with myself ... I thought, I am 50 – much of life over – I must think this thing through for myself – where am *I* to go. Should I not retire and determinedly give this way of living up and live with myself only in future? Face myself utterly and have only my mountains. But I cannot live without you; it is too utterly painful to contemplate such a thing ... and so I am almost desperate. What am I to do? Where can I go? Where can I lay my head? I am very weary of this endless journey.
>
> ... Would it not be better for me, and braver and more courageous, then, to make my peace with myself and leave this alone altogether ... alone in making of life what I can ... alone in accepting the fact that my way of wanting these things – love and faith – has been a failure.[35]

It is doubtful whether anything came of Bunchi's admission to Gautam, for it seemed that he was unable to disentangle the problems in his marriage from Bunchi's entry into Nayantara's life. As Bunchi astutely observed, Gautam wanted no more from his marriage than he already had; what he demanded was complete loyalty and fidelity from Nayantara. Real companionship or friendship, equality between partners, were secondary, if they were to be sought at all. Life and relationships, as he had encountered them, were matters of contract and competition; Bunchi and Nayantara personified almost the opposite. As if to assert his domination and authority, Gautam, on returning from Srinagar, announced to their children that he and their mother were separating because she was 'involved with another man'. The impact was stunning. Ranjit looked shell-shocked, Noni was speechless and Gita, not yet ten, simply lay down on the floor and howled.

Nayantara couldn't believe her ears, couldn't understand how a man could do this to his own children, couldn't forgive him for having shattered their emotional security so cruelly by choosing to inflict injury on them only in order to punish her. And having done so, he immediately departed for Europe on a business trip. As had lately been his wont, he gave no indication about how long he would be away or where he could be contacted; and as had lately been Nayantara's experience, his absence was both relief and suspense for he might walk in unannounced at any time. For now, she decided that reassuring the children, enveloping them with as much love and confidence as she could, was more important than worrying about him and the negotiations around a legal separation.

In the midst of her personal turmoil came news from Bunchi of war clouds gathering on the western front, with Pakistan infiltrating into Kashmir, making repeated attempts on army depots containing oil and ammunition, and the Pakistani army firing across the ceasefire line. Within a few days, after India crossed the CFL, the tension escalated and a full-scale war seemed imminent. On 6 August, D.P. Dhar sent Bunchi a cryptic note scribbled on a page torn out of his diary:

> Strictly confidential
>
> From D.P. for C.S,
>
> Intrusion in strength established. Our troops engaged in action. Kindly call I.G., Div. ComMr and D.I.G. to make unobtrusive but firm police arrangements to guard against sympathetic demonstrations. My hunch is that the matter is pretty serious. Love.[36]

In a note drafted by Bunchi on behalf of D.P. Dhar (then home minister, Jammu and Kashmir) for L. P. Singh, then home secretary in the government of India, they alerted Singh to the fact that well-armed and ration-supplied men had entered behind the Indian defence line, within three to four miles of Srinagar. They told him that in their assessment the ceasefire agreement with Pakistan had been violated, compelling India to defend its territorial integrity. They also thought that Pakistan would synchronise its action to coincide with the anniversary of Sheikh Abdullah's arrest on 9 August 1953.

Bunchi wrote to Nayantara later that day to say that two thousand armed men had already moved in, and that bridges in some isolated places in the Valley had been blown up. Rumours flew that Srinagar was surrounded by groups of armed men and Sadiq, the chief minister, telephoned Prime Minister Lal Bahadur Shastri for reinforcements. Shastri decided to send such reinforcements by air, even though night landing at Srinagar was inadvisable. Firing continued through the night of 10 August, and arson and daily attacks from near and far were reported. On 14 August, Batmaloo, a suburb of Srinagar, was set alight and two hundred and fifty houses were destroyed.

Two days later, sandbags had been placed and trenches dug at ministers' houses in preparation for what looked like a protracted conflict. Yet, schools and colleges were open, groups of girls could walk to them, and people shopped as usual. But Bunchi had a twenty-four-hour police guard at his house and his lawn too was dug up. Nayantara was worried sick as the crisis seemed to be escalating, with Pakistani Sabre jets screaming over Srinagar, and by the third week of August Pakistan had begun attacking across the CFL as well. Stray incidents of locals colluding with the infiltrators had been reported, and once Indian troops too crossed the CFL, Bunchi wrote to Nayantara to say, 'We are now irrevocably at war, when the whole genius of this country is alien to war. I see that every day.'[37]

To everyone's surprise, the tourist committee, of which Nayantara was a member, scheduled a meeting for 4 September, despite the fact that the city was under curfew from 8.30 p.m. every day. This being so, Bunchi insisted that she stay with him and Champa when she came for the meeting. It was a tense and difficult week. Bunchi was on call twenty-four hours of the day, the atmosphere at home was crackling with hostility from Champa, and outside, the city was scarcely any better. Not surprisingly, Nayantara and Bunchi had little opportunity to talk or meet by themselves, for even after-dinner walks were out of the question during the curfew. The danger of Srinagar being bombarded was real, and Nayantara's departure from there by helicopter, perilous. Accompanied by D. P. Dhar and Susheetal Banerji, additional chief secretary, Jammu and Kashmir government, also on their way to Delhi, they calmed their nerves with the whisky (and one glass) that D.P. Dhar had had the foresight to carry on board!

Nayantara returned to Bombay, also blacked out and under partial curfew, with no vehicles allowed to ply after 8.30 p.m., and to a letter from Gautam, written from Basel. 'I am withdrawing my objections to your desire for a freer life. I don't like the consequences, but that is not the question. Your point is conceded and that is that.' (undated) Despite its conciliatory tone his letter irritated Nayantara intensely. The country was at war, Ambala had been bombed, the Chinese had issued an ultimatum to India to 'withdraw' from the Sikkim–Tibet border – yet Gautam had opted to linger in Europe for the whole month, unmindful of what his family was going through. What was more, as soon as he returned at the end of September – the situation in Kashmir still tense, and her mind preoccupied – he dredged up the business of her friendship with Bunchi again, filling her with an enormous weariness. All those years of building a marriage, of making a family, of creating a home, coming to an end. All her attempts at keeping the peace, hoping for continuity and protecting the children – more or less in vain. She could, she knew, easily have it all back, the

Bombay Nov.23

10 a.m.

Too much has happened too suddenly since my return and I am still trying to get it into focus. I did not want to write to you about it until I had sorted it out somewhat in my own mind, but I am doing so in case you hear from Gautam (though I don't think you will) and are bewildered by anything he says. At the moment I am trying to feel my way through what once again seems to have become an impenetrable jungle.

I arrived here on the 20th night and Gautam met me at the airport. He had come straight from a party, had had quite a lot to drink, was affectionate, in good humour, glad to see me. All the way home we discussed his trip abroad. It had not been altogether smooth sailing and we talked about it from various angles. He was full of it, also very happy to be home. On arrival home I found he had arranged for champagne to welcome me back. We drank and talked some more, mostly about his trip. Up to now I had said nothing about my own trip except perhaps in passing. He did ask at the airport how you were and whether I had given you his message for the Director of Agriculture. Over the champagne he began to talk of two days he had spent in Yugoslavia, what a beautiful country it was, how much like India in some ways, and how warm and friendly the people. He found on the first evening that the business colleague he was with had arranged for two women to spend the evening with them. Gautam said he was not interested in this and that they should be told so, which was done. His colleague then apologized and said that people who came out on business usually couldn't wait for this sort of thing. Gautam said he thought it disgusting and that he could not think of anybody but his wife in these terms.

After telling me this he asked me what I would have thought if he had in fact slept with one of them. This question I dread because I have always and only one answer to it, which upsets him, and I particularly dread it over drinks. However, I said, as I always have, that I have never known the "right" and "wrong" of these matters, and that I would not have held it against him if he had. I knew what the next question would be. He asked me if I would go to bed with another man. I said as it happened I had a very satisfactory sex relationship with him, but that even if I hadn't I'd be afraid to do so because I was afraid of him. I said that his long inquisition had made me afraid. He said he could understand my being afraid on this score and that if he met that man today (the one I knew in '47) he would still want to kill him. He also said that the whole trouble with our marriage had been this man.

I don't remember what else we discussed but there was a good deal more talk during the course of which I know I told him I had been happy in Allahabad and felt closer to my childhood values etc. I think I also mentioned Shiv's letter which I had forgotten to bring with me, and he said he would write to Shiv. I asked him whether I need go to Delhi on the 29th and he said I must because he wanted me to be with him.

The next morning I spent most of my time with the children and the day passed pleasantly enough except that I felt Gautam looked a little preoccupied and unhappy and I began to worry about what was bothering him. All through the day he asked me questions: Where had you stayed Delhi? Where had you and I dined? I told him we had dined at your hotel on the 5th evening, that you had lunched with Kikook the next day, that I had taken you over to Lekha's for a drink, and that you had driven Kikook to Chandigarh. He asked me whether you had any physical relationship with Champa and I said you must have since, except for your involvement with Kaval, everything had seemed normal between you and Champa. He wanted to know where Khushvant Singh was, and I said in Delhi. He then asked whether things between you and Kaval were completely at an end and I said they were, but that you kept in touch with her and had the impression shelter and security and Gautam's frantic devotion, if she renounced Bunchi. And although she was afraid of what the future held, of how she would manage, how support herself, her decisions could not proceed from fear or on the basis of a negative reason.

Having come this far, a retreat now would be to abandon any possibility of recovery later.

The 1960s were not the 1990s in India, and unkind gossip and rumours about Nayantara were doing the rounds. The Sahgals were a high-profile couple, she was prominent in her own right, not only as her mother's daughter but as a writer, and Bunchi was a senior, highly visible civil servant. Social convention demanded submission on the part of the wife in order to uphold the sanctity of marriage. Clandestine affairs might escape opprobrium, but a woman openly insisting on equality and the freedom to forge relationships outside marriage, was highly suspect. The world's sympathy, Nayantara knew, would be with Gautam and Champa as the wronged parties, and she herself, as the 'other woman' would continue to be 'stoned in the marketplace'.

When Bunchi heard about Gautam's insistence on a formal separation he told Nayantara that he was willing to withdraw from their relationship altogether if that would save her marriage and her home. He even composed a telegram to Gautam to say:

> Have just heard that you are separating. Stop. Am shocked and never thought that this was possible or justified by the facts. Stop. Have decided that I will quit altogether

> and in future my relations strictly confined to the social and occasional letter. Stop. Please do not carry your plan to its unhappy and unnecessary conclusion. Stop.[38]

But the die, it seemed, had been cast.

All through October talk of their separation went back and forth between Nayantara and Gautam. Mrs Pandit consulted her lawyer, Gopal Swarup Pathak, Gautam informed his principals in Switzerland, wrote to their friends, Kaka (Dr HBN) Swift and his wife in Chandigarh – and confided in Morarji Desai, with whom the Sahgals had a warm and cordial relationship. Gautam had written to his mother-in-law suggesting that Morarji be the mediator in the marriage settlement; Morarjibhai was agreeable to offering advice, but clarified that the actual terms would have to be drawn up by a lawyer.[39] When Gautam went to see him, Morarji was shocked at the sight he presented: thin, ill-looking and completely distraught. His heart went out to him. Whenever angry, Gautam threatened court action, naming Bunchi as a co-respondent and creating a scandal that would embarrass everyone. In a letter of 12 October 1965 to Mrs Pandit, he implied that Nayantara had dealt shabbily with him whereas he had never transgressed decent behaviour. He also wrote:

> Your letter suggests that you have a fear that I am likely to deprive Tara of a reasonable living standard or that I might later on do something to hurt the children. You mention that provision should be made for the sort of education which will be provided for the children and the sort of marriage expenses that could be expected. This indicates that while you and Tara have their best

interests at heart and will continue doing so, I do not, and therefore must be tied down hand and foot. The children are mine as much as they are Tara's. It is in their interest that I have agreed to her taking care of them, but this does not in any way mean that I have abdicated my love for them or my responsibility towards them. I am not moving out of their lives and do not intend to do so. I cannot, therefore, allow anybody to step in between the children and me. Long ago when Tara and I were to be married, you wrote to my father that marriage should not be treated as a carnival and that unnecessary and ostentatious expenditure should be avoided. All of us agreed with you. When my children are married the same will apply to them and I shall give them whatever I am able to. After all, you must remember that if this separation question had not arisen, their futures were left to my good sense to provide for.

With regard to the financial settlement, I want to avoid any semblance of bargaining. It is my earnest wish that Tara should live well and comfortably. On the other hand, I am quite sure you will agree that I should not be bled white in the process, nor should I be expected to shoulder liabilities which are unreasonable and out of all proportion to my income. There can always be two opinions about the quantum to be fixed. This can give rise to the most bitter disputes and to the washing of dirty linen in public. It is for this reason that I particularly wished to avoid lawyers being brought into the matter. You are, of course, absolutely free to ascertain from whomsoever you wish if what I suggest below is unfair. I should, however, make it clear that I cannot do more. Morarjibhai has always been a close friend of ours and all of us have the fullest confidence in him. I consider it more than enough, therefore, for his opinion to be sought and for him to decide what is equitable and just.

I have taken careful note of all that you write and, in view of this, would like to be excluded completely from any say in Tara's financial future, once the settlement is finalised. In other words, I would like *all* her expenses to be met from the Trust as detailed below. This would mean that she will be entirely independent of me and would behave as if I did not exist.

I propose the creation of a Trust of which the ultimate beneficiaries will be Nonika, Ranjit and Gita. The corpus of this Trust will be created solely from the shares which my parents handed to Tara, plus those which were absolutely purchased by using the income from the original shares, plus those which were purchased from the sales proceeds of the original shares which were disposed of. I would like to make it perfectly clear that the shares which Tara has purchased from her own earnings, i.e., from her royalties, are *absolutely* excluded from this arrangement and she is free to do with them whatever she chooses. Similarly, any income she might earn from her writing or from any other source is also entirely excluded. All that I am concerned with is that the Trust should be composed exclusively of the shares which Tara received from my parents and the additions which were made from time to time from the income from such shares. I propose that the Trust gives Tara a gross annual income of Rs. 30,000.00. [Gautam's brother, Gogu, thought Rs. 2000 a month ought to be increased as it was hardly enough, with three children to provide for, but Gautam retorted that he wasn't about to 'subsidise' Tara and her affairs.] From this income she would have to meet all expenses including taxes, school fees, rent, living expenses and so forth. In addition, Tara

> will, of course, have whatever private income she gets from writing and other self-acquired shares. The income of Rs. 30,000.00 gross from the Trust is a secured income on the basis of present yields. You have misunderstood my remark in the notes I gave you about the Trustees arranging for temporary overdrafts to make good temporary shortfalls. Let me explain this. As you know, dividends are not received in equal monthly installments. In some months dividend receipts are heavy and in others they are light. As it happens, the major dividend receipts for the shares which will form the corpus of the Trust come in the period April-July. The Trustees will, therefore, have to cover any shortfall for the lean months by securing temporary overdraft facilities from the bank. This should not present any problem as the total borrowing will be infinitesimally small as compared to the value of the shares.

He concluded his letter with the statement that he would be 'more than content' to let Morarjibhai have the final say so that no 'interested' party be thought to exercise a bias either way.

As far as Gautam was concerned he had been wronged, and as a man wronged, he took the only decision open to him even though he knew it might destroy him. His excessive drinking, his heart problems and ill health all resulted from his wife's infidelity; the only solution was a complete break. When Nayantara asked him if he was happy with his decision, he said, of course not, but he had no choice and there was no going back on it. She acknowledged that this was completely consistent with his world view and had an integrity which she respected. 'For here is a man who has acted with courage in dreadful circumstances and not yielded or compromised over an issue he held sacred. And my heart goes out to him.' Her tragedy was her inability to go along with him. As she wrote to Bunchi,

> I have, I think, understood him gradually as I came to know him, but I have not understood him with love … I have in your words touched a human being 'without humanity' and that is a sin.
>
> Once more, as before in my relationship with him, I feel guilty … I feel I have spattered a clean surface with mud, destroyed what I ought to have nurtured … and I know now that I will never be free of my guilt towards Gautam, never cleansed of it, because towards him and in his eyes, I have done wrong.[40]

Bunchi urged her to reconsider, suggesting that she stay with Gautam, on his terms, believing that however heartbreaking and unsatisfactory such a choice was it would satisfy her more than breaking away. He, they, would accept it, would honour it, would still love and respect each other but observe their discipline. 'I do not say that *this* is the right answer,' he wrote, 'it cries out within me as incorrect in many ways,' but it offered the only way out.[41] How little he was persuaded that this was the 'right answer' was borne out by the fact that even Kaval Khushwant Singh advised him to 'take Tara away, do not allow her to go back to Gautam. Gautam has a cruel streak in him.' She told Bunchi, 'I have seen it. He will take it out on her.'[42]

In any case, by now, events had acquired their own momentum. When Nayantara arrived at the office of her lawyer, S.K. Handoo (Shri Bhai) to discuss the separation in December, he informed her that Mrs Pandit had consulted

Manubhai Shah, a Congress MP, who had been told about the separation by Morarji Desai, at the time a member of the cabinet. Her mother and sisters thought it the 'height of folly and unwisdom to see this crusade through' and it seemed to Nayantara that the very elements were ranged against her. Almost everyone thought her 'criminally insensible' to a husband's emotions, and there would be many who thought her a freak. By her side, supporting her, was only Bunchi, and perhaps he was a freak too.[43] At the lowest ebb in her life now, she saw with terrible clarity what the consequences of her choice would be. Her one hope was that, at some future date, when they were adult and faced with difficult situations of their own, her children would attach some significance to the fact that their mother had lived by her values, held fast to them.

Around her, in the flat in White House, her seventeen years of married life lay strewn around in packing crates and suitcases as she prepared to move to her mother's flat. Books, clothes, the children's things, it was like living in the middle of a blitzkrieg. Sorting, discarding, letting go, trying to keep a grip on herself, trying to keep Gautam calm as he blew in and out between trips to Delhi and Switzerland. On 4 December Nayantara wrote to her mother, saying that Shri Bhai had told her Mrs Pandit had sent two messages for her: that Manubhai Shah had suggested that Nayantara give up Bunchi for six months, at the end of which Gautam would be willing to reassess the situation; and that the PM, Lal Bahadur Shastri, was worried that their problems were becoming 'a national issue'. Nayantara said she was sorry the PM was distressed but that her marriage was her business, and although she was sure that both the PM and Manubhai were sincere in wanting to put things right, matters between her and Gautam had gone far beyond that point; it was no longer a question of patching up a superficial rift, but one of ideological differences.

A letter from her mother, received just three days before she was due to sign the settlement papers, offered sorely needed solace:

> I want you to know that I support you absolutely and that my love, so long as I am alive, will be your strength – afterwards it will still be with you. I have told you many times that I have great faith in you and I know, when the first hard months are over, you will build a good life for yourself and your children.
>
> My blessings always,
> Mummie
> *December 6, 1965*

On 9 December Nayantara went to court to sign the separation papers, and in the courtroom hung a large photograph of Nehru, who had signed her marriage certificate in 1949. This date, 9 December, in the year 1947, was also the day when she had met Gautam for the first time at a cocktail party; although she assured the court clerk that she had, indeed, read and understood the contents of the separation decree, she felt as if she was in quicksand all over again. When would the ground beneath her feet feel firm again? Back home that evening she told Gautam that she had signed the divorce petition, 'done the deed that you wanted me to'. He broke down and wept, took her hand and sobbed, 'I can't sign it, I can't sign it.'

For four years, between 1965 and 1969, Nayantara did not complete a single novel; what she did write was thousands of letters, especially from 1964 to1967, a selection of which was published in 1994 as correspondence between her and E.N. (Bunchi) Mangat Rai, entitled simply, *Relationship*. Although its publication followed all but one of her novels, I propose to discuss it here, as the letters constitute a significant output and mark a watershed both in her personal, as well as her writing, life. Their correspondence is also an unusual record of a sustained exchange between two very public, yet intensely private, individuals, discovering the exhilaration of an intellectual and emotional companionship while simultaneously negotiating one troubled, and one very turbulent, marriage.

Tara Sahgal and Bunchi Mangat Rai wrote upwards of six-and-a-half thousand letters to each other over a three-year period, often writing two or three letters a day, Bunchi remarking humorously that they had left the Barrett-Brownings far behind! Bunchi's letters could extend to twenty or more pages, often on onion-skin paper, written over two or three days or a week or even in a single day, begun in the morning, continued when he could snatch a few minutes from official duties, and completed at night. They wrote from wherever they happened to be – home, office, hotel, guest house, bedroom or bathroom – and in whichever city they were at the time – Srinagar, Jammu, Chandigarh, Delhi, Allahabad, Bombay ... Their letters are passionate, intimate, practical or philosophical, written without reserve or sophistry, testament to an abiding commitment forged primarily through them, and to a relationship as it was unfolding. Living in different cities, husband. This surprised him but he made no comment. I also told him you had not given her up easily but had tried to keep something of the relationship by suggesting that Kaval should spend a couple of months a year with you. Gautam said this was a most unorthodox proposal and I said you were an unorthodox man. He then asked me if I felt you understood me better than you had. I said we had talked a lot and got to know each other much better and that I felt you did understand me. He asked me if I had spoken to you about my '47 affair or about our break-up in '59 and I said I had not. He asked me, "Do you like Bunchi as a human being?" I said I did, that I loved you as a human being. He did not remark on this, since I had not said "as a man," and he said also that he liked you very much. He then said, "You used to think he was rather cold. Do you think so still?" I replied that you were not demonstrative, but also not cold, and that in fact I didn't know anyone who was as interested in people as you were. I said you were a person who lived close to your ideals and that this was what I liked in you, that in this I felt a resemblance between you and Mamu. He contradicted none of this and was friendly about it.

We went on to talk of Shiv and he wrote Shiv a very nice letter, to explain his own stand and try to win him back, also to ask him to join us for dinner at Claridges on the 30th. He said he had asked some others too, the L.K.Jhas, the Govind Narains, and Frank Moraes. I suggested asking Kikook and Jivat but he said he didn't think they'd fit into this crowd.

Sometime during the day the subject of old friends came up - perhaps through a mention of Shiv. I brought up the subject of Kikook again, said that she was an old friend too and it would be a good idea to keep up with her, see her now and then. We got onto 1959 and my "abominable" behaviour with the Dane. I told him I had done nothing abominable or that I was ashamed of, that I had been hungry for companionship, for conversation, and not for anything else. The recollection upset him and I pointed out that he had, after all, sought a similar satisfaction from Kikook's company during that period. And to bring that element in the conversation to a close I added that since he and she had seen so much of each other during that time it seemed odd not to see something of her now, and that we should both do so. He said he did not wish to see her because, as he had told me once before, her attitude toward me and our marriage had become too officious and somewhat unpleasant. I asked him in what way, and he said she had said nasty things about me. (He elaborated on this in the evening.) I told him that since he and she had seen so much of each other in Simla and again in Bombay when she was staying with us, and since she knew our marriage was breaking up, perhaps she felt entitled to talk to him frankly and say whatever she thought about me. He said emphatically that nothing he had ever said to her could have led her to believe she could say nasty thing to him about me. Furthermore, he had looked upon Kikook during that entire period as a man, someone he liked being with, but with no question of anything else between them. I said that from what I had seen of them together at the time I did not think she felt similarly, and he said, "That may or may not be. I am telling you how I felt." He added that she did her best to find out what was wrong with our marriage and that he never discussed any aspect of this with her or any aspect of his relationship with me. She went to his mother and sister then for information and came back to him with bits and pieces which he refused to discuss with her.

He told me he had dreamt the night before that I had fallen in love with another man. He had been terribly disturbed and wanted to wake me but did not. I then talked to him about the election and told him about the atmosphere in Allahabad, including how nice it had been to have you there.

In the evening he asked me if I wanted a drink. I was sitting thousands of miles apart and unable to meet freely, their letters were not just a means of communication – they were the medium through which they got to know each other, by virtue of a depth and breadth of sharing in their desire to be, as Bunchi said, 'whole with each other'.[44] This being the one way they could talk to each other, he said, 'I want and crave nakedness between us, the whole of what you can give, and I want to unload the whole of what I can give.'[45]

> I thought, I will have to love her with my mind, through the letters I write in answer to hers, live her fully and passionately with my mind, for that is the medium of communication on paper. And whatever I wrote would exude the strength and aura, the pervasiveness of the love I have for her, just as whatever she has written has brought me her love.[46]

In other words, they practically wrote their relationship into being, their letters becoming a dialect of love.

Bunchi had always been a prolific letter writer, earlier penning copious letters to Kaval Khushwant Singh (also more or less every day, for twenty years), but for Nayantara, this was a new experience. For the first time, she found a listening ear that was not judgemental and their correspondence enabled her to open herself to another human being and enter a space of mutual trust and caring. Bunchi drew her out, assiduously and relentlessly (as she put it), hungry for every detail of her everyday life and activities. And these were plentiful. As tensions in her marriage built up, she turned to Bunchi for succour and for advice. His responses were detailed and introspective, combining daily accounts of his working life and preoccupations, of administrative decision making and crisis management, with reports on the political developments of the day. Both he and Nayantara had a keen and probing interest in Kashmir politics, in particular, and the exchange of firing between India and Pakistan in 1965 afforded them an opportunity to comment publicly on it. Indeed, Nayantara's very first journalistic writing was on Kashmir, discussed and improved upon with Bunchi;[47] he in turn sent her his drafts of memos to the Union Government, speeches he wrote for Karan Singh, the Sadr-i-Riyasat, even an obituary he wrote on Partap Singh Kairon, erstwhile chief minister of Punjab, who was assassinated in 1965. Nineteen sixty-four and 1965 were crucial years in Jammu and Kashmir, with Abdullahites agitating against the Union Government, and Pakistan and China hemming the state in. Nineteen sixty-five was also the year that Congress politics were in flux. Nayantara's mother, Vijaya Lakshmi Pandit, indicated her wish to contest elections to the deputy leadership of the Congress party but was opposed by the Syndicate (as the party bosses were known); Lal Bahadur Shastri succumbed to their pressure and persuaded her to withdraw. Nayantara was bitterly disappointed, commenting that the current name for the PM was Lull Bahadur.[48]

None of this was out of the ordinary for two people so attuned to the political life of the nation; no, the letters are remarkable for the clarity with which their relationship to each other, and with and between their spouses, is analysed. In those incredibly long letters their respective situations were dissected minutely, with every gesture and nuance, every statement, every opinion, every doubt or anxiety discussed in sometimes excruciating detail – what

Nayantara called 'total attention par excellence, like being pinned to the wall like butterflies impaled on long needles'. So much so, that Bunchi would often write on the basis of points he put down on his scribbling pad which he would then tick off, one by one.

The shock of rejection by Kaval had induced in Bunchi a round of lacerating self-analysis that teetered on the brink of being maudlin. Not one but two women (Champa, now Kaval) had found him seriously wanting as a human being. Having experienced abandonment and devastation at Kaval's hands, he wondered whether he was doing the same to Champa – was he, like Kaval, a 'killer' and would abandoning Champa similarly amount to 'murder'?[49]

The awareness of how their relationship was viewed by society and of how it was affecting their marriages and spouses led to an exchange on the question of morality itself and how it was to be defined for oneself. Both agreed that they did not subscribe to the notion of sin, that what Nayantara called 'sex morality' held no particular charge for them. Thus, Bunchi maintained that having never kept the fact of his liaison with Kaval from Champa, he felt no need to repent or be punished for it. Kaval, on the other hand, had preferred to keep it hidden, clandestine, and he accepted 'her morality' because of the children. For him, his morality – or what he called his amorality – was raised to the 'convenience of a principle, a passion, an ideal ... I have an attitude, an emphasis about these matters, which does not accept the moral structure.'[50] A broken relationship to him was 'sin', whether with man, woman or God, for each depended on an unwritten code, an equation, that had to be honoured. This being so, there could be any number of patterns of morality between God and man, man and woman, even man and animal, and in each case the moral would be to honour the terms of each particular equation. Fidelity, then, would be a matter of keeping the faith and mutual trust, not a requirement based on social mores. It was this breach of trust by Kaval that was the violation, that led him to remark:

> From Kaval I received little strength – not because she did not have it, she does, and is more than normally a strong and determined person – but because it was not the kind I needed. It was not of the spirit, but of action only.[51]

What he meant, of course, was the strength and the courage of conviction; she expected nothing and would fight for nothing. The striking difference between his relationship with Kaval and the one with Nayantara was the fact that

> ... in my love for you there was no insistent need to break homes and get away with you as there was with Kaval ...
>
> The point I want to make is that I love you very differently, or at least that our love for each other has a different significance, which explains the decision that we maintain our homes ... It stems largely from the fact that *you* are a different person and that *you* love me in a way that Kaval could not. Your love for me is whole and I feel it as whole, a complete commitment of the spirit and yourself ...
>
> With Kaval there was the fact that she could not give wholly unless she stepped over wholly, she could not release herself unless she released herself from the contract ... at least that is how she defined it and believed

> it. And as the man who loved her wholly, had given myself to her wholly, there was an inequality ... the cure for which could only be that she came away and we break our homes to do so.[52]

With Nayantara, on the other hand, because they gave wholly of themselves, Bunchi believed that a much more constructive, more considerate comprehension of the well-being of everyone concerned, prevailed. While agreeing that breaking up homes was a terrible thing, Nayantara begged to differ on the rest. She had never, she said, been 'puritan-minded' as far as sex was concerned, never had the least inhibition before or aftertaste of regret. She had been fastidious, yes, but at the same time had a rather pagan view of it, as an all-by-itself thing with no strings attached. In this, she thought she had always been as straightforward and honest as a man, never put a premium on the body.[53] Despite this, she couldn't think of continuing to live with a man she no longer loved or could be wholly loyal to, accept the benefits of marriage without being wholly in it; or pretend to be faithful if she wasn't. She found Bunchi's rationalisation of his marriage abhorrent, was appalled by his relationship with Champa.

> You and Champa are faceless to each other. How do you *look* at each other? *Do* you look? ... It does not disturb you to lie to her or deceive her ... This whole edifice seems so blatantly false, such utter hypocrisy, because ... there is constant talk of frankness and openness ... There is the quality and the odour of wreckage about both of you ... I haven't found genuineness, nothing that rings true, only a slippery, hazardous surface and much unhappiness.[54]

In a similar situation she would feel 'dirty and deceitful', and 'so I broke away from the thesis of marriage preservation', felt that continuing with it would be tantamount to living dishonourably, like a coward. She told Bunchi frankly and bluntly that it was shocking to her that he had no difficulty living with two women – 'pulling it off', as he himself would have said – that it was not a matter of conscience for him. Nor did it pose practical difficulties, for Champa would never leave him and she, Nayantara, would not give him up, so he had the best of both worlds. A man's worlds.

Bunchi sent her a spirited, firm and eminently rational response, saying in no uncertain terms that if Gautam had given the slightest indication of relenting as far as they were concerned, Nayantara would have happily 'lived with two men', led a double life, practised what he called 'constructive compromise' and justified it to herself and to the world. He also thought that she was ascribing a decisiveness and determination to her actions that were, in fact, merely a response to Gautam's adamant refusal to accept a compromised relationship on terms he could not dictate; that the decision may not have been hers at all, if it had not been forced on them by Gautam.[55]

Moreover, he continued, although he did not believe he had sinned, he nevertheless felt great guilt towards Champa, not loving her, not needing her, not even really wanting to be with her – in fact, wanting very much to be free of her and their marriage, even had he not been involved with Nayantara.

Bunchi subscribed to what he called a 'higher morality', one that entailed talking about things that involved fundamental and basic loyalties. It could only be done rarely, and only in an exclusive relationship.

> But once that happens, it is the very law and instinct of that relationship that all is told without inhibition and restraint ... Higher morality involves a complete discipline in regard to such information being absolutely and entirely exclusive and not usable unless that is acceptable to both persons ... will you accept it between us?[56]

Yes and no, she responded. From one perspective this higher morality could be seen as the most outrageously and audaciously corrupt concept imaginable – and from another, the most extraordinarily courageous and pure.[57] For herself, she held dear those few principles that worked as well in the abstract as they did in real-life situations.

In Bunchi's life, there had been only three relationships in which he had vowed to be absolutely and wholly truthful – the first with Ronald Sampson, his closest English friend; the second, over a long period, with Kaval; and now with Nayantara. For her part, Nayantara felt she could talk with Bunchi. In his insistence on the discipline of inclusivity and on 'nakedness' in communication she found freedom, the freedom of no longer having to conceal, to keep things to herself. Not a little part of this sense of freedom came from the fact that he was the first man who had treated her not as a woman but as a person, 'who has not pounced on me and gobbled me up at the first opportunity'.[58] Intuitively perhaps, she recognised him as the 'feminist' he believed he was. 'It is one of my strongest beliefs,' he wrote to her, 'for a man aware acutely of women's inequality internalises that inequality and assumes greater responsibility with regard to their rights and claims.'[59] Very early in their relationship he could say to her,

> You are not, you cannot be, you should not be my equal. You are too precious, you must get on to *your* destiny, not mine – not that of the extinguished star, not the last flicker of the dying candle. BUT
> Let me be part of it
> A whole part
> A trusted and loved part
> Let the journey of your spirit be mine.[60]

Predicated as their relationship was on extreme uncertainty and insecurity, the almost total absence of possessiveness in it was remarkable. Even as they recognised the absolute rightness, the depth and mutuality of their love for each other, they understood too that they could be called upon to renounce it any minute. When it became clear to Nayantara, late in 1965, that she could no longer save her marriage, she wrote to Bunchi to say:

> This is the time to remind you, oddly enough, not of your bonds with me ... but of your freedom with and towards me. You must never feel hustled into doing anything on my account, never feel I expect anything from you – because I don't – never take any part of yourself or your life away from your own home, your own set-up, that you yourself do not expressly feel you must. I have no claims on you, none whatever.[61]

Unlike Gautam, Bunchi was a careful reader of anything Nayantara wrote and commented on it, often leading to an exchange that might take them far from the original. So it was that on reading *From Fear Set Free* Bunchi reflected on the question of non-violence, which was almost an article of faith with Nayantara. He thought, he wrote to her, that India could have responded with non-violence to the Chinese invasion in 1962, 'with results no different – though from the point of view of morale, much and significantly greater than what actually happened'. In his view, if India's borders had been defended non-violently with 'our bodies', the impact on world morality and on the confidence of the Indian public would have been tremendous. The number of people required for this, he maintained, would have been no larger than the armies deployed. What is important, he said, is '… the Indian people would have understood what they were doing, felt they had participated … and the whole campaign would have been one of organised unity …'[62]

Nayantara, having imbibed ahimsa along with the air she breathed from childhood, was in any case convinced that the only way to end war was through non-violence. Far from being a passive strategy it was an active force, synonymous with love. 'I could never be a pacifist,' she wrote,

> though I could with all my soul & my bones & marrow be a non-violent resister, because that means not taking anything lying down … it means putting one's whole self, moral and physical, against wrong … You utterly reject wrong, and every active force within you is released to battle against it.[63]

It required the greatest courage, she said to me later, to go into battle without a weapon except yourself, and she had used it time and again as a 'defence' with Gautam. Her refusal to be bullied was a training in non-violence,[64] in the face of his setting about 'to kill everything in me as Hitler set out to exterminate the Jews, with determination and a cold scientific attitude. I do not exaggerate this or its effect upon me, for there is no forgetting it.'[65]

The question of passivity, however, individual as well as civilisational, interested her greatly, not only as a trait of character but as the characteristic of a culture; and it was in this context, this matrix of active non-violence and civilisational passivity, that she located her understanding of Hinduism. But she rejected the doctrinaire and the dogmatic, the degraded 'Hinduism' that you wore on your sleeve, that clung to tradition in an obscurantist way; the Karan Singh variety, she remarked to Bunchi, who at the time was writing a speech for the Sadr-i-Riyasat. And he, good Christian that he was, replied that he was probably more Hindu than her, for he had a kind of 'nostalgia in the soul'.[66] Shrewdly, he observed that it was people like her and Gautam and their forbears who had dissociated themselves from the tradition, that resulted in its losing its natural intelligentsia; what choice then, except that it fell prey to the 'hocus-pocus of people with little education or opportunity'. Nehru had basically abandoned Hinduism, he wrote, and in modern historical times only Gandhi and Shivaji loved it from within and thus worked wonders in transformation. 'I am,' he said to Nayantara on one occasion,

> ... more Hindu than you are. I think I have the instinctive (and now intellectual) trait of separating truth from action; my conscience is more 'pliable' if you wish to be unkind. Such a characteristic is both a strength and a weakness, both a responsibility and a potential indulgence.
>
> ... You are much nearer the integrated conscience, you must do what you believe.[67]

Both his forbears and hers, he believed, were rebels, making Nayantara and him 'inheritors of a precious obligation to rebellion'. Hers were political rebels for liberty; his, rebels against spiritual and religious orthodoxy. This was debatable ground, he acknowledged, leaving him in a quandary – he did not know whether to choose truth or heresy.

These letter-conversations between them, what Bunchi called 'extensions of love to realms of rambling and of response', ranged over space and time, would break off and be resumed, and engaged equally with the trivial and the profound. Through them, they shared without reserve, sometimes voicing what they may not have thought even to themselves.

For Tara, they became her lifeline.

Endnotes

1 E.N. Mangat Rai to Nayantara Sahgal, letter dated 24 August 1964 (unpublished).

2 Ibid.

3 E.N. Mangat Rai to Nayantara Sahgal, letter dated 3 September 1964 (unpublished).

4 E.N. Mangat Rai to Nayantara Sahgal, letter dated 6 September 1964 (unpublished).

5 E.N. Mangat Rai to Nayantara Sahgal, letter dated 16 September 1964 (unpublished).

6 Nayantara Sahgal to E. N. Mangat Rai, letter dated 15 August 1964, in *Relationship: Extracts from a Correspondence* (New Delhi: Kali for Women, 1994), p. 7.

7 Nayantara Sahgal to E.N. Mangat Rai, letter dated 27 August 1964 (unpublished).

8 Nayantara Sahgal to E.N. Mangat Rai, letter dated 6 March 1966 (unpublished).

9 E.N. Mangat Rai to Nayantara Sahgal, letter dated 29 November 1964, in *Relationship*, p. 54.

10 Nayantara Sahgal to E.N. Mangat Rai, letter dated 1 September 1964 (unpublished).

11 Nayantara Sahgal to E.N. Mangat Rai, letter dated 18 September 1964 (unpublished).

12 E.N. Mangat Rai to Nayantara Sahgal, letter dated 25 October 1964, in *Relationship*, p. 47.

13 Nayantara Sahgal to E.N. Mangat Rai, letter dated 18 November 1964 (unpublished).

14 Vijaya Lakshmi Pandit, *The Scope of Happiness: A Personal Memoir* (New York: Crown Publishers Inc., 1979), p. 3.

15 Nayantara Sahgal to E.N. Mangat Rai, letter dated 24 November 1964, in *Relationship*, p. 52.

16 Ibid.

17 E.N. Mangat Rai to Nayantara Sahgal, letter dated 30 September 1964 (unpublished).

18 Nayantara Sahgal to E.N. Mangat Rai, letter dated 29 November 1964 (unpublished).

19 Nayantara Sahgal to E.N. Mangat Rai, letter dated 7 December 1964 (unpublished).

20 Nayantara Sahgal to E.N. Mangat Rai, letter dated 8 December 1964 (unpublished).

21 Nayantara Sahgal to E.N. Mangat Rai, letter dated 6 January 1965, in *Relationship*, p. 65.

22 Nayantara Sahgal to E.N. Mangat Rai, letter dated 14 December 1964, in *Relationship*, p. 60.

23 Vijaya Lakshmi Pandit to Nayantara Sahgal, letter dated 6 January 1965. Personal papers of Nayantara Sahgal.

24 Nayantara Sahgal to E.N. Mangat Rai, letter dated 19 January 1965 (unpublished).

25 Nayantara Sahgal to E.N. Mangat Rai, letter dated 2 February 1965, in *Relationship*, p. 84.

26 Nayantara Sahgal to E.N. Mangat Rai, letter dated 25 January 1965 (unpublished).

27 E.N. Mangat Rai to Nayantara Sahgal, letter dated 6 January 1965, in *Relationship*, p. 67.

28 Nayantara Sahgal to E.N. Mangat Rai, letter dated 26 January 1965, in *Relationship*, p. 80.

29 Nayantara Sahgal to E.N. Mangat Rai, letter dated 24 February 1965 (unpublished).

30 Nayantara Sahgal to E.N. Mangat Rai, letter dated 11 February 1965, in *Relationship*, p. 87.

31 Nayantara Sahgal to E.N. Mangat Rai, letter dated 5 February 1965 (unpublished).

32 Nayantara Sahgal to E.N. Mangat Rai, letter dated 9 May 1965, in *Relationship*, p. 121.

33 Nayantara Sahgal to E.N. Mangat Rai, letter dated 26 April 1965, in *Relationship*, p. 115.

34 Nayantara Sahgal to E.N. Mangat Rai, letter dated 9 May 1965 (unpublished).

35 E.N. Mangat Rai to Nayantara Sahgal, letter dated 24 July 1965 (unpublished).

36 E.N. Mangat Rai, *Committment My Style: Career in the Indian Civil Service* (New Delhi: Vikas Publishing House, 1973), p. 226.

37 Ibid., pp. 227–30.

38 E.N. Mangat Rai to Nayantara Sahgal, letter dated 11 October 1965 (unpublished).

39 Vijaya Lakshmi Pandit to Gautam Sahgal/Gautam Sahgal to Vijaya Lakshmi Pandit, letters dated 10 and 12 October 1965 (unpublished).

40 Nayantara Sahgal to E.N. Mangat Rai, letter dated 19 November 1965 (unpublished).

41 E.N. Mangat Rai to Nayantara Sahgal, letter dated 22 October 1965 (unpublished)

42 E.N. Mangat Rai to Nayantara Sahgal, letter dated 9 November 1965 (unpublished).

43 Nayantara Sahgal to E.N. Mangat Rai, letter dated 16 October 1965 in *Relationship*, p. 155.

44 E.N. Mangat Rai to Nayantara Sahgal, letter dated 27 April 1965, in *Relationship*, p. 114.

45 E.N. Mangat Rai to Nayantara Sahgal, letter dated 20 March 1965, in *Relationship*, pp. 100–101.

46 E.N. Mangat Rai to Nayantara Sahgal, letter dated 28 May 1965, in *Relationship*, p. 126.

47 Published in *The Indian Express*, 29 August 1964.

48 Nayantara Sahgal to E.N. Mangat Rai, letter dated 10 May 1965, in *Relationship*, p.122.

49 E.N. Mangat Rai to Nayantara Sahgal, letter dated 9 March 1965 (unpublished).

50 E.N. Mangat Rai to Nayantara Sahgal, letter dated 30 August 1964, in *Relationship*, pp. 16–18.

51 E.N. Mangat Rai to Nayantara Sahgal, letter dated 18 August 1965 (unpublished).

52 E.N. Mangat Rai to Nayantara Sahgal, letter dated 25 November 1965 (unpublished).

53 Nayantara Sahgal to E.N. Mangat Rai, letter dated 21 May 1965 (unpublished).

54 Nayantara Sahgal to E.N. Mangat Rai, letter dated 30 November 1965 (unpublished).

55 E.N. Mangat Rai to Nayantara Sahgal, letter dated 6 December 1965 (unpublished).

56 E.N. Mangat Rai to Nayantara Sahgal, letter dated 25 October 1964, in *Relationship*, p. 48.

57 Nayantara Sahgal to E.N. Mangat Rai, letter dated 29 August 1966 (unpublished).

58 Nayantara Sahgal to E.N. Mangat Rai, letter dated 21 May 1965 (unpublished).

59 E.N. Mangat Rai to Nayantara Sahgal, letter dated 6 December 1965 (unpublished).

60 E.N. Mangat Rai to Nayantara Sahgal, letter dated 18 November 1964 (unpublished).

61 Nayantara Sahgal to E.N. Mangat Rai, letter dated 6 October 1965 (unpublished).

62 E.N. Mangat Rai to Nayantara Sahgal, letter dated 7 February 1965, in *Relationship*, p. 86.

63 Nayantara Sahgal to E.N. Mangat Rai, letter dated 10 June 1965 (unpublished).

64 Personal interview, Dehradun, May 2008.

65 Nayantara Sahgal to E.N. Mangat Rai, letter dated 2 November 1964 (unpublished).

66 E.N. Mangat Rai to Nayantara Sahgal, letter dated 29 November 1964, in *Relationship*, pp. 54–56.

67 E.N. Mangat Rai to Nayantara Sahgal, letter dated 1 October 1966 (unpublished).

4
SINGLE AGAIN

Storm in Chandigarh
The Day in Shadow

ON 31 JANUARY 1966, NAYANTARA LEFT HER HOME IN White House and moved into her mother's flat at E 8, Mafatlal Park (Bhulabhai Desai Road), a building owned by the textile manufacturer, Arvind Mafatlal. The flat had been rented (at Rs 318 per month) by Mrs Pandit when she returned from London after her stint as high commissioner; like all those lucky enough to find a place in the city, she preferred to leave it vacant while she was away rather than give up her lease. It was a beautiful flat, light and airy, situated near the Breach Candy Club and with a magnificent view of the sea. Nayantara compared its grandeur and harmony to the view from her window in Anokha and of Kanchenjunga from Raj Bhawan in Darjeeling, where she had stayed when Padmaja Naidu was governor. It calmed her, despite her agitated and unsettled state, for the separation and move had been traumatic.

White House was at sixes and sevens, because she had had to leave half her belongings behind so as not to be charged with desertion by Gautam, and the children were reacting badly to their parents' break-up. Noni was alternately sulky and belligerent, Gita drooping like a wilted plant for she missed Gautam terribly. Nayantara herself was seriously unhappy. Anxiety about how she would manage on her own was compounded by a letter she had received from Bunchi, in which it seemed to her that he was withdrawing from making a firm commitment to their future relationship. She sensed in his mood hesitation and fear, a palpable absence of serenity about their decision to leave their marriages – or, at any rate, to leave his, since she had already more or less left hers. He worried about Champa whose blackouts had become more frequent, and seemed burdened by the very real problems and pressures surrounding Nayantara's divorce and the responsibility that this entailed. She recalled what he had once said about 'marriage not being a form of association that could make me flourish', that he preferred a commitment made with loyalty and devotion to any tying of the knot. Despite the fact that an apprehension of his hesitation induced in her a blank, staring frame of mind, that she felt she was living between two worlds, 'one dead, one powerless to be born', she wrote to him to say that he must, on no account, feel obliged to take the consequences of her decisions.

> I could never accept a life or a position that cost you so much to make possible. If there is no light in you about this commitment, if what predominates is fear and worry and unhappiness, then do not be afraid to tell me, and to withdraw from it
>
> ... And, Bunchi, do not be afraid, if ever you are, that I would abandon you. I have many faults, but betrayal is not among them. The one human being for whom I have risked everything, and for whom I would gladly, and with a song in my heart, risk everything again, should never feel the lack of my love and trust.[1]

Bunchi responded immediately and effectively, reassuring her, putting his concerns about them in perspective and reiterating his determination to make a life together possible. It would be a barren year for them, he warned, waiting for the divorce to come through, being very careful about meeting so as to avoid charges of adultery, and dealing with Gautam's mercurial changes of mood. But he was in no doubt that his future lay with her, that they would walk the earth together, and that she was already his wife and comrade. Later that January, she and Bunchi entered into an 'agreement' regarding a code of conduct for themselves, which in many ways anticipated the kind of pre-nuptial contracts that some couples draw up these days.

AGREEMENT BETWEEN US/23 JANUARY 1966[2]

Definitions

a) 'First year' means the period from now onwards ending with the date on which divorce by mutual consent is decreed for Tara and Gautam.
b) 'Second year' means the period following the 'first year' ending with the date when remarriage is legally permissible to Tara.

Objective

a) Tara and Bunchi have decided that their mutually accepted, desired and defined objective is to live together and make a home together as soon as possible.
b) They recognise and accept that depending on whether Champa will agree to a divorce, the objective at a) may mean that they are unable to marry at any time, and will in any case, should Champa agree to a divorce, involve a period of years when marriage will not be possible, owing to the time the

law prescribes for obtaining a divorce under the procedures applicable to Bunchi and Champa's marriage.

c) The objective at a) is thus with marriage when and if possible, and without marriage if this is not possible, and in any case for the period that it is not possible.

Procedures and Timing

a) Tara and Bunchi have not come to a final decision as to what would be the appropriate timing for Bunchi to inform Champa of the position, or the appropriate timing for Tara to inform Gautam, her mother and others concerned. This clause touches on some of the factors in the situation.

b) It is recognised that when Champa is informed it will be inevitable that Gautam and others concerned will sooner or later get to know also.

c) Considering all the factors in the situation and particularly any ill effect that premature disclosure may have in regard to the children, Bunchi and Tara have agreed that no disclosure of intention should in any case be made till Gautam has signed and put into court the paper relating to a petition for divorce from Tara, and signed the letter of intent, both of which documents have already been signed by Tara. They are also agreed that it would be advisable to wait thereafter till Gautam's attitude shows some indications of settling down to a pattern of acceptance of his decision in regard to the divorce, the children, and the letter of intent.

d) Tara and Bunchi are not yet decided whether after the conditions at c) are fulfilled, which it is hoped will be a matter of 2–3 months, it would be advisable for them to wait for the whole 'first year' or a substantial part of it, or to go ahead with making their intention clear to those concerned. This point will be considered by them when they meet next (in March 1966, it is hoped) and thereafter and from time to time, if necessary, till factors seem ripe for decision and action in the matter.

e) Tara and Bunchi are agreed that during the 'first year' they should not live under the same roof (without chaperonage, e.g., with Champa in the house) and when they arrange to meet it will be with independent places of residence. Tara will ascertain, at the appropriate time, her legal rights and proprieties in regard to living together in the 'second year'. It is presumed that she will have complete legal rights to do so in the period following the 'second year'.

f) In Bunchi's case a relevant factor in living together is extricating himself from his work in J and K State and retiring from government service. It is agreed that keeping the 1967 election in view the appropriate time to plan his retirement would be July 1967 earliest, or thereabouts, assuming elections are over before that date. It is also recognised that should circumstances make necessary he could press for an earlier date of release.

g) The firm decisions that emerge from the above are:
   (i) Tara and Bunchi will not live together in the 'first year.'
   (ii) They will live together as soon as the 'second year' has ended.

   In between (i) and (ii) they may do so depending on the resolving of the various factors mentioned in this clause.

   In the background of these decisions it is agreed that should, from now onwards, any occasion occur where Champa brings up the subject of future intentions, Bunchi may indicate that he is thinking on the lines of making a home with Tara, but not commit Tara to such a plan till various factors mentioned in this clause are clearer, and it seems appropriate to define the exact intention.

Exceptions

Apart from such dates and timings that are subject to final consideration, Tara and Bunchi intend that the substance of these decisions shall only be reconsidered in one or both of two circumstances:

a) If Gautam insists and presses a reconsideration of his attitude and particularly if such reconsideration has influence or effect on the position of the children and/or
b) If any new and entirely unforeseen fact emerges.

Should any reconsideration of these decisions be necessary for any reason whatever, it shall be done by mutual consultation between Tara and Bunchi and not by one of them alone, unless in relationship to a) above, a pistol-point situation is thrust on Tara which makes prior consultation with Bunchi impossible, in which case she will use her own discretion.

Fidelity

Any physical relationship between Tara and Gautam or Bunchi and Champa during the 'first year' shall not be considered infidelity as between Tara and Bunchi. The position regarding the 'second year' will be discussed and decided as plans and dates mature.

Signed
Nayantara Sahgal

Gradually, as Nayantara began to make the flat a home and the children settled into a routine of sorts – going to meet Gautam either on their way to or from school when he was in town – she felt the tension slip away and began to relax. Now, when she stood on her balcony to watch the sunset's matchless performance, the evening light filled her with a sense of peace. One month after leaving White House she wrote to her mother to say that in the space of thirty days she had gained immensely in self-possession. She had a fuller social life on her own than she had had with Gautam, was able to cultivate freely those whom she liked and avoid those she found tedious or hypocritical.

> I feel like the doors of my life have been flung wide open & that fresh air is flowing into musty rooms. For the first time since I was 21, I am making of my life what I like and want & it is a satisfying experience. Bombay was never like this before for me.[3]

Not that the going was easy. Also, for the first time since she was twenty-one, she had to take care of everything on her own: looking after the children as a single parent, paying the bills, managing household expenses, husbanding her finances. Making ends meet while maintaining a certain standard of living for herself and the girls became an unfamiliar preoccupation. The day she signed the separation deed in court, she came home, took off both her diamond engagement ring and the eternity ring Gautam had given her when Noni was born, and returned them to him. Over the next few days she also gave back every piece of jewellery she had received from her in-laws at her wedding; the shares they had bought in her name were managed by Gautam in any case, and he looked after all the dividends. She left without a single asset that had been hers as Gautam's wife; all she had were her own earnings from her writing and royalties from her books.

Having a livelihood became an urgent necessity. Her fortnightly column for the *Sunday Standard* brought in Rs 300 every month, and every now and then she was asked to do a radio talk for All India Radio (AIR), at Rs 150 per talk, or write a feature for a magazine. Much as she disliked the idea of a job and working full-time, she needed something more regular than sporadic assignments. Prem Kirpal suggested she apply to UNESCO for a job; Jamal Kidwai thought she could do something at or for the Indian high commission in London; Kuldip Nayar at UNI kept assuring her that a job was in the offing but never actually made an offer; N.J. Nanporia of *The Times of India* was frank enough to say she was better off freelancing; and R.D. Bhagat of the publishing house, B.I. Publications, sent her manuscripts to review in anticipation of his firm's tie-up with Prentice-Hall of the US, but stopped short of employing her. She had hoped that something might be forthcoming from their old friend, Peter Jayasinghe's Asia Publishing House, but from him there was not even the hint of a suggestion. She was disappointed, but in a funny way also somewhat relieved, as she would much rather have the time and mental space to do her own writing, if only she could find a way of augmenting her income, somehow. For, as she said to Bunchi, she was

> ... basically a home person, a woman who finds satisfaction in home tasks, in the comfort and security of home, in the daily process of making a home. That gives me real joy ... There is an art in making a home and a fulfilment from it.[4]

Socially, however, she was much in demand and became the object of many men's attentions. Attractive, intelligent, a published writer and without a husband in the background, prospective suitors flocked to her, competing for her favours. Ruefully she recalled what Uday Shankar had said to her when she and her sisters were students at his dance academy in Almora: 'Men will always break their hearts and each others' heads over you.' This, when she was only fifteen! Among those more serious was the Ahmedabad mill-owner, Madan Mangaldas (brother-in-law of the textile magnate, Gautam Sarabhai) whose company Nayantara enjoyed and with whom she could speak about her troubled marriage and relationship with Bunchi. They met on his frequent trips to Bombay where he retained a flat in Mafatlal Park, and she looked forward to conversations and adult company outside the drawing-room circuit.

Mangaldas was attentive and urbane, a man of the world with a way with women. For Nayantara, his was a shoulder to lean on, a hand to hold. As his pursuit of her became more ardent, however, and as Bunchi began to indicate a certain disquiet with regard to this friendship, she found herself holding back, even letting fall that she might be moving to Delhi; to which Mangaldas responded with great good humour, 'Please don't do that or I'll have to buy a mill in Delhi!' Too civilised to force himself on her he cautioned her about remarriage, and remained friendly throughout. To Bunchi, however, she felt she owed an explanation and wrote to him to say:

> I have faced 'attractions' like Mangaldas over and over again. There have been a number of such people in my life, wanting my time and company and attracted to me.

> I know exactly where I want such relationships to take me – nowhere at all, in terms of permanence or emotional involvement ... If I were the kind of woman who has affairs or takes advantage of fleeting encounters, I'd have had dozens by now ... But I'm not and never have been that kind of woman. I have no use for a casual affair.
>
> ... I'd like to remind you that I have *lived* quite a bit, in the sense that my life has had tremendous variety and much excitement and what you call 'glamour' ... I've had them all and in abundance and it was with all that behind me that I met you and valued you.[5]

Some of Bunchi's apprehensions might have stemmed from a tense and difficult meeting between him and Nayantara in March that year, in Bombay. There was an ugly replay of violence on Gautam's part when he accosted Bunchi and Tara at the Shalimar Hotel where Bunchi was staying, and gave him a sound thrashing. Bunchi suffered a cracked nasal bone, a black eye and facial bruising; for good measure, Gautam slapped Nayantara around too, threatening to kill Bunchi the next time he found them together. All Nayantara's fears and guilt resurfaced with a vengeance. Gautam had been difficult with the terms of the separation, mercurial about paying bills, and completely unhelpful regarding Noni's further education abroad. The children, particularly Ranjit and Gita, were still upset about the separation and she herself was riven with doubt about her future, as well as the possibility of a future with Bunchi. Her own family, moreover, thought she had acted rashly, thrown in the towel for no good reason. A kind of emotional paralysis came upon her and she found herself unable to work constructively at anything. Over and above this was the looming scandal of a divorce and public opprobrium. She ricocheted between defiance ('I'm at my best in situations like this') and complete inertia, afraid that Gautam would have her movements watched. Having waited and waited for a meeting with Bunchi, she found she was unresponsive even with him.

Bunchi, beset with anxiety himself about obtaining a divorce from Champa, was confused and bewildered, confessed that he felt wretchedly alone and lost and floundering, needed from her affirmation and intensity, not goodness and kindness. He wondered, he said, whether this relationship with him came up against 'a passion more subtle, less known, even dark and compelling and of driving force'.[6] Perhaps Gautam still held her in his grip? He said to her then that she should consider a third, very real, alternative that was open to her – to live neither with him nor with Gautam, but on her own. It would not exclude him, but it would mean that she need not assume she would always be 'hung with a man'.[7]

For his part, Gautam missed Nayantara acutely, but his way of dealing with his loss was to spend as little time as possible in Bombay. Europe, Delhi, Chandigarh, anywhere that she was not, for when in Bombay he was alternately solicitous and hectoring. He asked her repeatedly whether she intended to marry Bunchi, told the children their marriage had ended because she was with another man, told *her* he wanted nothing more to do with her. Friends of his informed Nayantara that he was looking drawn and wretched and spending wildly, throwing hundred-rupee notes around, buying up bands in hotels for the evening, living recklessly. Shock and pain haunted his eyes.

Their emotional see-saw continued, compounded now by concern over Champa's frequent blackouts which could have been psychosomatic or physiological. Bunchi confessed that he felt as if 'shades and shadows of imprisonment' had closed in around him. Their together-yet-separate life could continue indefinitely should Champa refuse to give Bunchi a divorce, as she could easily do under canonical law. This meant that Bunchi and Nayantara would have to devise a living arrangement that might entail co-habiting adulterously under one roof, or living separately, but on the understanding that they were 'married'. But where would they live? Which city would be most hospitable? Bombay, with Gautam, was clearly not an option, nor was Chandigarh, where anyway Bunchi had already served as chief secretary and could go no higher. Delhi was a possibility, but for Nayantara the thought of Delhi was terrifying, like being thrown to the wolves in a jungle. Perhaps they could live outside India. An invitation to a university abroad offered Bunchi the possibility of taking time off to write his book on Kashmir, but if Nayantara was unable to accompany him the offer would have to be declined. His priority, he said, was being together, he was not willing to chase two moons. Nevertheless, they took some initial steps towards a life lived together by jointly investing a sum of Rs 10,000 to which both had contributed, and which they augmented over the year. In the midst of all the uncertainty and tension there arrived a forecast for Nayantara made by the pandit of their old Allahabad family friend, Rashid Shervani, which read as follows:

> From 20.4.1966 to 17.6.1966 your emotional desire will be at peak, but otherwise it is not a good period. You should be careful about your own self. From 17.6.1966 to 29.11.1966 this is a period of good enjoyment and good life. More interest in politics or in literary works and a craving for power is also indicated. From 29.11.1966 to 18.1.1967 this is an uneventful period. You should be careful of your enemies. From 18.1.1967 to 9.4.1967 is a period of awakening. You will leave no stone unturned to achieve and other spheres are normal. From 9.4.1967 to 6.6.1967 ... you should be very careful otherwise life will be doomed.[8]

Although she sent it as a sort of joke to Bunchi, one little corner of her mind grudgingly acknowledged the reality and power of cause and effect in life's course.

> An act has endless and continuing repercussions (she said) and each day might reveal a new, unseen, even undreamed of factor. If that is true with reference to externals – & I have faced so many 'externals' – then it is doubly and trebly true of 'internals', of the way we all react in feeling at any given moment when up against some facet, suddenly revealed, of a 17 year old relationship.[9]

And so their arid year wore on, with intermittent breaks for her in Delhi, occasional meetings with Bunchi, increasingly difficult encounters with Gautam over practical arrangements and legal provisions, and frustration regarding a job for herself. In October that year she calculated that she had made about Rs 9,000 from royalties and her columns, quite a respectable sum for 1966, but her financial insecurity continued to preoccupy her.

Bunchi, during this period, was responding both to Champa's intuitive fear of being abandoned and to Nayantara's depression as the reality of her separation and uncertain future began to sink in. His letters to her were, at once, an insistent affirmation of their love and an anxious apprehension of her unhappiness. Again and again he reminded her of the 'ultimate principle' on which they had taken the decisions regarding their spouses. His cause for concern was real; in January he and Nayantara had reached an agreement regarding their future plans, in March she was racked by doubt. In April she was absolutely certain she would never return to Gautam but by September she was in two minds.

Bunchi called this the 'NOT YOU' aspect of her personality, one that he felt could take over her rational, reasonable self.

> You go on and on returning to points and corners we have turned, and I go on and on being influenced and frightened by this ... Could we not try and work something out between us, and together, and go ahead with it finally and fully?[10]

He worried that Nayantara might find Gautam difficult to resist, that he would unbend just enough for her to relent, to be able to assuage her guilt at his obvious distress. He wrestled with his despair at what he feared was her emotional vacillation, but with his inherent sense of fair play he could not impose his will or his need on her, or compel her to make a commitment she did not wholly volunteer. That he felt unfairly dealt with by her he did not hesitate to tell her, saying even that he felt she used double standards in her assessment of his disquiet regarding Champa and his marriage.

On 19 October 1966 he sent her a thirty-four-page analysis of his reading of the changed situation and its implications for their relationship. Ever the bureaucrat, his note was drafted in the best traditions of the profession, down to a blank half page on one side for 'notations' by its reader. It was an extraordinarily detailed exposition setting out the evolution of the problem, its development, pros and cons and likely trajectory. In the process he analysed Nayantara's motivations and compulsions – conscious and subconscious – her confusion and contradictions, his own puzzlement and pain. And his vulnerability in the face of her loyalty to her 'kinsman', to her marriage, to convention. His note was ruthless in its clarity, remarkable for its compassion and understanding, unfaltering in its even-handedness. It spared neither Nayantara nor himself; while never doubting the integrity of their love he nevertheless accepted that there may be considerations larger than it for her. 'For me', he noted in his diary, 'I know that I will never have a friend, and a woman, and an equation as fulfilling and blessed as with Tara. So this may well be the end of my story in the realm that I value most.'

Earlier that month Nayantara had written to him to say that she was consicious of the fact that she had dithered, that it had not been possible for her to stand firm and provide him with the rock-like certainty he needed. There were many things she could say in explanation – a whole new life lived and a whole new person in herself discovered, difficulties experienced and revealed, fears felt, the pressures of opinion, the questioning in her mind, over and over and over again, about years of effort wasted and undone.

These nagging doubts had taken a terrible toll on her writing, the one activity that anchored her, the only 'work', really, that she wanted to do. Although she had begun thinking about her next novel it was tough going; she found the beginning, getting the process rolling, the most difficult and discouraging, the prospect of what she was about to embark on, daunting. The sheer size of what she was contemplating was scary. 'No, I can't possibly cope with that,' was her spontaneous reaction, 'I'll never make it.' The plot was too complicated, she would never be able to bring it to life, it just wouldn't work. Nevertheless she would

> ... go on squeezing out paragraphs so that finally I get into it, into the very thing I am trying to avoid, and then am able to go safely on. I am not 'rolling' till I have about 10,000 words before me – something solid on which to build.[11]

In December that year Nayantara left for Chandigarh with the children, for what would be their last winter vacation at Anokha. Her sadness over this leave-taking was compounded by the general disapproval she experienced from the Chandigarh crowd regarding her relationship with Bunchi. An air of sullen resentment, fuelled by gossip and an impression that she had been led astray by an older, more experienced man, discouraged her from participating in the usual social round over Christmas and New Year. Among the friends they had in common, only Kaka and Prem Swift seemed sympathetic to her situation, with Balbir and Sarla

Grewal and Eulie and Jugal Chowdhury openly aligned with Champa. As Nayantara herself remarked perceptively, a couple becomes the possession of a community, and injury to it becomes a community loss. Moreover, Champa was a familiar and popular Chandigarh figure, integrated more organically with the city and its small professional and bureaucratic society, while Nayantara remained an occasional visitor.

Within her own family her mother, though loving and supportive, was worried about her future and how she would manage alone with the children. Early in her marriage, Nayantara had decided never to discuss her ups and downs with Mrs Pandit or reveal any weakness or indecision in herself, knowing that her mother had very little inner stability to keep her serene and steady in the face of adversity. Lekha, on the other hand, practically inclined and in a less-than-happy marriage of her own, offered sound words of advice and could be relied upon to be discreet. This was more than could be said about her younger sister, Rita, and her husband, Avtar, to whom her behaviour was shockingly immoral. Apart from which he thought her completely foolhardy and reckless to be throwing in her lot with Bunchi. 'As regards you,' she wrote to Bunchi, 'I know I am completely alone and will never have any support.'

Nayantara returned to Bombay in January 1967, depressed and at a very low ebb emotionally. At home, Noni, going through a rebellious teenage, perhaps, clashed often with her mother who recognised that this was more than just adolescent angst – in Noni she felt she was encountering Gautam's temperament and rigidity of attitude. Recognised too that Noni was deeply attached to Gautam, missed him but was uncertain about his on-and-off relationship with them, and was now beginning to hold her mother responsible for the rupture in the family. Here was a child, Nayantara knew, desperately seeking love and understanding, yet she herself was unable to respond to either her friendships or interests. A year or two at an educational institution abroad would do her a world of good, she believed, and her preference was for the Badminton School in Bristol, where Indira Nehru had studied. But Gautam stonewalled all discussions on the subject, taking refuge in the strictly controlled foreign exchange regulations of the time. In any case, he maintained that what Noni needed was a finishing school, ideally one in Switzerland, for which he thought he could arrange financing. Neither Nayantara nor Noni were agreeable, however, although this may, with hindsight, have been a good option. In the event Noni enrolled in Elphinstone College in Bombay, having spent the intervening five months learning French, shorthand and typing.

In February that year, Vijaya Lakshmi Pandit decided to contest the Lok Sabha seat from Phulpur, her old constituency, although both Lekha and Nayantara had their reservations about the wisdom of doing so. Relations between Mrs Pandit and Indira Gandhi were far from cordial, had in fact been rather frosty ever since Mrs Gandhi became prime minister after Lal Bahadur Shastri's death in 1965. Consequently, Mrs Pandit received no help from the All India Congress Committee when she announced her candidacy – 'Not a rupee or a jeep or a kind word from anybody, and complete silence from Indu'.[12] This time, unlike 1964, Nayantara was reluctant to help her mother in her campaign, uneasy about leaving the children, but she was at the same time alarmed by her mother's accounts of anti-Congress violence in Allahabad while electioneering. Mrs Pandit's car was stoned, students from the university were out in strength shouting, 'Congress ka nash ho! Sarkar ka nash ho! Indira ka nash ho!' instigated, Mrs Pandit believed, by the Lohiaites and the Socialist Party.

> The stone-throwing at Indi has rightly been condemned by all parties (she wrote to Nayantara) but not in Allahabad. Oh, no – the public is so busy hating her that it is really frightening. Yesterday the SSP candidate opposing me said in a speech at Hamidia, 'Jaise Sarupnakha ki lambi naak kat gayi thi vaise hi pradhanmantri ki lambi naak kati hai. Jaise Ravan jala, vaise Congress jalegi aur Bharat ki janata holi khelegi.'[13]

Voting was held on 19 February 1967 and Mrs Pandit won by 37,000 votes, down from her 60,000 majority in 1964. Across the country the opposition parties – especially the Jana Sangh – did well in the north and south, with the communists and the Dravida Munethra Kazhagam (DMK) triumphing. As it turned out, Mrs Pandit's was a pyrrhic victory, for when the cabinet was formed Indira Gandhi pointedly ignored her; in a backhanded gesture she offered her the ambassadorship to France, which Mrs Pandit politely declined. In a letter to Nayantara written in early April, she commented wryly that among the four ministers of state positions being considered, the names doing the rounds were Maharani Patiala, the journalist Romesh Thapar, Yashwant Kapoor, Mrs Gandhi's secretary – and a fourth from the south. Appalled by the goings-on, she was seriously considering resigning from Parliament where the ratio of ministers to members was 1:5 – or in the words of L.L. Desai, '52 cards and a joker (Satya Narain)'.

After the 1967 elections, Nayantara for the first time began to see herself as an 'observer' of the Indian scene, rather than identifying with it completely, 'it & I in a magic circle'. Where earlier she had accepted everything about the country in a fundamental sense even though she knew much was wrong, now the ground beneath her feet had shifted. This realisation was almost unbearable and in time, it would set her on a collision course with far-reaching consequences.

Nayantara and Gautam's divorce came through on 1 March 1967, in a record fifteen months. (Considering, she said later, that it took many more months to get a ration card, one year to buy a Birla car and five to get a Fiat!) Both were required to stand in the witness box and answer routine questions, after which the divorce decree was passed. When they came out of the courtroom Gautam put his arm around Nayantara's shoulder and said he would drop her home in his car, their last ride together as a couple. In the car, Nayantara kept her eyes averted, knowing with complete certainty that Gautam was still in love with her and would go on being in love. Unable to control herself after seeing Gautam put on his dark glasses to hide his tears she began crying too, a signal as it were, for him to start upbraiding her, blaming her for bringing their marriage to this pass. Subdued, they reached Mafatlal Park and Nayantara suggested he come in with her to meet

Vijaya Lakshmi Pandit, in Bombay to be with her daughter. He stayed till about 12.30 p.m., chatting desultorily with them, and after he left Nayantara went into her bedroom and collapsed, slept, got up to eat a sketchy lunch, then lay down and collapsed again.

Gita went to see her father that evening and returned with him, and the whole family went to dinner at the Rendezvous. Gautam was attentive and loving, spoke warmly and at length with Noni, enquiring after her exam results and plans for college. On the way back he took Nayantara's hand and said to Noni, 'Your mother is very beautiful, I should like to date her. Would you mind that?' To which she replied, 'Mind? No, I'd be thrilled.' As if on cue, Nayantara was assailed by the old familiar feelings of guilt and regret, mixed in this time with nostalgia and a kind of tenderness towards Gautam. She felt strangely comforted by his presence; by the fact that he was yielding somewhat to the children, being affectionate and cheerful, a normal family man. And she experienced again the impossibility, yet strange durability, of her relationship with him, haunted by the desire that they could, somehow, establish a regularity of friendly contact as parents for the sake of the children, as well as for themselves. In him she sensed a change that, oddly enough, was a consequence of the divorce, as though having vindicated his honour he could now love her without owning her. 'I have myself, a real need to re-establish a healing relationship with him,' she wrote to Bunchi, a day after their divorce.

> And more than anything else I have a desire to get the look of him back to some semblance of the gaiety and

> sparkle he once had. Well, that is the human side. And there is the practical side ... as usual with G-me, I am afraid to lose the ground recovered and the goodwill established. I have felt such a tremendous burden roll off me as regards the children ... and I feel a different person because of it.[14]

Back and forth she went, relieved that a troubled marriage had ended but wracked by a peculiar dying sensation with reference to Gautam, a memory that could not be banished of the life there once was with him. 'It's all very hard to bear, Bunchi, very hard, and I can hardly bear it.' Nor could she have borne it if she ever found that the children were getting alienated from her as a result. Caught in an emotional twist, she both welcomed and dreaded their pendulum swing towards Gautam – were they to go over to his side altogether she would consider herself a criminal for letting her own life come first. Everything would become a mockery if they rejected what she stood for; she had only herself to give and if that wasn't good enough, she had nothing else.

Bunchi's reactions to Nayantara's outpourings were desperate in their bewilderment and perplexity. Everything she said about her response to her divorce felt like an earthquake to him, shaking their relationship to the core. How, he asked, could he assume that they would live together as a couple if she believed that Gautam was still very much in love with her and that, given half a chance, she would gladly embrace a stable and reassuring relationship with him? Where did that leave him? For the first time in many years, he found he couldn't sleep and was smoking heavily. Although he had written to Champa about Nayantara's divorce, he nevertheless had the gravest misgivings about her and her attitude, felt in fact that she had less and less interest in him as a person. Never had a relationship been worked at so hard as theirs, he said, and for so long and so single-mindedly. Every situation, every setback, every eventuality had been discussed threadbare, they had spared no effort or energy to do so. How could she expect him to take this latest shock in his stride?

In despair he confided in Kaval, sought her opinion about how he should deal with this newest development. Kaval, down-to-earth as ever, believed that Nayantara would come through eventually, but that great forbearance would be required of him in the meantime. She guessed shrewdly that Nayantara was susceptible to Gautam's sheer exuberance, something Bunchi couldn't ever match – he loved differently, quietly, in a lower key. And she told him quite frankly that she thought she herself would have been better for him because she could laugh ('sheer exuberance is so much a part of me!') but she didn't think Tara could.

Lekha arrived in Bombay a week after Nayantara's divorce and lent not just a sympathetic ear and a shoulder to lean on, but also offered a great deal of no-nonsense advice. On no account should Nayantara encourage Gautam's overtures; on the contrary she should actively discontinue meeting him and maintaining contact. Not only would it complicate matters terribly otherwise, it was also unfair to him as he was evidently still involved with her, whereas she was clearly planning a life with Bunchi, whose own divorce proceedings would soon be set in motion.

Ironically, the very divorce that had triggered an emotional tumult in Nayantara brought her face-to-face with its hard reality in the form of the Consent Terms that she and Gautam had agreed to in order to file for divorce by mutual consent. At issue was the question of an alimony to Nayantara in the form of maintenance, to be met by income from shares and securities invested in her name by Gautam. At the time of their divorce Gautam's estate was valued at Rs 8 lakhs, a considerable sum in 1967. According to the Consent Terms, Gautam would pay Nayantara Rs 2,000 per month as maintenance, which amount would be drawn from the share income. This allowance would cease in the event of her remarriage, although the children would continue to receive Rs 500 each. Upon reaching the age of thirty years, each child would get a one-third share of the invested money in their own right. The sting in the tail was that the entire share income would be added to any income Nayantara might earn on her own, and her tax liability be calculated on the combined income. In effect, Gautam's tax shelter (a common enough strategy for tax avoidance) would become her tax burden, for she could neither touch the share income nor trade in the shares.

Nayantara reacted to the full import of these terms with stunned disbelief; that she could have been naive enough to sign a document as crucial as the Consent Terms without fully understanding them, and that Gautam could, deliberately and with cold calculation, have foisted something so unjust and potentially crippling on her. Nor could she find it in herself to excuse Shri Bhai, a trusted advisor, for having misled her. Her attempts to redress the situation and persuade Gautam to review the terms or consider alternatives, drew a complete blank. Gautam refused to budge. Creating a trust in the children's name, he said, would attract a heavy tax payment, and defraying Nayantara's taxes from the share income itself would entail cutting off her alimony – he couldn't afford to do both. In any case, he didn't think this an unfair arrangement as her tax liability would increase only if her own income exceeded a certain amount.

There began an anxious and frantic correspondence on this impasse between Nayantara and Bunchi, and between her and her mother and Lekha, whose husband, Ashok Mehta, suggested that she seek another opinion on tax regulations. Bunchi, true to character and training, drew up detailed notes for her, together with rates of taxation, permissible deductions, rebates and penalties, with which to present her case. Gautam's accountants, as well as Shri Bhai, while deferring to her concern, remained non-committal. Early in April 1967, Nayantara wrote to Gautam informing him that Shri Bhai had told her he had 'misunderstood' the implications of the Consent Terms and thus given her an incorrect assessment of her tax liability. This being so, she put forward a couple of suggestions for his consideration:

1. I have all along maintained that you should create a trust. I do urge this again. You would have an initial tax burden, but in the long run it would be the wise course. There would be no further complications or mix-up regarding the money, and it would no longer stand in my name, which I would welcome.
2. I cannot make myself liable for taxation at the high rate which the share income imposes on me. The shares and securities are, after all, in my name only for your convenience. It is very unjust that I should be liable for a much higher rate of taxation simply because they stand in my name. If you cannot

> create a trust – and I still feel that you should – then two tax calculations will have to be made every year: one on my personal income only, and the other on the personal income plus the share income, with the difference between the two payable by you. My liability should be strictly confined to my personal income. And the same principle should apply to annuity and wealth tax.

She received neither a reply nor an acknowledgement from Gautam, although he let it be known to the children that the divorce had reduced him to 'poverty'. Worried about the fact that she would soon have to file her tax returns, Nayantara stayed awake nights, unable to sleep or to write. Her new novel was in limbo, not even half-written. Her brother-in-law told her quite simply that, as the shares were in her name, she should exercise all the rights of ownership but, as it turned out, custody was in their joint names, hers and Gautam's. Moreover, as they were held in trust for the children she would do nothing to jeopardise them. There was a slim chance that a legal review of the Consent Terms might work in her favour, but as she had voluntarily signed on the dotted line moving the courts didn't hold out much hope. Nevertheless, she sought out an old acquaintance from her Dil Pazir days, the lawyer Muhsin Tyabji, and entrusted him with the facts, such as they were.

Nor was there much joy on the personal front. Offers of work were fleeting and remained elusive, and Bunchi's desire to retire from government service and join the private sector met with little positive response. Industrialists like Lala Bharat Ram were friendly but non-committal, and businessmen like Garware merely wanted a point man in

Delhi to liaise with the government. As he had already served as chief secretary in Jammu and Kashmir as well as in his home state, both were no longer available and a posting in Delhi, commensurate with his seniority, would not be easy especially for someone with a reputation for integrity and independence. Meanwhile, initiating divorce proceedings of his own he encountered an unexpected obstacle: an application for divorce could not, by law, be filed in the state of Jammu and Kashmir as it was not governed by the same laws as the rest of the country. He would have to do so in Chandigarh, then live under the same roof as Champa for thirty days before the application could be registered and their period of separation commence legally. This would entail an extended leave from Srinagar, which he may or may not be granted. Everything, it seemed, was conspiring against them proving, Bunchi said, that he was right – he was doomed to survive. Nayantara replied,

> We both are, and must, and because survival alone will not do, we must do better. But for the first time in my life I have found effort & will not enough, the knowledge of love & comradeship not enough, doing the best one can, not enough. And for the first time I have needed God – not to pray to, but to keep with me ... to keep my feet firmly on the road and my actions true.[15]

On 2 July 1968, a little over one year after their divorce, Gautam married Rosemarie Wilhelm, the daughter of Dr Arthur Wilhelm, then vice chairman of Ciba and the man who had hired Gautam in 1951. She was twenty-eight, sixteen years younger than Gautam, a divorcée with two young children whom she left behind in Switzerland to be looked after by her parents, while she returned with Gautam to live in Bombay. Their marriage came as a complete surprise to Nayantara, who heard about it a week later from her daughter, Noni, whom Gautam informed; but the romance was, by all accounts, already at least a year old. In July 1967, at the height of the Arab-Israeli war, Gautam had made a rushed trip to Cairo to rescue Rosemarie, then divorced from her first husband. He brought her back to safety in Switzerland, and although he may not exactly have been in love with her she was attractive in other ways, not least as a step up in his career. She, however, was completely infatuated with him, swept off her feet by his personality. But for Nayantara and Bunchi, the long wait for remarriage had just begun, five years at the very least. Christian law required that the divorcing couple wait three years after their application was registered; another year before a decree was passed; and one more year before remarrying. As Bunchi and Champa's application for divorce had still to be filed his marriage to Nayantara was very much in the future. But divorce proceedings had already been initiated and he found he was at the receiving end of unkind cracks from all, including his family. 'I suppose the ICS are like the maharajas,' his sister Priobala said, 'they put aside one woman and take another.' And Champa wondered whether Bunchi should be likened to Hitler or Caligula or Al Capone.[16]

Storm in Chandigarh, Nayantara's third novel, dedicated to Bunchi, was completed in July 1967 and published in 1969 by W.W. Norton in the US, and Chatto & Windus in the UK. Written at the height of her marital problems and during one of the most traumatic periods in her life, the subtext of the novel is so close to her own life and situation as it unfolded during 1965–66, as to be unmistakable. 'I still have no title for it,' Tara wrote to Bunchi when she finished it, 'and I am dissatisfied about not having made enough of it. I greatly regret my mental pressures and strains of the past months ... my total inability to unwind.'[17] But it was done, she sent it off to her agent, William Morris in the US, and put it out of her mind.

Set in Chandigarh, *Storm in Chandigarh* is like an elegy for the city, a kind of farewell to a house, a life and an environment that Nayantara knew would no longer be available to her. Despite her initial unease in Chandigarh society, leaving it was definitely a wrench. As early as October 1965 she could write: 'I have been thinking this evening of how much I shall miss Chandigarh – miss having it as my home, as being mine, and it did become mine over the years.' She would miss the view of the hills from her window, the walks by the lake, the brilliant sunsets, the sound of the children's laughter as they raced up and down the infamous ramp. More than these, though, Chandigarh had become something of a symbol in her marriage and her life. It was here that Gautam and she had started life together again after the 1959 crisis, in a new house, and it was here that the first blow-up between her, Gautam and Bunchi took place in December 1964. She had decided after *This Time of Morning* that her next novel would be set in Chandigarh so that she could relive some part of her life, recreate some of the city's particular character.

The events in the novel take place some time around the

mid-1960s against the backdrop of the division of Punjab in 1966 into Punjab, Himachal Pradesh and Haryana. United East Punjab's chief minister, Partap Singh Kairon, had just been assassinated, and Master Tara Singh's agitation for a separate Sikh-dominated state had been successful. The demand for a separate state was as old as pre-independence India, with Master Tara Singh declaring, 'We want a province where we can safeguard our culture and our tradition.' It received a fillip with the setting up of the States Reorganisation Commission in 1953, but the Akali resolution asking for a Punjabi Suba was rejected by the Commission in 1955. Kairon himself, chief minister of Punjab from 1956 to 1965, was strongly opposed to the linguistic division of states, going so far as to place a blanket ban on the publication of all reports about the Akali agitation.[18] A committed secularist, he referred to Master Tara Singh as 'a fool with a capital F',[19] and the Punjabi Suba was Enemy No. 1. Kairon was convinced that division spelt ruin for the people and for the progress of Punjab. Tara Singh pressed on, insisting on the demarcation of a territorial unit where, on the birthday of the gurus, armies of Sikhs might march in the streets and a Sikh flag fly with the national flag.[20] Negotiations with the Union Government continued for a good ten years, till 1966, when Punjab was finally divided. The new state of Punjab now had a population that was 54 per cent Sikh and 44 per cent Hindu, and a shared capital with Haryana – Chandigarh.

In the novel the chief minister of Punjab, Gyan Singh, is a swarthy, aggressive, no-holds-barred go-getter, bent on appropriating maximum control over, and benefit from, hitherto shared resources and infrastructure. His counterpart in Haryana, Harpal Singh, is the opposite: mild-mannered, soft-spoken, deeply unhappy about the division of the state. *Haryana*. The word stuck in his throat, struck no chord in him. He had never wanted it to exist. Hadn't one division, in 1947, been enough? What could possibly be gained by breaking it up again into three separate states? He had no use for sanctifying another language, spouting another nationalism. Uneasily, he recalled that he and Gyan Singh shared a past – in the awful killing violence of Partition Harpal had been a desperately fleeing refugee on a bus driven out of Pakistan by Gyan Singh. Since then, Gyan had made his way in the world through a cunning combination of guile and muscle. The last thing Harpal wanted was to tangle with him. Now, as if to confirm his worst apprehensions, government employees had called for a statewide strike in response to Gyan Singh's threat to take over control of the dam at Bhakra Nangal in Punjab. The air was electric with tension, labour was restive, and Chandigarh residents and businesses braced themselves for an indefinite disruption in their power supply.

The central government put its foot down with a firm hand – Bhakra was a national facility, managed and run by its own authority; it could not be held to ransom by a wilful chief minister. Into this stand-off between Gyan Singh and the Union home minister steps Vishal Dubey, a civil servant with the highest credentials and a reputation for successfully handling the most difficult situations. He accepts the challenge, much against his better instincts, and arrives in Chandigarh, little realising that his own life is in for a huge change.

Vishal Dubey is modelled on Bunchi, down to the last

verbal flourish and his belief in a 'higher morality'. Like Bunchi, he is a civil servant with a reputation for honesty and the ability to deliver; like him, he had helped in post-Partition rehabilitation in the Punjab and earned his juniors' respect and loyalty. Unlike Bunchi, he is a widower, albeit with a similarly unhappy marriage behind him. He has been handpicked by the Union home minister, Old Bones, for the job of persuading Gyan Singh to call off the strike, something even the home minister knows is like tilting against windmills.

Vishal arrives in Chandigarh and the intersection of his personal life with the official and political sets the stage for how the story develops. Jit and Mara, and Inder and Saroj, are old Chandigarh residents who take Vishal under their wing. They are part of the small non-official community that, together with the displaced and resettled refugees from Pakistan and sundry professionals who have relocated, make up the capital's business and social community. Inder owns and runs a factory – nylon, the new textile of the 1950s and '60s; Mara, Jit's wife, runs a school; Jit is semi-retired and Saroj is a housewife and mother, now expecting her third child. Both marriages are dysfunctional; Inder and Mara are involved in a half-hearted affair while Jit and Saroj look on, unhappily and somewhat helplessly. In this foursome Jit is the opposite of Inder, and Mara of Saroj.

Unexpectedly, and to his surprise, Vishal finds himself responding to Saroj's trapped stoicism and vulnerability, seeing through it to a resilience born of a fundamental sense of self-worth and faith in the ultimate triumph of goodness and decency. This enables her to withstand Inder's ferocious jealousy, his unpredictable and violent outbursts which an appalled Vishal is witness to. Almost involuntarily, or so it seems to the reader, Saroj begins turning to Vishal for a few simple pleasures – a walk by the lake, a friendly conversation, a listening ear. The inevitable happens.

Unhappy marriages recur like a leitmotif in Nayantara's novels, confirming her own belief that marriage fared pretty well if one thought of it as an institution, but fell flat if one examined it as a relationship. Her own parents apart, most of the marriages around her, family as well as friends, were unsatisfactory, held together by convention and fear of social sanction. Of all the women in her novels so far, however, Saroj is possibly the most timid, enveloped by a suffocating, oppressive domesticity. Yet Faubion Bowers, reviewing the book in the *Village Voice* wrote:

> Somehow Mrs Sahgal makes passivity a source of excitement ... the unnatural pall of a go-slow action, the only kind of a situation impossible to handle ... is as much a source of excitement as the violence of the strike when it *starts* to begin.
>
> It is a masterpiece ... it grips like snow tires on an icy road.

Although Nayantara maintained that the characters of Saroj and Inder are a type, the parallels between their marital situation and her own are striking. Like Gautam, Inder cannot either forgive Saroj for her premarital affair, or forget it; like Nayantara, Saroj finds herself hemmed in by her marriage but unable to break out of it; and like her, again, the promise of emotional support from Vishal/Bunchi gives her the courage, eventually, to walk out. The shadow of her own troubled marriage hovers over every page of the book, becomes the template on which she plots her narrative. Yet, of all the characters in the novel, Nayantara says the one she would rewrite is Vishal, because he is too recognisably based on Bunchi. She would allow him to be more himself, develop a personality that did not mimic Bunchi's. (Bunchi himself thought Vishal was 'more a presence and an idea than a person', and that the novel would have benefitted from 'a break in the breathlessness' of its conclusion.)[21]

Vishal is the thread that ties the two parts of the story together, which otherwise unfold quite independently of each other. Inder is tangentially a part of the political story as his factory is gutted during a labour strike, but this is incidental. The organic meshing of the personal and political that characterised the earlier two novels is elusive here, with the political story gaining in credibility. As characters, the two married couples are only partially realised, and the relationship between Vishal and Saroj is strangely without vitality: one is hard put to see what exactly Vishal is attracted to in Saroj.

By contrast, Gyan Singh and Harpal Singh, though typecast, are more fully developed and have both a personal and a political history which progresses to its logical conclusion. They are, in fact, what keeps the story going. The strike is called, two thousand workers surround the dam, all road junctions are blocked by the strikers. Vishal, implementing the Union government's order to keep the works going, has posted four hundred men at the site with instructions to ensure uninterrupted power supply to the city. As darkness falls that evening lights begin to twinkle across Chandigarh and Harpal Singh prepares to go home, a happy man. On his way out of the office Vishal hears that his one rock of support at the Centre, the home minister, has passed away; and Gyan Singh calls off the strike as a token of respect to the departed leader. But before the old man can be laid to rest winds of change have begun to blow in the corridors of power – Vishal is chided by the cabinet secretary for sticking to his guns, for not compromising with Gyan Singh and somehow averting the strike. The time for principled action, for the Gandhian example of every act proudly performed in the sunlight, would be buried with Old Bones.

In May 1967, L.P. Singh, then home secretary in the Government of India, phoned Bunchi in Srinagar to tell him that he had been appointed as special secretary to the ministry of petroleum and chemicals at the Centre. For the first (and last) time in his career, Bunchi had requested a posting in Delhi as it seemed to be the most neutral city in which he and Nayantara could begin a life together. An initial meeting with the then cabinet secretary, D.S. Joshi, had prompted a comment by him regarding Bunchi's drinking habits. Bunchi was taken aback but held his own, following up his interview with a letter on the subject. There was silence from Joshi. Bunchi mentioned the matter to L.P. Singh as well as to G.M. Sadiq, both of whom dismissed Joshi's objection as irrelevant. Still, mindful of the fact that with Indira Gandhi in power his chances of being accommodated were slim, Bunchi also sent out feelers for jobs outside government. And so, when L.P. Singh called to inform him about his appointment, he was both surprised and relieved.

And not a little sad.

Kashmir was a difficult state, almost predictably on the brink of eruption, politically, at any given moment. As chief secretary, Bunchi was on his toes as a matter of routine, responding to the differing styles of Sadiq and Mir Qasim and their different political and strategic responses to crises. Centre–state relations were also delicate, with D.P. Dhar (then state home minister) having frequently to take Bunchi into confidence and act if Sadiq and Mir Qasim were reluctant to 'take the plunge'. Then, as now, perceptions in the Valley regarding critical developments and policy responses to them were at great variance with the Centre. One such, within a year of Bunchi's taking over as CS, was the August 1965 war with Pakistan. The view in the state government had been to deal decisively with the infiltrators, cross the ceasefire line and attack Pakistani positions. 'The only solution to Kashmir is now in our hands,' Sadiq had said on 25 August. 'Let us not lose it or hesitate. This is the only answer. Let us win or lose, but nothing midway.' But Indian Army generals were reluctant – because, in Bunchi's view 'we are deeply pacifist' – so that when, eventually they did cross the CFL the next day, Sadiq remarked, 'India will fight this war to the last policeman.'[22] In this instance, at any rate, Sadiq stood firm as a rock. For Bunchi personally at the time, the circumstances were at once poignant and worrisome, for staying with him then in Srinagar were his sister, Priobala, and his mother-in-law, Mrs Singha, both Pakistani nationals.

Despite the tensions that were part of the warp and weft of his time in Kashmir – the 1965 war, Sheikh Abdullah's release from jail in 1964, Nehru's death soon after and its implications for the state, and sundry local skirmishes – leaving Kashmir was a huge wrench for Bunchi. He had been happy in the state and had been able to initiate certain long-term administrative changes that would professionalise the services and better integrate the state within the Indian Union. He liked and admired many of his colleagues and superiors and was trusted and well-liked in return. And the physical environment was unsurpassed; he loved the hills, and Srinagar was where he and Nayantara had discovered in each other a kindred spirit; his deepest regret was what he called 'the lack of faith within India'. Gandhi and Nehru might have put through the secular idea but India had not achieved it in fact. No Muslim could feel he belonged. The Sikh may, the Christian may, but the Muslim was not accepted. A wave of nostalgia swept over him as he prepared to leave, uncertain of how he would adapt to Delhi. He was, by inclination and experience, an officer of the provinces where he preferred both the people and the work, the smaller canvas where his abilities could be best used.

And so it was with a feeling of great sadness and apprehension that he packed his bags in July 1967. Things were likely to be emotionally upsetting on the home front, as he and Champa were to submit their application for separation, prior to divorce, as soon as they arrived in Chandigarh on 7 July. Champa was unhappy at leaving Kashmir, did not want to return to her teaching job in Chandigarh, and told him repeatedly that he was paying a very heavy price for his infatuation, for what was in the end just a 'bit of fun and games'. On the drive down to Jammu and from there to Chandigarh, she remained either silent or reproachful. When they reached home, the state of the house reflected their turmoil. Their tenant, Mehta, was still resident, the place was a mess, dusty and unkempt, and it was raining heavily. The weather was sultry, hot and humid, and Bunchi felt as if they were stranded on a railway platform. A horrible change from Kashmir.

These minor irritations apart, they now had to come to grips with the reality of their divorce and the anxieties around it. Champa had shown considerable restraint thus far – and perhaps on account of it had a recurrence of sleeplessness and blackouts, on one occasion experiencing six in one night. What she had thought might be a temporary affair on Bunchi's part was looming before her as a radical change in her life and circumstances, one that she projected onto him as ruinous for him as well. 'This is your home,' she said to him, 'openness to all who come, laughter and goodwill – no one has crossed this threshold without some degree of acceptance.' She deplored the change that had already come over him: narrower, smaller, not himself. There had been other men in Nayantara's life, she said, her divorce from Gautam was inevitable. Why did he have to get caught up in it? 'Kaval was alright, a straightforward Punjabi. But here you will be cat's paw, a speck eventually on the horizon of a woman much younger than you, who will do what she likes and keep you in your place.' She found an ally in Priobala who arrived unannounced in Chandigarh shortly after they had. She advised Champa against agreeing to a divorce, confident that 'T's family are not likely to countenance it'. To Bunchi separately, she said he was being a fool, that wives and marriages couldn't be cast aside on mere fancy.

And indeed, Bunchi himself conceded that he had experienced much warmth in their marriage, a gregariousness that had come about largely through Champa's outgoing and sociable personality. She attracted friends and sought out a variety of acquaintances who, left to himself, he may not have pursued. Twenty-three years of marriage entailed certain claims, placed responsibilities on him that could not be shirked. Nor would he shirk them; but equally, he would not surrender his personal freedom – the fundamental truth by which he sought to live – to a relationship that he could no longer honour, that, on a daily basis, repudiated the values by which he wished to live, and be. But for Champa, his 'truth' was 'academic, theoretical, even cruel, certainly unnecessary', and she couldn't accept it emotionally.[23] Nor could she reconcile to the eventuality of a divorce – and yet, just such a break had been a very real possibility with Kaval three years earlier.

On 7 August 1967, Champa signed the application for divorce in an atmosphere tense with unhappiness and, on Bunchi's part, guilt and superstition – 7 August being what he had earlier designated as the birthday of his heart. Priobala was unrelenting in her hostility and disapproval, and he felt quite shattered by what he was inflicting on Champa and what the future held for her. 'It's not the money or anything like that,' she had said, 'it is the company and companionship – how can one live without that?'[24]

And again, what really could he offer Nayantara that would be whole and wholesome?

Bunchi arrived in Delhi on 8 August, immediately after he and Champa had signed the application for separation, and went straight to Prem Kirpal's home on 23, Safdarjung

Road. They had agreed that he should stay with his friend and contribute to household expenses till government accommodation for him came through. Bunchi was relieved at not having to look for digs right away, but the feeling of being unsettled all round did not leave him. At work he was having to familiarise himself with the workings of a ministry he knew little about – petroleum and chemicals – and the realisation that his position, though on par with that of a secretary to the government, was quite dispensable. For although he could deal independently with his subjects under orders from his minister, in matters of policy he would have to work under the secretary – he had neither the power nor the responsibility to advise.

Outside the work situation, his main preoccupation was finding a suitable flat for Nayantara when she moved to Delhi in December with Gita, to join him. His old misgivings about their living under two separate roofs rose to the surface again as he contemplated the To Let ads in the papers and made the rounds of flats in Jor Bagh, Sundar Nagar and Defence Colony. A modest flat in a decent colony would be in the Rs 600 – 800 range, a rather large sum for Nayantara who was on a tight budget. Running two households, keeping two sets of domestic help, allowing for transport between their two homes – it was all adding up alarmingly.

Ever the administrator, he made up a list of monthly expenses for them that added up to just about what they could afford on her allowance of Rs 2,000 p.m. and his salary, after he had paid for Champa.

Expenditure for both of us per month and the children:

1.	Servant	Rs 250/-	Including dhobi, casual cleaning up, etc.
2.	Rent	Rs 650/-	
3.	Electricity & Water	Rs 150/-	
4.	Food	Rs 700/-	
5.	Miscellaneous		a) Transport is likely to be a heavy item in Delhi, with school, office for me & living under 2 roofs.
	a) Transport	Rs 300/-	
	b) Drink & tobacco	Rs 100/-	
	c) The rest	Rs 500/	c) The rest means everything else – toilet, occasional clothes, writing & reading material, occasional travel.
6.	The children in so far as they are not included in the above items	Rs 750/-	This includes fees, books, clothes, extras, etc
	Total	Rs 3500/- p.m.	

I realise this can only be a rough estimate and we may even save on some items like nos. 5 & 6. Please consider how far this is real.

But how would they deal with the unexpected? Another list of combined resources was drawn up which, at its most optimistic, included share income, Nayantara's earnings from her writing, bank/ post office savings, and totalled Rs 4,600/- p.m.

The practical option, he believed, would be for both of them and the children to live in the house that would be allotted to him, but Nayantara was adamant: two roofs, not one. And so, many flats later and after consulting with Lekha and Mrs Pandit, Bunchi finally settled on C 316 Defence Colony for Tara, at Rs 650 p.m., and signed an eleven-month lease on her behalf.

Meanwhile, Champa and Chandigarh were never too far away with friends reporting that she was lonely and unhappy, and she herself writing to him to say,

> Wouldn't it be best of all if my life came to an end. General handclaps all round and my sick heart at rest. I have the bottle [of sleeping pills] I took away many years ago from Eulie, all intact, unopened, bearing its 25 tablets. Enough for 2 elephants. Why should a person live who is unhappy and knows there's nothing due to be till death?[25]

Nor was Nayantara's state of mind any easier. She and Bunchi might have decided to live in the same town, but the children were none too keen on the move. Noni was openly against it, especially as it became clear that she might have to repeat a year in a Delhi college; and Gita minded terribly a home reduced by half and school friends left behind. And then there were the vexatious Consent Terms and a tax situation that she was trying valiantly to overcome.

In August that year, at her mother's urging, Nayantara went to England to consult a specialist for a medical condition and spent time in London as well as in Paris and Rome, a break that both she and Vijaya Lakshmi Pandit felt would help reduce the stress of the last many months. Despite the fact that this time she was in London without her mother's presence at 9 Kensington Palace Gardens, the official residence of the Indian high commissioner, the change was welcome and enjoyable. This time too she made a special point of meeting and seeking out Bunchi's close friends and acquaintances, in particular Ronald Sampson and his family, whom she visited in Bristol, and Inder Bhattacharji in London. But the highlight of her trip was a weekend in Fleury with Nicky and his wife, the first time she would have an opportunity to spend time with him alone after 1948.

Paris was enchanting, she fell in love with it all over again as soon as she arrived on 5 September. The city in autumn, the trees gold and brown, was extraordinarily beautiful with its perfection of architecture, cobbled streets, stone courtyards and lacy, wrought-iron balconies. The week she spent in France rediscovering neighbourhoods and bistros, lingering in galleries and museums, eased the tensions that had never quite left her, even in London. And then there was Fleury.

Nicky and Sabine's country home, an hour away from Paris, was French aristocratic, situated in acres of garden and trees. The house was old, high-ceilinged and gracious, though filled with the kind of heavy furniture that tended to dwarf the rooms. Sabine busied herself with household chores and with her family, her mother and sisters who lived close by, leaving Nayantara and Nicky to reminisce by themselves. He was as elegant, gracious and gentlemanly as ever, affectionate and solicitous, but Nayantara thought she sensed in him that unhappiness without a name that hovers just beneath the surface. Memories of their spontaneous and mutual – and in his case, long-cherished – attraction for each other rushed unbidden to her now, filling her with nostalgia and concern for him. Perhaps even for what they had lost. It was, she told Bunchi, the one and only time her mother had unequivocally voiced her strong disapproval, telling Nayantara that if she had even the faintest idea of breaking her engagement to Gautam, she would be responsible for calumny being heaped on Nehru, and that the scandal might even cause his government to fall.

Nicky had been bewildered and broken by her decision to renounce him, told her now that he had worn the ring she had given him then till it began to cut into his finger and he had to take it off. She confided in him about her divorce (He said, 'You had so much character and personality, how could you suddenly become so subdued? I never understood that.'), about Bunchi, and though she hoped for a similar confidence from him, he held his reserve. 'When you make up your mind to make another person happy,' he said to her, 'that can be a twenty-four hour job, and then there isn't time to think of the self.'[26] She tried in more ways than one to draw him out, to tell her about himself, but he was cautious, deflecting her queries gently but firmly. And so she came away feeling sad and incomplete, yet glad that they had finally had an opportunity to meet without constraints.

Back in Bombay, she was soon immersed in the seemingly endless process of relocating and resettling in Delhi, and in the protracted and unfinished business of shares and taxes and a reasonable resolution to the problem. In the end, Gautam agreed to an Association of Persons being formed which was in the nature of a family agreement, by which the shares would be transferred to the children in graduated stages in order to both reduce the burden on Nayantara and avoid any gift taxes that this might attract.

Nayantara left for Delhi with Gita on 6 December 1967, having arranged for Noni to continue at Elphinstone and lodge at Sophia College. She was glad now to be on her way, to end the long separation between herself and Bunchi and begin a new life in a city new to them both. Relieved in a way to be leaving Mafatlal Park that had, in any case, been like a transit flat. And yet it had become a home in which she had lived as an independent woman, in which moreover, she had shared a space with Bunchi, however briefly and infrequently. He felt it too, a palpable regret at shutting the door on a place that he identified solely with her, that he could, as he said, immediately see her in when they were apart. The phone by her bedside, the desk she worked at, the balcony they sat on, the many dinner table conversations they had as they sipped their brandies.

But even before Nayantara arrived in Delhi and they began living in the same city, the strains of doing so came to the surface. Together but not married; two roofs not one; social and family pressures, especially for Nayantara; divorce and work anxieties for Bunchi. Doubts and unhappiness, some hurtful disagreements about how to cope with these stresses and, for the first time, a feeling of fear between them. Of hurting each other or the children by this unconventional decision, or hurting her mother politically. For her part Nayantara was terribly aware of Bunchi's misery and lack of buoyancy, of how the light had gone out of him ever since her divorce. Troubled herself, she became brittle and distant, unable to respond to his needs and insecurities. The week he had been in Bombay, 10–17

November, had been, she knew, one of tearing, unreasoning hurt for him, a pure ordeal. 'In me it has created the ghastly feeling that I am in the dark with you – or somewhere outside your dark – that I can't reach you.' Having burnt their bridges, however, they had no option but to press on.

Nayantara arrived in Delhi with a mountain of luggage, reached Defence Colony and was filled with dismay; the flat was small, there was hardly space enough for her and Gita, let alone all the furniture and personal belongings. Tensions ran high, with Gita miserable at her new school, Mater Dei Convent, and Bunchi unhappy with the continuous to-ing and fro-ing between Defence Colony and Safdarjung Road. They bickered constantly; he was scathing about her reluctance to move into a house with him, she was worried about the scandal that would ensue. Differences between them on this reached such a point that Nayantara began feeling that the relationship couldn't work, seriously wanted to get out of it. Writing was at a standstill, and although she had accepted a commission from the National Council of Educational Resources and Training (NCERT) to write a supplementary reader on the national movement for them, she was too distracted to attempt anything of her own.

Sometime in April 1968 Bunchi was offered a house in Lodi Estate and a decision had now to be made about whether he should accept it – as it was in a grade lower than his designated category – or wait for what was his due. He would take it only if Nayantara moved in with him; and so it was that after considerable hesitation and fearful of what this living together might mean for Bunchi's divorce, she left Defence Colony for 44 Lodi Estate.

Much to Nayantara's surprise and to her great reassurance,

Gautam's family were neither disapproving nor distant; they were warm and friendly, visited often, thought of the house as her home and behaved as normally as before. As she set about organising it and reconciling herself to the shift, as friends and family, nephews and nieces moved in and out of the house, she found in the domesticity a calming and stabilising influence. Never quite a Delhi person, her circle of acquaintances grew as she resumed her newspaper columns; and though she remained as always, largely solitary, she settled into a rhythm that had a tenor more even than she had known for some time.

Also to her surprise and relief – and it must be said, a little heartburn, as well – Noni and Gautam's new wife, Rosemarie, got on like a house on fire. Close enough in age, they enjoyed each other's company, did fun things together, went shopping and to the movies. Noni spent weekends with her father, and when he was away, with Rosemarie. Those flashpoints of irritation and rebellion that marked her relationship with her mother were completely absent with Rosemarie, who obviously was nowhere near as demanding or disciplining, so that now when Noni came to Delhi during her holidays, she was in a sunnier frame of mind than Nayantara had anticipated.

Gita too was much happier after she was withdrawn from Mater Dei and admitted to the British School, then run from a small house in Defence Colony with one inspired and charismatic principal, Mrs Shankland, one teacher and a handful of students. Although still a far cry from the Cathedral & John Connon School in Bombay which Gita had left behind, it was liberal and flexible, child-centred in a way that suited her perfectly. In 1972 she left

India to continue her education at yet another progressive school, Atlantic College in Wales, then the only institution that offered the International Baccalaureate. Set up by Kurt Hahn (who had started Gordonstoun in Scotland) with active support from Dickie Mountbatten, it provided the kind of intellectual environment that opened up new and vast vistas for Gita, much as Wellesley had done for Nayantara. But it was expensive, beyond Nayantara and Bunchi's budget. Mountbatten stepped in; said it wouldn't be 'right' to offer Gita the Nehru scholarship, but that other aid would be sought.

Atlantic College was internationalist in the sense of throwing people from different social and cultural backgrounds together, in the belief that understanding difference through dialogue could forestall hostility at a national level; and it encouraged its students to engage in some form of socially useful work in the community as well. After her IB, Gita joined the School of Oriental and African Studies in London for her undergraduate degree, which is where she was when India's Emergency was declared – frightened for her mother's sake.

The Day in Shadow, Nayantara's fourth novel, was dedicated to her three children and published by Norton in New York (1971–72), London Magazine editions, London, and Vikas in Delhi, also in 1971. It is set in the capital, and the story revolves around Simrit, a recent divorcée, and Raj, a member of parliament, who is slowly falling in love with Simrit while tackling the growing corruption, double dealing and power politics within the bureaucracy in the capital. It is the most explicitly autobiographical of Nayantara's novels, and possibly the least successful.

Simrit and her young children live in a barsati flat in a new south Delhi colony, where she is trying to cope with life as a divorced woman, saddled with a set of terms regarding her financial liabilities that are so unfair and crippling as to leave her with one hand tied behind her back. Her difficult material circumstances are compounded by her worst apprehensions regarding her son coming true before her very eyes. The teenaged Brij cannot resist the allure of his father's wealth and power, or the promise of an education abroad and all the attractions of a life of privilege. His father, moreover, exerts a magnetic influence on him, with all the trappings of success on seductive display.

> Each time Brij entered his father's office, something delicious happened to him. Everything about the office was controlled and immaculate. The temperature for one thing. Whatever it was like outside, here the air was exactly right. The sounds were subdued office sounds. In the main room where the secretaries and stenographers sat with frosted glass partitions between them, typewriters discreetly punctuated the silence. There were brand new journals on technology and engineering symmetrically placed on a round table in the visitors' section of the room. Not a scratch or a smudge on any glossy wood or glass surface. The chairs were upholstered in moss green leather framed in dark teak. There was a coffee-coloured pile carpet. Brij breathed deeply. It was beautiful.[27]

Simrit knows she is losing him to a lifestyle and values that she abhors, that she herself has turned her back on, but knows also that this will be a losing battle. Brij is torn between loyalty to his mother and admiration of his father, now an irresistible force in his life, and in order to ensure his survival, opts for a path of no-confrontation with either of them. A path of non-violence, one could say.

Simrit's life and marriage with her ex-husband, Som, is recounted in flashbacks and mimics the author's own, almost to the last detail. Som works with a European multinational company, is ambitious and driven to succeed, the blue-eyed boy of his German principals. Simrit is increasingly disconnected from this corporate life, unable to participate with the enthusiasm that Som clearly expects from her.

> 'I'm worried about Simrit,' he says to his German colleagues, 'she's not herself.'
>
> 'How do you mean that?' Vetter required interestedly.
>
> 'I don't know,' Som replied, 'I have no idea.'
>
> Then,
>
> 'I'm busy ... I'm away a lot – it's part of the game ... I can understand that upsetting a woman, but she called it destruction.' He laughed ruefully. 'Oh, not of our marriage. I could even understand that. She doesn't need me to spend more time with her – she's very complete with the children and her writing and the rest of it – she wants me to spend more time with *myself*. You know, sit and contemplate about goals and so on.'
>
> Vetter said something Simrit did not hear.
>
> 'No, no, not literally, but – you know – think about things. Think with a capital T, and about matters not connected with what I have to do from morning till night. Tell her she's got more to give the children because of the business and the life I lead – more money, more

> extras – and it's just so much water off a duck's back. She just doesn't care.'[28]

Similar conversations had taken place between Gautam and his Swiss principal, Dr Kapelli, regarding Nayantara; Kapelli, who was very fond of her, had suggested more than once that she travel to Switzerland for a complete medical check-up, which he would personally arrange for her.

Simrit blames herself for the divorce, for breaking up a home, and Raj is, willy-nilly, drawn into picking up the pieces with her. Brij, anxious to somehow keep the lines of communication open between his parents, tries to intercede with his father about the 'tax problem' but just can't muster up the courage to do so. Besides, Som has already told him that he will inherit huge amounts of money from him – 'You're going to be a millionaire, boy' – and that he is planning to send him abroad for further education.

Simrit can see her son slipping away from her, slowly but surely.

Against this family drama there unfolds, via Raj, a story of sleaze, bribery and venality in the corridors of power, as opposing forces jostle for control over the resource of the future – oil. Licences for drilling this black gold are to be given out by the government, and rival claimants backed by their governments are lobbying with ministers and civil servants for contracts. The Russians are in the fray, as are the Americans, already present in the country through their petrol companies. Once again, the smooth-talking, manipulative minister outmanoeuvres his opponents, and a deal is struck that compromises the country's interests.

Raj is, of course, Bunchi, Simrit is Nayantara, and Brij is Ranjit. During the time that Bunchi was special secretary in the petroleum ministry, India was embarking on a programme of Indianising oil explorations and the oil companies, via oil imports from the Soviet Union and the setting up of the Indian Oil Corporation. Not surprisingly, the American oil giant Esso and the Anglo-Dutch Burmah Shell were far from pleased at these developments. Esso – the Rockefeller-owned Standard Oil Company – lobbied vigorously with the US government against the Indian government's policies, hoping to use India's dependence on the US for foodgrains to pressurise it. At the time Bunchi was already involved in tough negotiations with Phillips Petroleum over a joint venture in Kerala, the Cochin Refinery, and it was clear to him that no one was going to retreat in a hurry.

In the novel, the wheeling-dealing minister, Sumer Singh, signs a contract for oil exploration with the Soviets, raising a furore in parliament. Raj, as MP, objects, saying that parliament has a right to documents and information, that the minister could not withhold these, citing 'public interest'. Sumer Singh, however, was giving public notice of a very different event, of a departure from a twenty-year-old policy of non-alignment. 'We have to decide where we stand,' he declared, 'the West is in decay, they know it themselves – we have to look in a new direction.'[29]

Critics responded to Nayantara's skill in portraying Delhi as a 'kind of floating amalgam of ambition and administrative chaos' and praised the novel's emotional and intellectual maturity. Maurice Wiggins, writing in *The Sunday Times* (London) said the story had 'a sort of wistful wisdom which distinguishes it from the general run of immature psychological solipsism'.

Inasmuch as the fictional characters are based on real-life personages, there are no surprises in *The Day in Shadow* – by now this had become a recognisable feature of Sahgal's novels. What is unusual is the presence of Brij/Ranjit, the first time that one of her children figures in her books – in fact, the only time.

'My father had a *huge* influence on me,' Ranjit Sahgal told me when we met in Chandigarh at Anokha, 'and I hero-worshipped him as a child. He would tell me, "Sahgals have broad shoulders, Sahgals don't cry, Sahgals don't lose, we always win."'[30]

Gautam became Ranjit's role model. He followed in his father's footsteps professionally, joining Ciba (a decision he made while still at school) and working his way up the organisational ladder; even, like his father, living abroad for the most part of his working life and marrying a European. Unlike his sisters, his relationship with his father never soured, never reached a point of no return. When his parents separated, Gautam kept asking Ranjit whose side he was on, told him he couldn't ride two horses at the same time. Ranjit replied that there was no question of his choosing either one or the other parent, said, 'If your emotions tell you you have to abandon me, so be it – that's your choice, not mine. I worship you both.' His parents' divorce hit him badly and he was never able to reconcile himself to it. 'It took a piece out of me, and it's never been replaced ... I developed a dislike for life, a hatred of it ...'[31]

But he knew where his father was coming from, and

anger apart, Gautam never abandoned him, as he did his daughters, who he believed were in their mothers' camp.

> I was his only friend when the rest of his family distanced themselves towards the end ... I was his reference point, not only his son ... Right to the end, he hadn't reconciled himself to the separation or the divorce or anything else that happened afterwards. In me, he saw a lot of my mother, I think ...
>
> Every argument we had, every disagreement, was emotional, and it was always about the divorce ... But we never disconnected, I never abandoned him.[32]

And, 'I'll never let him down,' pledges Brij in the novel, 'never as long as I live.' Pa turned towards him and his look, warm, possessive, electric – the only look in the world – went right into Brij.[33]

Endnotes

1 Nayantara Sahgal to E.N. Mangat Rai, letter dated 24 January 1966 (unpublished).

2 Agreement dated 23 January 1966.

3 Nayantara Sahgal to Vijaya Lakshmi Pandit, 28 February 1966.

4 Nayantara Sahgal to E.N. Mangat Rai, letter dated 27 March 1966 (unpublished).

5 Nayantara Sahgal to E.N. Mangat Rai, letter dated 5 May 1966 (unpublished).

6 E.N. Mangat Rai to Nayantara Sahgal, letter dated 28 March 1966 in *Relationship: Extracts from a Correspondence* (New Delhi, Kali for Women, 1994), p. 186.

7 E.N. Mangat Rai to Nayantara Sahgal, letter dated 4 April 1966 in *Relationship*, p. 189.

8 Nayantara Sahgal to E.N. Mangat Rai, 13 May 1966 (unpublished).

9 Nayantara Sahgal to E.N. Mangat Rai, letter dated 2 June 1966 in *Relationship*, p. 196.

10 E.N. Mangat Rai to Nayantara Sahgal, letter dated 4 October 1966 (unpublished).

11 Nayantara Sahgal to E.N. Mangat Rai, letter dated 12 August 1966 (unpublished).

12 Vijaya Lakshmi Pandit to Nayantara Sahgal, 20 January 1967.

13 Vijaya Lakshmi Pandit to Nayantara Sahgal, 13 February 1967.

14 Nayantara Sahgal to E.N. Mangat Rai, letter dated 2 March 1967 (unpublished).

15 Nayantara Sahgal to E.N. Mangat Rai, letter dated 5 January 1967 (unpublished).

16 E.N. Mangat Rai to Nayantara Sahgal, letter dated 7 August 1967 in *Relationship*, p. 232.

17 Nayantara Sahgal to E.N. Mangat Rai, letter dated 29 July 1967 in *Relationship*, p. 232.

18 V.N. Datta, *The Tribune 130 Years: Witness to History* (New Delhi: Hay House India, 2012).

19 E.N. Mangat Rai, *Committment My Style: Career in the Indian Civil Service*, p. 177.

20 Rajiv Kapur, *Sikh Separatism: The Politics of Faith* (London: Allen & Unwin Ltd., 1986), p. 212.

21 E.N. Mangat Rai to Nayantara Sahgal, letter dated 24 November 1967 (unpublished).

22 E.N. Mangat Rai, *Committment My Style*, p. 230.

23 E.N. Mangat Rai to Nayantara Sahgal, letter dated 30 July 1967 (unpublished).

24 E.N. Mangat Rai to Nayantara Sahgal, letter dated 10 August 1967 (unpublished).

25 Champa Mangat Rai to E.N. Mangat Rai, 30 August 1967.

26 Nayantara Sahgal to E.N. Mangat Rai, letter dated 11 September 1967 (unpublished).

27 Nayantara Sahgal, *The Day in Shadow* (New Delhi: Vikas Publishing House, 1971) pp. 66–67.

28 Ibid., pp. 77–78.

29 Ibid., p. 152.

30 Ranjit Sahgal to Ritu Menon, personal interview, Chandigarh, November 2008.

31 Ibid.

32 Ibid.

33 Nayantara Sahgal, *The Day in Shadow*, p. 217.

Nayantara Pandit, ca. 1939.

Bronze head of Nayantara Pandit by Isamu Noguchi, New York, 1946/47.

Nayantara and Chandralekha Pandit, photographed for *Vogue*, New York, 1943.

Nayantara and Chandralekha Pandit, on arrival in the US, 1943.
(Blackstone Hotel Studio)

Nayantara and Rita Pandit in Mexico City at the home of
Miguel Covarrubias, 1946. Photograph by the well-known artist, Tamayo.

Rita Pandit, Bob Hope and Nayantara Pandit in Hollywood, 1946.

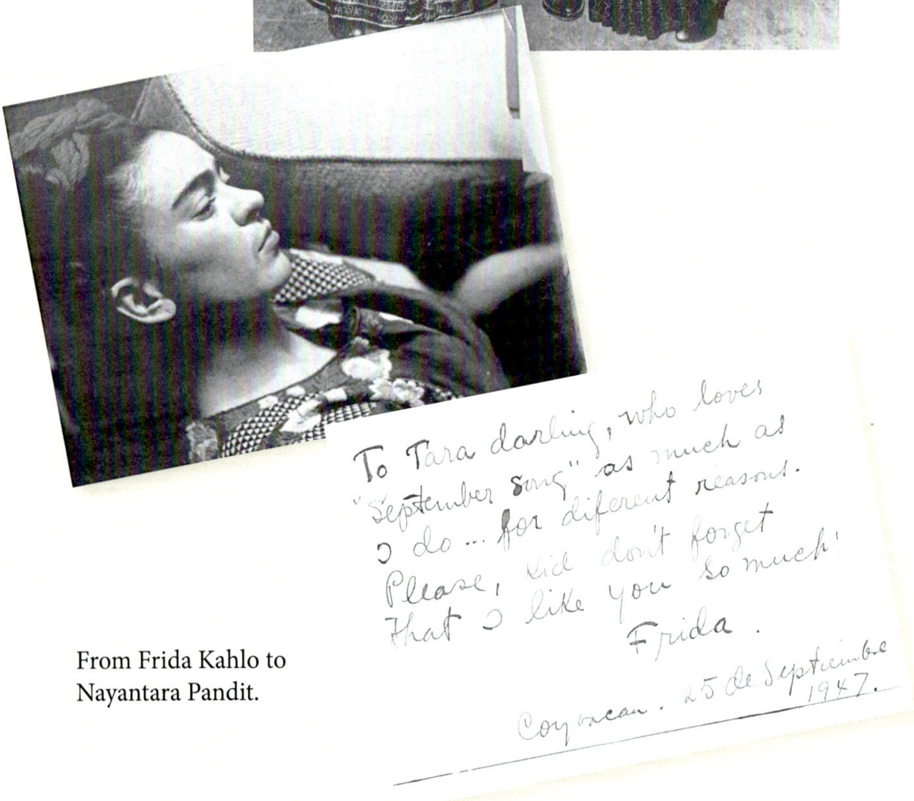

To Tara darling, who loves
"September song" as much as
I do ... for diferent reasons.
Please, kid don't forget
that I like you so much!
Frida.

Coyoacan. 25 de Septiembre
1947.

From Frida Kahlo to Nayantara Pandit.

Feroze Gandhi.

Indira Gandhi, ca. 1950-51.

Chandralekha Mehta, Vijaya Lakshmi Pandit and Nayantara Sahgal, at Teen Murti House, New Delhi, 1950s. (P.N. Sharma)

Nayantara Sahgal, Vijaya Lakshmi Pandit and Rita Dar in New Delhi, 1952.

Nonika, Nayantara and Ranjit Sahgal in London, 1955.

Ranjit, Nonika and Gita Sahgal in Srinagar, 1959.

Nayantara Sahgal at work.

With Lady Duggan and the daughter of the head of Twentieth Century Fox (sister of Marilyn Silverstone).

From Ho Chi Minh to Nayantara Sahgal, 1958.

Rita Dar, Chandralekha Mehta, Vijaya Lakshmi Pandit, Nayantara Sahgal and Padmaja Naidu in New Delhi, 1968.

Ranjit Sahgal, Rajiv Gandhi, Sonia Gandhi and Priyanka Gandhi in New Delhi, 1987.

Nayantara Sahgal with Prosser Gifford (second from left), Director of the Woodrow Wilson Center, Washington D.C., 1981.

Nayantara Sahgal at the award ceremony for the Commonwealth Writers' Prize, 1987. On her left is Ben Okri. (Martin Cole)

Githa Hariharan and Nayantara Sahgal at the Neemrana Festival, 2002. (Courtesy: Roli Books)

Ruchir Joshi and Gita Sahgal in South Africa, 1991.

Nonika Sahgal.

E.N. Mangat Rai and Nayantara Sahgal in Washington D.C. , 1981.

Nayantara Sahgal and E.N. Mangat Rai in Dehradun, 1986/87.

PART TWO

1968–2005

5

POLITICAL . . .

Political Columns

The Sunday Standard

Everyman's Weekly

BY A CURIOUS CIRCUMSTANCE OF HISTORY, BOTH PERSONAL and political, Nayantara relocated to Delhi at the same time that her cousin was embarking on recasting the Congress party in her own mould. And by the same curious circumstance, but this time more personal than political, Nayantara began writing the political columns that would reconfigure her relationship with Indira Gandhi, unalterably and permanently.

Nayantara Sahgal was probably the first woman political columnist in the country, beginning with the *Sunday Standard* in Bombay, and continuing in Delhi after she moved there in 1967. (At the time, Nandan Kagal was the editor of the Delhi edition, which sold for the princely sum of 18 paise.) She may not, however, have been a columnist by choice. Financial constraints following her divorce and the expense of managing on her own, in a way, forced her hand. Then, as now, a writer couldn't hope to live off her royalties and so, for a good many years, her fiction and journalism proceeded more or less in tandem, albeit with considerable difficulty; it meant snatching time from her other preoccupations, from householding and parenting. Nayantara wrote a regular political column for close to fourteen years for the *Sunday Standard* (of the Indian Express Group), as well as for Jayaprakash Narayan's *Everyman's Weekly* before the Emergency of 1975, when she reported on the student movement in Bihar. Among others, and on occasion, she also contributed to *The New Republic*, *Atlantic Monthly*, *The Times* (London) and *The Far Eastern Economic Review*.

What connected her fiction and non-fiction was, quite simply, politics, and politics is what triggered her imagination. To write politically was the only way for her to proceed. 'I approach fiction that way,' she told me.

> To write a sort of apolitical novel wouldn't have come naturally to me. The thing is, whether I wrote fiction or non-fiction my connection with politics was my emotional mainspring, not an event happening out there. I have been profoundly affected by it, one's laughter and tears, everything was connected with it, and there was no getting away from the emotional element in politics ... I've never grown a hard shell about *that*.[1]

Her emotional engagement apart, Delhi provided the kind of grist for a political mill that entailed continuous appraisal and analysis; from 1969 onwards, events unfolded in such an unexpected manner and at such speed that Nayantara was soon in the thick of it. Early in the year, she noted that the national mood was at a low ebb, that a party that had been committed to austerity had been reduced to horse-trading and self-aggrandisement. The Opposition, ineffective though it may have been, was waiting to fill the vacuum, while the most militant and organised outfit had coined the dangerous slogan of Hindi-Hindu-Hindustan. In February 1969, mid-term elections in five states indicated a downhill slide for the Congress; within the party, meanwhile, signs of an imminent rupture between the old guard and a tilt in favour of Mrs Gandhi could no longer be wished away. Deftly, she neutralised the Syndicate and as the year wore on, Mrs Gandhi's grip on the party and on government policy became more secure. She revived two key provisions of her earlier 1967 Ten Point Programme – bank nationalisation and the abolition of the princes' privy purses. Nayantara's columns on both the party and her cousin's policies and tactics became increasingly critical and unequivocal. The stronger faction within the party, she wrote, exhibited 'unparalleled crudity', the only consideration being power and its maintenance. The winning side's victory was unprincipled, the cultivating of real politik a dangerous strategy. In her view, the mass rallies that Mrs Gandhi had taken to organising outside her house were reminiscent of the Nazi and fascist propaganda of Hitler and Mussolini, not befitting of an elected representative. The leadership, she said, had 'unleashed a violent atmosphere in which those without scruples can take charge' (*Sunday Standard*, 7 September 1967).[2] The nationalisation of banks, she wrote, was a populist initiative with little substance, and rural credit a complex issue that could not be simplified via loans to small entrepreneurs. She saw these trends, political and economic, as signalling the end of the Nehruvian era, the end of the liberal values he stood for.

Nayantara was not alone in her denunciation; commentators like Frank Moraes and Nandan Kagal deplored Mrs Gandhi's ends-justify-the-means rationalisations, as well as her lack of responsibility towards her party and colleagues in parliament. In November 1969, Nayantara's criticism became even more strident, blaming the Congress directly for the deterioration of standards in politics. 'The government,' she wrote, 'has put up a performance worthy of the best gangster tradition in politics.' The party had no space for criticism, assiduously cultivated personality rule, and eschewed any kind of accountability at all. A party that didn't respect its own constitution could hardly be relied on to uphold the Indian Constitution or abide by its principles. By the time the Congress split in December, Nayantara's pessimism was near-total. The breakaway Congress, her cousin's faction, had nothing new to offer; the majority in the party were go-getters, what service could they perform for the country? She charged the party with instigating anarchy in Bengal and communal frenzy in Ahmedabad, both 'signposts of calculated disorder'. This was a mockery of revolution: 'It looks very much as if deception, disguised as revolutionary fervour, is being practiced on the Indian people.'

'As a political writer I was up against the establishment,' she told me.

> I was not writing political commentary at a time when all was well in the country. It was a period when the government, the prime minister, was seeking authoritarian powers. This was over a period of time before the Emergency, leading up to it ... so all of this I was recording, and coming up against authority in a very shattering way.[3]

She was warned repeatedly that if she didn't fall in line, all would not be well. When she tried to get accreditation as a journalist, to which she was entitled, she was told not to bother. This meant she couldn't belong to a professional fraternity or seek protection from a journalists' union. She was always alone, always on her own.

Throughout the early 1970s, Nayantara took up those issues that impinged most directly on the country's economic and political life. In her March 1970 column on the budget, she slammed the proposal to club husbands' and wives' incomes for tax purposes, saying it would deal a body blow to women seeking employment. It was 'an error on government's part not to treat women as independent financial entities', and deny them their right to keep a legitimate portion of what they earned. A recurring theme throughout this time was her concern about the erosion of democratic principles and the suppression of all dissent. The country was witnessing a growth of authoritarianism, so much so that 'it is not a matter of conjecture what the situation will be a few years hence. Whatever it will be is already happening.' She deplored the inability of Indian intelligentsia to organise against this trend, to resist the encroachment of the powers that be on their fundamental rights. Educated Indians, she maintained, played no role in influencing the direction India took – in order for this to happen, a more engaged, deliberative and active public was called for.

Her misgivings were shared by others too; a couple of months earlier the *Economic & Political Weekly* commented that:

> It is maintained that Indira Gandhi's colleagues, fearful of taking positions contrary to the PM, have gradually and almost gratefully fallen into the habit of referring matters to the boss ... Questions are being asked whether this method of functioning is at all healthy and whether it doesn't lead to a durbari atmosphere.[4]

Of Mrs Gandhi's landslide electoral victory in 1971 (even before the triumph of the Bangladeshi war of liberation) Nayantara said that any party with a two-thirds majority deserved to lead, and that Mrs Gandhi's singular accomplishment in this election had been to convince the electorate that 'she has nothing to do with the past, that she stood for something different. Perhaps Mrs Gandhi will be India's answer to Mao, the alternative she herself believes she is, who will be able to combine progress with a commitment to democracy.'

But she was unwavering in her scepticism regarding socialism, going so far as to think that Nehru's faithful adherence to Fabian socialism was 'economic emotionalism', quite impractical for India. Of the Indian brand, Nayantara believed that as long as the essential needs of people – health, food, shelter and education – remained unmet, it would remain mere tokenism. The government was not interested in working towards real socialism; even the Left parties, she wrote, were concerned with a more-radical-than-thou rhetoric rather than with socialism on the ground.

Looking back at 1971–72, Nayantara wrote that the victory in Bangladesh and Mrs Gandhi's mature foreign policy with regard to India's immediate neighbours were the two achievements of that period. On the negative side, class war had intensified, there was growing sympathy with the Naxal movement, and politically the country had seen a shift towards centralisation and a weakening of the federal structure. The government's call to 'end disparities' sounded hollow, because 'disparities' between the ruling class and ordinary citizens had never been greater. She called politicians, well taken care of by the state, 'nationalised individuals', who had no idea of the difficulties faced by the common man.

By the mid-1970s, Nayantara was openly comparing the promise and potential of the Gandhi–Nehru era with what she called the degraded political culture of the new Congress. Notwithstanding the Indian National Congress's many shortcomings, its romance with the masses was genuine; that romance was now over, and in its place was a 'shady affair in which there is not the compassion of Gandhi, the vision of Nehru, or the realism of Patel'. The Congress president, she wrote, blamed the corrupt bureaucracy for preventing the implementation of policies, a strange complaint given the corruption within the Congress itself. Accusing it of 'double-speak and double-think', she said Nehruvianism was now in full retreat, with Congress in the hands of a ruthless clique. 'Far from being "democratised" after the split, the party functions under a single line of command, where every chief minister, every person in the top hierarchy, knows that they owe their position to the PM and hold it at her pleasure.' Nothing, she said, could be farther from this state of affairs than governance under Nehru, when opinions were expressed, debate was welcome, and even his own son-in-law was free to expose corruption and venal politicking.

It is hardly surprising that Mrs Gandhi was displeased.

Unlike Nayantara, and for better or for worse, she had entered the political fray, and for a decade or more had encountered and weathered the rough and tumble of Indian politics. Also for better or for worse, she had tried to set in motion certain reforms that were in line with centre-left politics, reforms that she had argued for even while Nehru was alive. As early as 1959 she had told a Conference of

Provincial Congress Committee Presidents and Secretaries that

> It must be made clear that the persons who do not see eye to eye with the objectives of the Congress and its economic programme and are not in a mood to keep pace with the progressive section, who are determined to work for the establishment of democractic socialism, should have no place in the organisation.[5]

And later, 'The task of building up a powerful cooperative movement must be taken in hand immediately ...' (Nayantara recalled that when, after Nehru's death, she asked Indira why she had resigned as Congress president after just one year, her cousin replied that it was because she couldn't do what she wanted to.)

Having proven her mettle now and wrested control of the party from the old guard, and having, moreover, won the elections by a huge majority, Mrs Gandhi would have felt justified in purging the party of those vested interests that were an obstacle in her path.

This was anathema to Nayantara.

> I spoke out against my cousin *because* she was my cousin – how could she, of all people, betray the freedom and democratic ideals we had fought for ... I was defending my uncle's values, it was inconceivable to me that India could betray her tryst with destiny.[6]

Over thirty years later, Nayantara said she would write her columns differently now, that her emphasis would change. On abolishing the princes' privy purposes, for instance, while in no way endorsing their feudal privileges, she nevertheless believed, like Nehru, that 'a government doesn't break its word', that it was important for it to stick to its covenant. And on bank nationalisation, she acknowledged that she didn't know too much about it herself but, according to Morarji Desai, nationalisation of the Imperial Bank meant social control had already been attempted in the rural areas by extending credit to those in need; taking over the other fourteen banks didn't necessarily further the desired objective. She believed Indira Gandhi 'had done the wrong thing for the right reason'. Wanting to break away from the Syndicate was a sound reason because, Nayantara told me,

> ... she didn't want the socialist legacy destroyed – even in Shastri's time, I think she felt this was beginning to happen. But she went about it the wrong way, she could have achieved the same thing without these gimmicks.
>
> But all this is hindsight.
>
> I didn't have the maturity then, and what I did with my political writing was that I destroyed myself. I went all out ... went hell for leather when I saw what was an authoritarian trend taking over.[7]

Her columns had great impact and gained her a large following, but all this came at considerable personal cost. The break with Indira was a great loss for Nayantara, especially as they had been so close at one time; even politically, she realised she could have been less judgemental.

> I should have kept my mouth shut, I couldn't. I thought leaning towards the Soviet Union was a betrayal of non-alignment, but in hindsight, how else could we have kept our distance from America? How would I have dealt with it? And I saw how the signing of the treaty with the

> Soviet Union was greeted, the enormous popular impact it had ... so I was mistaken.[8]

On 13 October 1971, and without any prior indication, Bunchi received a courier notice from the Central government, relieving him of his duties in the ministry and placing his services at the disposal of the Punjab government 'with immediate effect'. No reason was given for this sudden decision but on enquiry, Bunchi found that he had been implicated in a particular case, referred to as 'the pipeline case', under investigation by the Takru Commission. The fact that he was nowhere on the scene during the period under investigation and that his own conduct was not the subject of enquiry, suggested that the Commission was being used as an excuse to banish him from the Central government. As no position for a person of his seniority was available – or was made available – in Punjab Bunchi decided to resign after thirty-three years of exemplary service, and put in his request for premature retirement. He was only fifty-seven on the day he left the Government of India, 19 February 1972.

It would have been a difficult and painful decision for someone of Bunchi's reputation and calibre, but the decline in service conduct and standards had been apparent to him for some time. There were very few signs of team spirit within the services, he noted, but many of doing the very best for oneself. Later he would write of this in his account of his career as a civil servant; of his last few years in service he said:

> It was an isolated and lonely game, lacking affection, loyalty and adventure; often devoid even of humour.

> The politics of power, present and potential, seemed to have gone deep into the working, and now the soul, of bureaucracy; it was neither policy nor public principle that determined action, but whatever maintained and enhanced personal position.[9]

Nayantara was convinced that a good part of the reason for his sudden transfer lay in Bunchi's relationship with her and her own uneasy relationship with Mrs Gandhi. She and Bunchi moved out of 44, Lodi Estate and stayed for four months in journalist Rahul Singh's flat in Sujan Singh Park, before moving to rooms in Massey Hall, the YMCA's property, on Janpath. Bunchi became adviser to a German institution in Faridabad, and this was where they had their home for the next twelve years. A new phase in their lives had now begun.

Among the friends and acquaintances that Nayantara and Bunchi had in Delhi was the cultural counsellor at the US Embassy, Margaret Clapp (formerly president of Wellesley), at whose home they met Tom Arpe, then the head of the English department at Southern Methodist University in Dallas (Texas). Would she consider spending some time as writer-in-residence at SMU, Tom asked Nayantara. To say that she was taken completely by surprise would be an understatement – the whole idea of being a writer-in-residence was a novelty. As someone who had never considered herself a Writer with a capital 'W', she wondered what she would do as one in residence at a university. Dallas, in any case, she associated with Kennedy's assassination and could hardly bring herself to thinking about going there. But then, here she was in Delhi where Gandhi had been shot dead, and surely that was much closer home. And so, in the autumn of 1973, Nayantara and Nirmal left for Dallas, where they stayed till the summer of 1974.

It was a wonderful break. Away from the dailiness of life in Delhi, in an academic environment of teachers and students and with just a light teaching load – that too of a creative sort – the whole sojourn was relaxed and fun-filled. The entire English department was made up of people from the east coast, not a single Texan among them, and all of them were lively and engaging. Never having taught in her life, Nayantara invented the course as she went along, concentrating more on teaching her students *how* to read, and only then attempt writing. But although she was meticulous in discharging her responsibility and their stay became a pleasant interlude, she didn't really enjoy her experience of teaching – the environment was culturally too alien and writing, not teaching, was her thing. This she couldn't do at SMU, and so she declined Tom Arpe's offer to extend her time at the university for another year.

The 1970s in the US, like the 1950s in Bombay, were a time of great literary and creative churning in theatre, the arts, dance; yet, despite all the opportunities offered to her to meet writers and other literary personalities, especially in New York and Cambridge, Nayantara was curiously unadventurous in this regard. She visited museums, yes, saw plays, met people like the John Kenneth Galbraiths, old friends like Dorothy Norman and others she had known earlier, even Isamu Noguchi, but she didn't seek out the writers of the time. Never wanted to, she said, unless she was particularly taken with their work. At SMU she embarked on a serious reading of the southern writers – Eudora Welty, William Faulkner, Tennessee Williams – which she found enormously rewarding, but it remained just an individual journey of discovery.

In 1974, it was Nirmal's turn to be invited by his old friend, Morris-Jones, now director of the Institute of Commonwealth Studies in London, to spend some months at the Institute, writing a book. The subject was administration, and Nirmal, having served under the British, pre-independence, and later the Indian government, was well placed to write about the two systems of governance. They lived in a small flat in Mecklenburgh Square, by London University, but as soon as they arrived, Nirmal was hospitalised with pneumonia. London was bitterly cold, the flat was inadequately heated and cramped, and Nayantara was plunged into housekeeping and coping, in addition to making daily trips to the University College Hospital to be with Nirmal. The contrast between London in winter and Texas, with its vast expanses, sunny weather and the extreme comfort of the campus, couldn't have been greater. It was also a huge change from Nayantara's earlier visits to London when her mother was high commissioner, living in the luxury of 9, Kensington Palace Gardens, and being wined and dined by a succession of socially and politically prominent people, meeting the most interesting minds of the time.

Their stint in the city now was much more modest or ground level, with England herself in some turmoil. The miners' strike meant coal shortages in an already severe season, there were demonstrations against nuclear stations being built, and students were protesting, among them her younger daughter, Gita, then a student at SOAS. It was not an altogether happy visit. Of course, there were old friends, hers and Nirmal's, with whom they spent time, the Sampsons, Louisa Service and Anne Money-Coutts and others, and both of them were writing their books. *A Situation in New Delhi*, a novel Nayantara had begun at the Southern Methodist University, she now worked on at the small dining table in their flat, and more or less completed while in London.

By the time they returned to India in August 1974, the country was heaving.

It is always difficult to say, afterwards, when and how a flashpoint is reached or when the sparks ignite, and so it was with what came to be known as the JP movement. Within the space of six months, between July–August and December 1974, what had begun as a trickle of protest by students in Bihar against a corrupt university system became a flood of opposition – initially to the Congress chief minister of Bihar, Abdul Ghafoor, and very quickly thereafter, to Mrs Gandhi's government itself.

The year 1974 would later be remembered for three main events that triggered a crisis for Mrs Gandhi's government. The great railway strike, which was forcefully crushed in April 1974; the Nav Nirman movement in Gujarat, which toppled the Chimanbhai Patel government; and JP's movement for the restoration of democracy in the country.

Strikes, skirmishes and gheraos had become a common feature in the country in the 1970s, but the railway strike was something far more serious. The workforce of the railways (the largest employer in the country) belonged to more than one hundred unions, big and small; on 7 May 1974, one million of them went on strike demanding permanency of jobs, a fair wage and better working conditions. The government had invoked Defence of India Regulations to declare the strike illegal and by 8 May 60,000 strikers had been arrested. Despite being dealt with brutally, with Mrs Gandhi personally supervising the repression, the strike lasted twenty-two days. It was broken finally, but Mrs Gandhi's troubles were far from over.

In Gujarat, a students' protest in Ahmedabad against inedible and insufficient food at college hostels may have been small compared to the railway strike, but it nevertheless managed to unseat the ruling Congress government in the state. It was almost as if the students had responded to Jayaprakash Narayan's challenge of 9 December 1973:

> Will our youth continue to look on idly at this strangulation of the democratic process at its very birth? Surely there cannot be a more important issue which should move the youth to action ... What form their action should take, it is for the youth themselves to decide. My only recommendation would be that in keeping with the spirit and substance of democracy, it must be scrupulously peaceful and non-partisan.[10]

Jayaprakash Narayan then was a frail seventy two year-old, not in very good health, and recently bereaved of his beloved wife, Prabhavati. An old Congressman, he was a fellow-traveller with Nehru as well as with Nayantara's parents and, naturally, Gandhi. As early as 1934, however, differences between the more radical members of the

Congress – the socialists – and the others, as well as the calling-off of the civil disobedience movement in May that year, led to the socialists breaking away and forming the Congress Socialist Party; it included Acharya Narendra Dev, JP, Ashoka Mehta, Achyut Patwardhan, N.N. Goray, Minoo Masani and M.L. Dantwala.

As far as JP was concerned, this initial split was the beginning of his formal break with party politics, post-independence; the gap between what was professed and practised, between the perceptions and policies of those in power and the ground realities, was too great for this man of conscience to accept. By 1952, three weeks after he underwent a self-purificatory fast in Poona, he gave up organised politics altogether. Having been attracted to one tested-and-tried political ideology after another and found them wanting, he saw that none of them was fully or wholly in support of freedom and liberty.

> For many years I have worshipped at the shrine of the goddess, Dialectical Materialism, which seemed to me intellectually more satisfying than any other philosophy. But while the main quest ... remains unsatisfied, it has become patent to me that materialism of any sort robs man of the means to become truly human. In a material civilisation man has no rational incentive to be good.[11]

Yet, although he had opted out of party politics, his engagement with the country's political, economic and social life remained deep and abiding. Bhoodan, gramdan, self-help, self-government, decentralisation and devolution of power became a viable, alternative politics for him, a practical means of accomplishing a social revolution; of evolving from rajniti to lokniti in order to achieve genuine democracy.

JP became the natural magnet for the agitating students of Bihar, frustrated, angry but without a real focus for their agitation. JP himself, having toured in various districts of Bihar, could see at first hand how rising prices, drought and endemic corruption had immiserised huge sections of the rural population. At public rallies the students responded lustily to his transparent style and integrity, and cries of 'Loknayak Jayaprakash Zindabad!' began to rent the air. He responded cautiously but confidently, told the students to abandon their studies for one year and form action committees in every high school and college. They should arouse public opinion against corrupt ministers or legislators, and begin the process of screening candidates for the next elections.

On 9 August 1974, JP held a public meeting at Monghyr where half the population of the city turned up to hear him. He recalled 9 August 1942, when the Congress had launched the Quit India movement; now he called upon the crowd to ask the Congress to quit its throne for it had betrayed its promise to the people.

On the same day, Mrs Gandhi addressed a huge gathering of students in Delhi; Congress governments in the states had sent contingents by bus and train to swell the crowd in the grounds outside parliament. She drove in, escorted by fourteen Youth Congress outriders on motorcycles, and exhorted the youth of the country not to be taken in by phony revolutions bent upon subverting democracy. But these students were not of the same ilk as the ones supporting JP, nor had they the same motivation as those of the Nav Nirman student movement in Gujarat. The battle lines, it seems, had been drawn, although a head-on confrontation suited neither JP nor Mrs Gandhi. But the movement snowballed, drawing in supporters, sympathisers, activists and politicians of many stripes, not all of them wholly desirable.

Almost before she could catch her breath, Nayantara was plunged in at the deep end with the resumption of her column, and Dallas and London were now a world apart, literally and figuratively. 'Home,' she wrote, 'had changed completely.' Peaceful black-flag protests were brutally dealt with by the police or not allowed to take place; the collapse of Abdul Ghafoor's government in Bihar was imminent; Youth Congress louts were flexing their muscles at JP's followers; and on 26 September Atal Behari Vajpayee was arrested under the Maintenance of Internal Security Act (MISA) and taken to Bhagalpur jail. As a result, JP called for trains and buses to be halted, exhorted policemen and civil servants to disobey orders, and urged the common man to 'Paralyse Bihar'. The Bihar Satyagraha was scheduled to commence on 2 October, Gandhi's birthday, and JP said he feared arrest. Students called for a three-day hartal, demanding the resignation of the chief minister and the dissolution of the Bihar assembly. By 4 October, there was a total bandh in Bihar and three people were killed in police firing. Life in the state ground to a halt with all communication links broken. On 6 October, the final day of the bandh, five towns were placed under curfew and four people died in the Patna violence. On 7 October, thousands of people rallied in support of JP in Delhi, and although he feared attempts on his life, he nevertheless called for a 'people's assembly' to be formed in Bihar, based on elections in all 318 constituencies. But the Congress was hard-pressed to find a replacement for Ghafoor as inner-party wrangling had tied its hands.

By the end of October that year, it was becoming increasingly clear that the JP wave was gathering force, and that the counter-offensive – calling his supporters reactionaries or left adventurists or questioning the source of his funds – would likely boomerang. On the moral plane it would be difficult to challenge him or to dismiss his claim that the country had seen a serious erosion of democratic values. Rather than addressing the issue, Congress president Dev Kant Barooah gave the party's state units the green signal to work together with the Communist Party of India (CPI) to fight JP's movement in Bihar. On 27 October, five agitating leaders in Bihar were externed from the state for sixty days, and the following week Mrs Gandhi declared that she would resign rather than bow to pressure from anti-nationalists. On 4 November, four hundred people were arrested on the eve of the Delhi Bandh, with the prime minister saying that JP's stir was 'incompatible with democracy'. The following day JP was hurt in a lathi charge, the police tear-gassed a crowd of demonstrators, and JP went on an eight-hour dharna in a police van.

By mid-November JP accepted the PM's challenge of an electoral battle, and a conference of opposition parties convened by him decided to mobilise one million people from across the country to march to parliament in support of the Bihar movement. The following month, the Jana Sangh alerted its state units to launch a Bihar-type stir, provoking Mrs Gandhi into saying that the Bihar movement was being conducted by the Rashtriya Swayamsevak Sangh (RSS).

Like Indira, Nayantara had seen JP as a young girl, in and out of Anand Bhawan, in and out of jail with her parents, whom he addressed as Bhai and Didda. Direct contact had more or less ceased after independence, but when in September or October 1974 JP sent her a message (via their mutual friend, Rashid Shervani of Allahabad), saying he'd like her help, she agreed immediately. That November, Nayantara visited Bihar at JP's request to see for herself what his movement was about and how it was being dealt with by the government. Subsequently, she travelled to Bihar three or four times in order to write for *Everyman's Weekly*, and a couple of times to report on the situation there for *The Indian Express*. In Bihar she was accompanied by a young Lohia-ite who took her around in a battered old Ambassador donated to JP by the industrialist, Ram Nath Goenka. (Earlier that year, Nayantara later reported in *Everyman's Weekly*, Goenka had been approached by an emissary of the ruling party to withdraw his support from JP and to modify the editorial policy of *The Indian Express*. He declined, saying he would not interfere with the paper's editorial independence, and that he considered it a privilege to be associated with Jayaprakash; in December 1973, a group of Congress and CPI MPs introduced a privilege motion against Goenka in parliament *Everyman's Weekly*, 2 February 1975.) JP told Nayantara apologetically that he could only pay her Rs 250 per article, which she declined, saying, 'I'll do it for love.' But JP would have none of this and so she accepted, reluctantly. She visited towns and districts, returning in the evening to spend time with JP and staying with a family arranged by him.

From October 1974 to May 1975 Nayantara contributed seventeen articles to *Everyman's*, the paper started by JP and edited by the well-known Delhi journalist, Ajit Bhattacharjea. 'Some words recur in the history of suffering,' she wrote in her very first column, 'and one of them is Bihar.' Bihar had seen terrible famine, floods, drought, earthquakes and communal violence, to say nothing of smallpox and hunger. A grim list of natural and man-made disasters. But in 1973 Bihar acquired a new distinction, one that held out great hope for the whole country because of JP's movement. It had reminded the people of their precious obligation to rebel when faced with injustice and authoritarianism.

Her columns were a blunt and brutal attack on the Congress, not only for its misdeeds and its alliance with the CPI, but for its wilful blindness in its reading of the political mood. 'An earlier, more sensitive and humanitarian Congress might have seen in such a movement an ally, a source of strength to itself,' she wrote, but its failure to see what was happening in the country was an indication of its alarming distance from its electorate. She was unrelenting in her criticism of Mrs Gandhi and the hangers-on around her, quoting her own words back to her and impaling her on them. Mrs Gandhi, she said, had told the Congress in 1972 that she didn't believe in leadership; yet she had gone about working for a leaderless society in a queer way, 'by exacting dire penance from those who do not conform, and reacting with a sharp attack of nerves' if she felt her power was being threatened.

For Nayantara, JP represented a return to the selfless, people-driven and people-oriented politics of Nehru and Gandhi; he himself was incorruptible, with 'a strange kind of purity' as a politician, working tirelessly to recuperate an ethical politics. In him, she found an alignment of her own principles and, like him, she believed in the power and moral force of non-violence and satyagraha as an alternative political strategy in the face of repression and brutalism. And so she pulled out all the stops in her support for his movement, saying later that 'it was something that had to be done, because democracy was under threat'.

Yet she was naive to think that 'Sangharsh' was 'India's opportunity to achieve a revolution without violence, an invitation to a peculiarly Indian Long March with all the peasant patience and endurance that we have in reserve'. Even then, at the height of the resistance, this would, at best, have been political wishful thinking; at worst, it was a romantic idealisation of the kind of alliance the JP movement had forged. There was also something inexplicable about Nayantara's distaste for the CPI and her almost petulant dismissal of them, notwithstanding their later wholly indefensible support of the Emergency. She deplored their 'pernicious influence' on policy, and rebuked her cousin for 'echoing the absurd Pravda jargon' about 'fascists' and 'reactionaries' when referring to those, including some of her own partymen, who supported JP. 'With her particular background,' Nayantara said, 'Indi should have known better'.[12]

Mrs Gandhi could have been left in no doubt about where her cousin's loyalties lay.

Events moved rapidly between January and June 1975, a combination of political activity and spontaneous responses; or, put differently, immovable object meeting irresistible force. Lalit Narayan Mishra, Union minister of railways, was assassinated in January; a series of 'accidental deaths' of people investigating cases with important political repercussions occurred around the same time. The Nagarwala case was the most prominent, but others related to licences being awarded to favoured business houses, or to smuggling and so on, added to the scandals besetting the government.

A ragtag opposition (referred to as a 'motley crowd' by Mrs Gandhi) made up of disparate groups, including the Jana Sangh, the socialists and dissatisfied Congressmen, began to coalesce around JP; it was not necessarily a salutary development. JP agonised for a long time about letting what was essentially a students' movement be infiltrated by political parties but, according to Nayantara, 'he said he had to allow it since its (the movement's) aims were political, and at the time there was a huge Opposition groundswell against the government'. She herself thought it was a 'big mistake' to let the Jana Sangh in 'because it not only compromised his (JP's) position, it gave respectability to the Sangh which it would never have gained otherwise'.[13] She recalled meeting Nanaji Deshmukh often in the course of the movement and mentioning to him, once, that Mrs Pandit was under surveillance in Dehradun. Deshmukh said to her, 'Main aap ki mataji ki raksha ka prabandh karoonga, koi ghabrane ki baat nahin,' and she remembered thinking that her mother would have got the shock of her life if she suspected that the RSS was protecting her! 'We would never, in any circumstance, want to be associated with that lot of people. So there were all these paradoxes.'

As early as 1967, when the Jana Sangh made significant electoral gains in the country, Nayantara warned in her column that 'linguism and religion have come out into the open as political forces', and went on to say:

> The Jana Sangh, perhaps the most disciplined and highly organised of our political parties ... commands a militant youth movement, harbours a nostalgia for tradition and encourages a revival of the Hindu mystique ... The way could easily be open for a backward march, always too easy for India ... It needs to be asserted again and again that India is not, and never will be, a Hindu nation.

Influential members within the Congress tried to persuade Mrs Gandhi to hold a dialogue with the Opposition on an agreed basic programme for the country; she did the opposite, throwing out those within her party who dared to differ – Mohan Dharia, Krishan Kant and Chandrashekhar among them. She chose to confront rather than conciliate.

In February, JP addressed a meeting of government employees at the Boat Club in Delhi, and reminded them that their duty as public servants and their loyalty were to the country, to the people and to the Indian Constitution, not to the prime minister, the home minister or the government – obeying illegal, partisan or immoral orders was against the country and the constitution. His appeal to the army and police was similar. When asked to explain himself, he replied:

> If any party, government or party leader intends to use the army as a means to further their party and power interests, it is the clear duty, to my mind, of the army not

> to be so used ... If all this amounts to committing treason, I shall not mind being prosecuted for this offence. [14]

In March 1975, the Opposition planned a huge march to the capital, to which the Congress bigwigs reacted by stopping the entry of buses into Delhi, and by disconnecting water hydrants on the route of the march. Writing in *Everyman's*, Nayantara reported that the march 'was a triumph of organisation, peaceful purpose and heroic commitment ... the most massive protest ever organised against misrule'.

Later that month, she wrote a long comment on JP's call for civil disobedience in her *Indian Express* column:

> Satyagraha is a moral principle, only employable when the cause is just. Its essence is that truth, be it represented by the individual or the mass, can shake an empire ... In a purely religious context the message of Christ on the cross is somewhat the same, for how could the suffering and death of one man save millions unless the truth He stood for had the power to affect and influence beyond Him?
>
> ... In British times we broke laws we considered unjust, made by a government to which we did not give our allegiance. Today we have a Constitution and laws of our own making and a government elected through them, but one which almost daily violates them either in fact or in spirit. We ... do not wish to depart from either the Constitution or the laws, but to see that they are observed by those in authority. The aim of satyagraha today is to demand their proper observance. We are in the very curious position where the government of the country needs this reminder.

> ... The politician or his mouthpiece must be disobeyed when he plays fast and loose with the laws or with decent practices and conventions. The civil servant who is told to arrest 25 people who are squatting in a peaceful demonstration knows very well that there is no ground for arresting them, that the demonstrators are breaking no law, and that the executive order is arbitrary and unjust. In such a case the civil servant is not bound to carry it out. There are too many such cases nowadays where the civil servant, particularly the young and sensitive, fresh from their training or their first experience of field work and earnest about their responsibilities, are thrust into terrible situations of being driven to act against the law and against their own conscience. The ritual enactment of MISA must put this kind of strain on many an official conscience, as it must also on the police, who must at times be confused and bewildered at what they are asked to do. The ferocious use of force, or on the other hand the total absence of the police when they are urgently needed, are signs of confused, and at times unscrupulous, executive orders.

In April, Morarji Desai informed the prime minister that unless correct constitutional procedure was followed and an election announced in Gujarat, he would commence a fast unto death. She replied to say an election would only be held after the monsoon session of parliament, following which Morarji began his fast. She then scheduled a date in June for the Gujarat polls but, as events unfolded, June was to be her nemesis month. Maverick Bharatiya Lok Dal MP, Raj Narain, had filed a petition in the Allahabad High Court charging Mrs Gandhi with offences during the 1971 elections; he prayed that her election be held invalid on grounds of misusing government resources and services during her election campaign. The Allahabad High Court and Justice Jagmohan Lal Sinha ruled, in a landmark judgment, that Mrs Gandhi was guilty, unseated her and debarred her from holding office and contesting elections for the following six years.

Mrs Gandhi was stunned. The entire nation held its breath, at once elated by and apprehensive of the verdict's consequences. Predictably, the Youth Congress poured out into the streets, declaring that 'we will not accept the High Court judgement'. The Congress Parliamentary Board passed a resolution saying that their 'considered view' was that Mrs Gandhi's 'dynamic leadership was indispensible to the integrity, stability and progress of the country'. Two chief ministers advised that she should take steps to limit the jurisdiction of the courts in the matter of election petitions; and Mrs Gandhi herself decided to challenge the judgement in the Supreme Court. Judge Sinha allowed an appeal that stayed his order for twenty days, but on 25 June JP announced that, beginning 29 June, he would organise a week-long protest outside the PM's residence.

That same night, at 11.00 p.m., Mrs Gandhi drove to Rashtrapati Bhavan with a document that the president was to sign, the proclamation of a national emergency. Accordingly, on 26 June, Fakhruddin Ali Ahmed informed the people of India that 'a grave emergency exists, whereby the security of India is threatened by internal disturbances'. But before this, in the early hours of the morning, the country's top Opposition leaders had been arrested, and the national press was blacked out through a series of presidential ordinances that imposed total censorship and suspended civil liberties. There was a blanket ban on strikes and demonstrations, and a complete wage freeze.

The nation was in shock. But the CPI, which backed the Emergency, stated that 'a blow had been struck against counter-revolution, and against neo-colonialist, reactionary, communal and fascist forces'. For this, it earned itself the jibe, Communist Party of Indira.

In June 1975, Nayantara's son Ranjit married Franca Dal Bianco whom he had met in London when they were both students. Franca's family was from Padua where Nayantara travelled with her mother to attend the wedding. Afterwards Nayantara and Mrs Pandit left Italy for London where they stayed at the Indian Students' Hostel wing of the YMCA. The following morning, as Mrs Pandit waited in line at the cafeteria for her breakfast, a young man standing next to her asked if she had heard that an Emergency had been declared in India. She could hardly believe her ears. A posse of journalists had collected outside, waiting to interview her, but as she knew nothing about the circumstances that had led to this, she declined to comment. Later that day, she and Nayantara went to the Indian high commission where they learnt that JP, Morarji and dozens of others had been detained under MISA; and so, although she and Nayantara had planned to spend a few weeks in England they decided to cut short their visit and return immediately to India. Soon after they landed, Ajit Bhattacharjea called Nayantara to tell her that the police had raided the offices of *Everyman's* and shredded its last issue.

An estimated number of 38,630 people were detained without trial during the Emergency under MISA, and 72,000 under the Defence of India Regulations (DIR). Those arrested included professors who were critical, activists of the right and left, CPI (M) members, intellectuals, students and trade unionists.[15] Hundreds went underground, fearing a similar fate. In jail, JP's health deteriorated rapidly. His brother went to see Nayantara more than once about this, and on one occasion showed her a letter he had drafted to Mrs Gandhi; in it, he said it would be bad for the government if JP died in custody. In confidence he told Nayantara that the deterioration had been so marked that he believed it couldn't be due to natural causes. She helped him redraft his letter to the PM, and JP was shifted to the All India Institute of Medical Sciences in Delhi. Nayantara went to see him with Ajit Bhattacharjea and was appalled at his condition. 'His brother said that to kill JP when in that state, all you needed to do was to add extra salt to his food. That would be poison enough.'[16]

At a party where he met Nayantara's sister, Rita Dar, Siddhartha Shankar Ray (Mrs Gandhi's hatchet man for the Emergency) told her, 'We can pick her (i.e., Nayantara) up any day under MISA.' The fear in the family was that even though Indira Gandhi might refrain from arresting her, the same could not be said for Sanjay Gandhi.

With censorship in full swing, Nayantara's column in the *Sunday Standard* came to a virtual halt; the then editor, S. Mulgaonkar, told her she was welcome to write on any subject bar the political, which for a political columnist was tantamount to being silenced.

In June 1976, the Bunting Institute at Radcliffe College

in Cambridge, Massachusetts, awarded Nayantara a six-month fellowship to work on a book of her choice, and she and Nirmal left for the US, where they stayed for the next twelve months.

In hindsight, it is difficult to say that the JP movement offered a real ideological alternative to the Congress; indeed, JP's call for Total Revolution seemed to be almost as rhetorical as Mrs Gandhi's exhortation to Abolish Poverty. His political project of decentralisation and devolution had some merit – and Nayantara reported on one such experiment of a Janata Sarkar in Khadigram in Bihar, with ninety delegates representing twenty-one blocks in the state in April 1975 – but whether it would have broken the stranglehold of big business and big farmer interests remains an equally big question mark. Nayantara believed there were two aspects to what JP was doing: Sampurna Kranti (i.e., devolution and decentralisation) and building an opposition against authoritarianism in Delhi; of her own involvement with the movement she said:

> I felt a strong Opposition was a good thing because Congress had been in power a long time and Mrs Gandhi had outlawed it altogether. For me, personally, it gave me the chance for the first time in my life to see the Opposition at work, to get their point of view ... But it's true, it never amounted to a really effective movement.[17]

Looking back, she felt that JP and the socialists could have served the country better by remaining within the Congress rather than leaving it as they did in 1948, when

JP was general secretary of the Socialist Party. The most the Opposition could have achieved, she saw now, was to build on people's frustration with the government, to consolidate its strength and keep up the pressure of its protest.

Endnotes

1 Personal interview, Dehradun, October 2008.

2 Except where otherwise stated, all quotes are from Nayantara Sahgal's column in the *Sunday Standard*.

3 Personal interview, Dehradun, October 2002.

4 *Economic & Political Weekly*, 14 March 1970.

5 Zareer Masani, *Indira Gandhi: A Biography* (London: Hamish Hamilton, 1975), p. 108.

6 Personal interview, Dehradun, October 2008.

7 Ibid.

8 Ibid.

9 E.N. Mangat Rai, *Committment My Style: Career in the Indian Civil Service*, p. 264.

10 Ajit Bhattacharjea, *Jayaprakash Narayan: A Political Biography* (New Delhi: Vikas Publishing House, 1975), p. 142.

11 Ibid., p. 25.

12 Personal interview, Dehradun, October 2008.

13 Personal interview, Delhi, March 2009.

14 Nayantara Sahgal, *Indira Gandhi: Tryst With Power* (New Delhi: HarperCollins, reprint, 2012), p. 208.

15 Tariq Ali, *The Nehrus and the Gandhis: An Indian Dynasty* (London: Picador, 1985), p. 188.

16 Personal interview, Delhi, March 2009.

17 Ibid.

6

. . . AND PERSONAL

Indira Gandhi: Her Road to Power

At the heart of Nayantara and Indira's relationship, both personal and political, was Jawaharlal Nehru, who embodied both the personal and the political in his individual relationship with the cousins, one of whom was his daughter; the other for whom he became surrogate father.

Radiating out from this central figure, however, was a complex web of relationships that encompassed Nehru, his sisters and his young wife; Nehru, Kamala and their daughter; Kamala Nehru, Vijaya Lakshmi Pandit and Nehru; Feroze Gandhi, Kamala Nehru and Indira; Nehru, Feroze and Indira; Indira, Nayantara and Mrs Pandit; Nehru and Indira; and Nayantara, Indira and Nehru.

Growing up together in Anand Bhawan, and growing up often in the absence of their parents who were in jail, the cousins were really close. The three Pandit sisters and Indira Nehru basked in the warmth and expansive paternalism of their grandfather, Motilal, and the enveloping love of his extended household as friends and relatives streamed in and through it in and all their growing years. They shared childhood's little joys and upsets, birthdays and death days, the company of strangers and brothers, and the ripples and eddies of momentous events unfolding in the very home they lived in, though they may not then have understood their full import. And then there was Jawaharlal, beloved father and uncle around whom, it seemed, revolved the sun, moon and stars, for he drew into his embrace not only the children, but their parents as well. Both Vijaya Lakshmi and Ranjit Pandit were devoted to Nehru, comrades in politics and unquestioningly loyal. Indi was the adored older cousin, older by ten years to Nayantara, who, even before the latter was born, had already been to school in Switzerland, learnt French, travelled in Europe with her parents, and returned with romantic tales to tell her cousins.

In January 1932, Vijaya Lakshmi Pandit, Nehru and Ranjit Pandit were all in jail and Kamala Nehru was lying ill in Bombay; there was talk of Anand Bhawan being confiscated and the four girls were sent to a boarding school in Poona at Gandhi's suggestion. Nayantara was then five years old, Chandralekha eight, Indira fifteen and Rita just three. The Pupil's Own School was run by a nationalist Parsi couple, Jal and Coonverbai Vakil; the school had just twelve boarders who lived like a family in a bungalow surrounded by a garden. Classes were held, Santiniketan style, on the veranda or in one of the rooms, and the children were encouraged to be multilingual – they spoke Hindi, Gujarati and English. Every morning they went on prabhat pheris, walking the silent streets of the silent town, singing bhajans and nationalist songs. Occasionally, they even swept the streets, the Vakils being not only nationalist but Gandhian.[1]

But all four girls were miserable, separated from their parents and far from home. Indira cried herself to sleep every night and Tara and Lekha were unbearably homesick, but just as they had been told never to cry in front of the police when they came to arrest their parents, so they suppressed their sadness and tears beneath their pillows. Stoically, Indira took her young cousins under her wing, helping them in their lessons and keeping their spirits from flagging.

Fortunately, their stay in Poona was short-lived. After their parents were released fifteen months later, the Pandit sisters were withdrawn from the school; Indira continued there for another couple of years till her matriculation in 1934, after which she was sent to Tagore's Santiniketan. Poona might have been difficult, especially after her cousins left, but Indira believed that Coonverbai Vakil 'had a very great influence on me, and it was really through her that I learned to work on the ground floor'.[2] In March 1935, Indu wrote to her aunt from Santiniketan, asking her to send Chandralekha there for the Spring Festival. Vijaya Lakshmi, Chandralekha and Ranjit all went and found Indu looking better than she had been for a while, happily settled in the community and speaking Bengali like a native.[3] Soon after Santiniketan, however, she was sent to the Badminton School in Bristol to prepare for her Oxford entrance exams, and the Pandit sisters went to Woodstock, an American missionary school in Mussoorie – one that admitted Indians but ignored India, Nayantara said! School holidays meant they were all back at Anand Bhawan again, at least for the first couple of years, for after Mrs Pandit became a minister in the UP cabinet of the interim government in 1936, vacations for the Pandit sisters were spent in Lucknow. Indira had now completed her schooling at Bristol and was at Somerville College in Oxford.

To the ten-year-old Tara, Indi was sophisticated beyond belief, at home in London and Paris, and now when she came back, she brought with her the kind of magazines and books they had not been exposed to, and exciting stories about plays and concerts, both of which Indi consumed avidly. The sisters hung on her every word, although it would be a while before they heard about her romance with Feroze Gandhi, then a student at the London School of Economics. But she told them about Krishna Menon and the India League where she helped out, raising funds for India's Spanish Aid Committee or the China Aid Committee (of both of which her father was president), and about life as a student at Oxford. One reason she had chosen Oxford was that Feroze was in England, a link with family and India.

In London, through Feroze and other young students like Bhupesh Gupta (later with the Communist Party of India), Rajni Patel and Mohan Kumaramangalam (a minister in her government in the 1970s) Indira was exposed to left politics and activism, gradually developing a political personality of her own. She joined Victor Gollancz's Left Book Club, became a member of the Labour Party's youth wing and attended Labour rallies. Still in mourning after her mother's death in 1936 and alone in a foreign country, she turned more and more to Feroze Gandhi, who became her constant companion.

In 1940 Indira suffered from an attack of pleurisy that was serious enough for her to be sent to Switzerland. Doctors in London, familiar with her mother's medical history, were worried that the condition might worsen, and advised a period of recuperation in the sunny and therapeutic climate of Leysin, where she stayed for almost one year, from December 1939 to November 1940.

The war in Europe was now getting into stride, and what should have been a short spell away from her studies extended to several months. Returning to England was now ill-advised as Germany had already targeted the country; and so, early in 1941, Indira decided to return to India. She went first to London by air, then travelled to the south of France, Spain and Portugal, avoiding northern Europe and Italy where German troops were advancing steadily. In London the blitz was in full swing, with air raids and bombing; as chances of completing her degree at Oxford became more and more remote, Indira set out for India, accompanied by Feroze.

Indira Nehru and Feroze Gandhi were married in March 1942, and set up house independently in Allahabad. Within a few months, on 8 August, the All India Congress Committee passed the Quit India resolution in Bombay and Nehru, Gandhi, Raja Hutheesing and Ranjit Pandit were arrested. Feroze slipped away quietly to do underground work in Lucknow, and Indira boarded the train for Allahabad[4] where the three Pandit sisters were now alone again in Anand Bhawan. Very soon thereafter, Indira courted arrest when local college students invited her to a flag hoisting, which she knew was forbidden. There was a lathi charge, she was struck on her back and arms as she held the flag aloft, and fell as the blows hit her. But the flag was hoisted, and a few days later Indira held a public meeting at which she addressed a large crowd, dispelling the rumour that Gandhi and her father were being removed to the Central Jail in the Andaman Islands. She was arrested, of course, together with Feroze, who had come to Allahabad secretly to see her. Earlier, on 30 August, Lekha Pandit had also been arrested while demonstrating against the government; hurriedly, but also excitedly, putting together a small attaché case for prison, Lekha wondered what she could take to read. 'Don't take novels,' advised Indi, 'they finish quickly.

Take something that can be reread.' And she handed Lekha a volume of Shaw's plays, Joad's book on political theory, and an anthology of modern poetry.[5]

With Indi's arrest, all three adult women at Anand Bhawan – Vijaya Lakshmi, Indira and Lekha – were now in Naini Central Jail, in the same barracks. Relieved though they were to be together, the dreary jail routine had somehow to be made less boring; so Indira named her part of the barracks Chimborazo, Lekha's was Bien Venue and Mrs Pandit's, Wall View! In the evenings, Lekha and Indira would read aloud from plays, each performing a different role, with Mrs Pandit as their audience. They wrote in their prison notebooks, supplied by the prison authorities, each page numbered so that no pages could be torn out. Indira wrote hers in French to frustrate the matron's prying eyes.

Nehru, whom Nayantara thought of as her third parent, loomed large in her emotional, literary and, later, political landscape. He was the much loved uncle who joked and clowned around with them as children, standing on his head to amuse them, pulling their legs, marching around Anand Bhawan with them, singing nationalist songs at the top of his voice, then making them sing his Harrow School songs: 'Jerry, You Duffer and Dunce' or 'When Grandpapa's Grandpapa was in the Lower Lower First.' As they grew up and grew into the freedom movement, his was the face of the struggle and of future freedom, and the example he set became their inspiration. When little Rita and Nayantara unfurled the national flag on the balcony of Anand Bhawan because no adult was around, they did so with Mamu and their parents in mind. When Lekha arrived in Naini Jail to serve her term, beaming and bearing garlands, it was as if she had qualified for admission to an exclusive political cadre. Their growing up, Nayantara has said, was India's growing up into political maturity, on the basis of an ideology made up of self-sacrifice, compassion and non-violence.

After her father passed away in 1944, Nehru became Nayantara's emotional anchor, the parent she turned to for succour and advice, for direction or support when in doubt. When she returned from Wellesley in 1947 she went straight to Nehru's house on 17 York Road, as her mother and Lekha were in Moscow at the time. Indira came and went from Lucknow where Feroze was now with the *National Herald*, glad that Nayantara was at home to look after her father. Indira might have been a fleeting, intermittent presence at York Road, but Nayantara remembered the affectionate concern with which Mamu enquired after Tara's well-being, often when he was retiring for the night himself, long after midnight. If he saw a light under her door he would wander in, his arms full of books for her to read. 'Here are some books that arrived recently,' he would say, 'they might interest you. I haven't had time for them yet.' And it was while she was still at York Road that the shocking news of Gandhi's assassination came to them. As she wrote to her mother and sister:

> Darling Mummie and Didda – It is hard to know what to write. We had just to begun to breathe freely after Bapu broke his fast when this terrible news came. Even now, after the cremation, it is impossible to believe that he is not with us. On Friday the 30th Indi and I were having a

late tea alone, as the others (Masi, Padmasi, Mamu and Feroze) were all out. We were in an unusually gay mood. Uncle Syed and (M.O.) Matthai came in and we all became very hilarious. Then suddenly Seshan rushed in with the news that Bapu had been shot at and was dying. We were stunned, but did not for a moment believe that he would die. You see, just a few days before, there had been an unsuccessful attempt on his life. Uncle Syed, Indi, Matthai, and I immediately went to Birla House, leaving word at the office to inform Mamu and the others – but we did not know where Padmasi and Masi were, or how to reach them. Bapu died just as we reached there. He had been shot while going to prayers by a man (Hindu) standing barely a yard away from him. Afterwards the assassin tried to commit suicide but did not succeed and was caught. Bapu's body was covered with blood. Even then we hoped against hope that some miracle would revive him. Where he is concerned it is possible to believe in miracles.

Sardar Patel and Maniben were in the room beside him, among others. Indi and I controlled ourselves till Mamu came in, and then it was impossible. He came in and knelt down beside Bapu and sobbed. I had never seen him so grief-stricken before, like a lost child. I had a dreadful nauseous feeling when Sardar Patel put his arm around Mamu and tried to comfort him. What did he know what the loss meant to Mamu?

Masi and Padmasi came later and then, of course, everyone came in hordes. Birla House was surrounded by gigantic crowds. To get rid of them Bapu's body had to be shown to the people from a balcony upstairs. At 8:30 the same evening Mamu and Patel broadcast. I don't know if you heard it. Mamu spoke most beautifully and it was heartbreaking to listen. Even now I cannot bear to look at his face, though he has been wonderfully controlled and brave. Patel's talk was another show of hypocrisy. It seemed a sacrilege that he or anyone else should speak after Mamu.

On the 31st, yesterday, Indi, Mamu, Feroze, Padmasi, Masi and I went to Birla House at 8:00 a.m. Mamu and others had been up till all hours the night before, planning the route of the funeral procession, and precautionary measures against crowds. Bari Masi [Sarojini Naidu] and Rita were due to arrive at 8 a.m. but their train was late and they came at 10:30, fortunately before the procession started. Bari Masi, as you can imagine, was completely broken up. The procession left Birla House at 11:45. Bapu's body, draped in the flag, was on top of a car. Patel and Mamu were to sit beside it on top, but Mamu walked most of the five miles. It took nearly five hours along the dusty, hot, densely crowded road to walk to the cremation grounds. Bari Masi with Amrit Kaur and Hansa Mehta went ahead by car, as did many others, but we agreed with Padmasi that we would all walk since it was the last time we would walk with Bapu. It was a terrible ordeal for the healthiest person, so you can imagine what it was like for Padmasi who never gets any exercise or is at all inconvenienced. The crowds were something I've never seen before. It is impossible to describe. On the whole they were orderly, but at times would get so violent that we were in danger of our lives.

When we got to the cremation ground at 4:30 the crowds lost control altogether. They trampled on each other to get to Bapu's body. It was a terrifying scene. I lost sight of the others completely and was dragged along and squashed to pieces. Bijji Mami who faints at the slightest provocation was with me clutching my arm. I couldn't make her let go. As it was, the shock of Bapu's death was a terrible blow to her, and then the insane crowds made it worse. We managed to get out bruised but alive, and later found the others. All the precautions taken by the police and the military amounted to nothing. All the cordons were broken as if they'd been made of thread. There was no dignity or beauty about the ceremony as there ought to have been, and I was revolted by the show of animalism where there ought to have been respect and silence. If all the people acted out of genuine love and sorrow for Bapu, they could be forgiven anything, but Indians are not guided by any such genuine emotion. It seemed the majority just came for cheap sensationalism. And even now, the atmosphere seems not laden with grief so much as with political tension. There is the constant feeling that Bapu was SHOT, and one can't forget it somehow. The assassin was caught but there must be others. What madness is this that has taken hold of the country, and what hope of checking it now that Bapu has gone?

Only the day before he died we had gone to see him, and we can't stop thanking God for the opportunity. It was a wonderful interview. He was sitting out in the garden in the sun, in a large straw hat which immediately fascinated Rajiv. Bapu was in a gay mood, munching radishes, and received us (Indi, Masi, Padmasi and myself) as his harem! We talked of all sorts of things – it was rare good luck to be with him alone. He said it was a good thing we had found him alone, because next time we would see him in a crowd. As we were leaving he asked me to come and see him sometime alone, as he had

> not had a chance to speak to me. At least we have that last chance to be grateful for.[6]

Bapu and Mamu, two sides of a coin, indivisible in Nayantara's mind. With Bapu gone, and for the next several years till his passing away in 1964, Mamu became the embodiment of everything that was unique and noble about the Indian experiment with democracy. Nehru's political ideology was the barometer by which she gauged the practice of this democracy, post-independence; his idealism and integrity with regard to political principle was the lodestar which guided her own commitment to India and the political developments of the day.

Her strong and passionate interest in Indian politics notwithstanding, Nayantara chose to keep aloof from party politics, even as she continued to observe and comment on it through her writing, and via her mother's active involvement in it. Indeed, it was after Nehru's death, when Mrs Pandit decided to contest as a Congress candidate from Phulpur, that the first real cracks in the family façade began to appear. When Mrs Pandit wrote to Indira to say that she had been told about Mrs Gandhi's unhappiness at her candidature and that she would willingly withdraw, unconditionally, Indira replied:

> I do not know who has been talking to you but there is absolutely no foundation in the remark that I am not happy at your being in Phulpur ... It may seem strange that a person in politics should be wholly without political ambition but I am afraid that I am that sort of a freak ... I did not want to come either to Parliament or to be in Government. However, there were certain compelling

> reasons at the time for my acceptance of this portfolio. Now there are so many crises one after another that every time seems to be the wrong time for getting out ...[7]

Nevertheless, Mrs Gandhi was coolly distant as far as her aunt's political presence was concerned, indicating early on that Mrs Pandit couldn't presume on the relationship. Letters between Mrs Pandit and her daughters, and from Nayantara and Lekha to each other, trace the declining affection between them and their cousin. In November 1967, Nayantara went to see Indira when she was in Delhi; as she wrote to Bunchi, 'it was a deadening experience, with as much warmth as an Egyptian mummy's embrace. The deadness and coldness of the woman,' she went on to say,

> ... and her extreme removal from even the barest humanness chilled me to the marrow. She was washing her hair when I arrived (9:45 pm) & came out with a towel wrapped round her head & sat down & said, 'Yes?' & waited, in the tone of someone conducting an extra interview that was not in the schedule. I said, 'I didn't come to see you about anything, I just came to see you.' 'Oh, I thought you wanted to discuss something.'

She then enquired disinterestedly about Nayantara's children. Nayantara informed her that she was moving to Delhi and mentioned the problems she was having with her taxes. Mrs Gandhi neither sympathised nor offered to help. 'She just didn't give a damn. I thought,' continued Tara,

> ... that in different, more human & interested circumstances, I could have talked about you, at least mentioned the subject, but there was not even the flicker of any aliveness

> from her. I was damned if I was going to hand her anything of worth just to be given that fish-like stare in return. I came home, thoroughly extinguished. I don't know why I even try with her any more ... The contrast between the days when Mamu's home was so much home & now, is so colossal, I could cry about it. Something is really dead & gone.[8]

Even before the Congress split in 1969 and Mrs Gandhi emerged as its undisputed leader, Mrs Pandit withdrew from Congress politics and the Nehru family's political legacy now came into Indira Gandhi's sole possession.

Unlike Nayantara's unqualified love for Nehru (Noguchi once asked her if she was 'in love' with her uncle because she couldn't stop talking about him!), Indira's relationship with him was always mediated and complicated by her deep and constant love for her mother, and what she sensed about her unhappiness in her marriage. Kamala's ill health and early death in 1936, when Indira was barely eighteen years old, contributed to the intensity of an attachment that was made up – perhaps even born of – in more or less equal measure of loneliness, anxiety, protectiveness and fierce love. 'We were very close to each other,' Indira told Promilla Kalhan, her mother's biographer, 'I loved her deeply, and when I thought that she was being wronged I fought for her and quarrelled with people.'[9]

After her mother's death she seemed, almost bizarrely, to have inherited her ill health, and was required to spend long periods in hospital in England and Switzerland in order to recover. From Leysin in 1940, she wrote to her father almost every day and he responded similarly. Her letters were warm, full of affectionate concern (for Nehru was often in jail), spontaneously cheerful or not, but never distant. They discussed everything. Books. Politics. Family matters. The looming war in Europe. Her health, of course, Congress and nationalist affairs, Nehru's travels, poetry. Signed off always with effusive expressions of love. The letters open more than a window into their minds and hearts and to how they responded to their particular circumstances.

Yet, not once did Indu mention Feroze or her growing attachment to him, not even casually, although it is more than likely that he would have visited her in Switzerland. And so the announcement of their engagement by her, almost immediately on her return to India in 1941, came as a complete surprise to Nehru; her keeping this relationship from him is curious, given the openness with which they discussed everything else.

When Indira returned to Bombay via a troop ship that sailed around the Cape of Good Hope, Nehru was still in prison in Dehradun. As she was still recovering her strength she spent the summer in a rented cottage in Mussoorie with her other aunt, Krishna Hutheesing and her two sons, both in order to recuperate and to be near her father. The news of her engagement was greeted with much the same consternation in the family as Tara's would be a few years later, and largely for the same reasons: they were very young (Indu was twenty-three when she decided to get married, Tara twenty), had been little exposed to life and society and other suitable young men, and could afford to wait. But Indira displayed a resoluteness of purpose and a determined streak that was almost adamantine. On an early visit by her father to England she declined to return with him to India during her vacations, preferring to remain in London with Feroze. Nehru insisted, at which she told him that if he forced her to go with him she would not speak to him for the duration of her stay. She was as good as her word. She remained silent during the journey home, uttered not a syllable when they were back in Allahabad, so that, sometime later, her father was compelled to accept defeat and buy her a ticket back to London. When it became clear to Nehru that she was determined to marry Feroze, he suggested she speak to Gandhi about it as Bapu's advice was sought on many personal matters. Indira told Nayantara later that though she agreed to consult Bapu, she had no intention of doing anything he said – she had made up her mind. So too when Krishna Hutheesing advised her to wait for a while before making a lifetime's decision; Indira retorted, 'You and Raja Bhai knew each other for only ten days when you decided to get married. I have known Feroze for a number of years, and I know him well ... Besides, I wish to marry him.'[10]

She had, in fact, already said yes to him on the steps of Montmartre in Paris.

News – or rather, rumours – of Indira's engagement to Feroze leaked out and the family was besieged with anonymous letters from Hindu and Parsi orthodoxy, objecting to an interfaith marriage; so much so that Nehru was obliged to make a public statement:

> A marriage is a personal and domestic matter, affecting chiefly the two parties concerned and partly their families

> ... I have long held that though parents may and should advise in the matter, the choice and ultimate decision must be with the two parties concerned. That decision, if arrived at after mature deliberation, must be given effect to, and it is no business of parents or others to come in the way. When I was assured that Indira and Feroze wanted to marry one another, I accepted willingly their decision and told them that it had my blessing.[11]

A great deal has been made of the emotional and intellectual mismatch between Jawaharlal and Kamala, and of the incompatibility of their vastly different upbringing and lifestyles. It would have been completely natural for a young and bewildered Kamala to feel out of place in a household of strong, vigorous, articulate and assured women, particularly her older sister-in-law (the younger, Krishna, was only nine at the time) who already shared an extremely close relationship with her brother. Nehru himself was acutely aware of Kamala's discomfiture:

> I was 26 at the time and she was 17, a slip of a girl, utterly unsophisticated in the ways of the world. The difference in our ages was considerable, but greater still was the difference in mental outlook ... and there was a want of adjustment. These maladjustments would sometimes lead to friction and there were many petty quarrels over trivialities ...[12]

'Everybody is maladjusted in early married life,' Indira said of her parents' marriage, and for her mother, adjusting to the anglicised, unorthodox family into which she had married, was a great strain. She and Vijaya Lakshmi avoided each other; Jawahar, after the first four or five years, was often in jail and Kamala was forced to cope alone. 'She was unhappy,' Indira said to Kalhan, 'but some of it was avoidable and perhaps there was no cause for it. You know, in our household a lot of people carried tales.'[13] Her mother felt neglected, she believed, because crowds of people would come to see her husband and she would be lying alone on the veranda upstairs at Anand Bhawan. Kamala herself wrote to Nehru, sometime in 1921 or 1922 when he was in prison, about her difficulties with Vijaya Lakshmi and Ranjit regarding the temporary, makeshift 'hospital' she had set up in Swaraj Bhawan. During her absences from Allahabad, when she was either in Bombay or Calcutta for medical reasons, its running was entrusted to Ranjit. Differences arose on how the hospital should be managed and who should be responsible for it. She wrote to say:

> There are many things I want to talk to you about but I do not always get an opportunity to do so and things remain unsaid in my heart. The sort of things happening here (Allahabad) require of you in fairness to be acquainted with both sides of the picture. At the moment you know only what Ranjit and Sarup tell you. It is therefore becoming difficult for me to work here.
>
> ... I do not wish to write all this because I am learning self-sacrifice, but I am unhappy that some people talk irresponsibly and they are believed.[14]

Like Ranjit Pandit and later, Feroze Gandhi, Kamala realised that marrying a Nehru entailed marrying the freedom struggle, but in her case, this was actually quite welcome. Embracing swadeshi and plunging full-time into politics, the Nehrus had turned their backs on a life of ease and plenty; the enforced simplicity suited Kamala quite well and, in a sense, she was perhaps more attuned to it than the others. When her husband decided to throw in his lot with Gandhi and heated words were exchanged between Motilal and Jawaharlal, it was Kamala who supported him. She might even have intuited that this was an activity and a cause she could share with him, one that would bring them closer.

In an article written for a school magazine in 1957 Indira Gandhi said:

> Many people know the part which was played by my grandfather and father [in the freedom movement]. But in my opinion, a more important part was played by my mother. When my father wanted to join Gandhiji and to change the whole way of life ... it was only my mother's courageous and persistent support and agreement which enabled him to take this big step which made such a difference not only to our family but to the history of modern India.[15]

Moreover, it was Kamala's foray into politics in Allahabad that brought her into contact with Feroze Gandhi, then a student at the university. As president of the Allahabad District Congress, Kamala led a demonstration sometime in 1930 and picketed the college where Feroze was studying. In the course of the sloganeering and shouting she fainted and fell, and Feroze rushed to her aid. Shortly afterwards he became a Congress volunteer and worked closely with her, as her hectic activities kept her on the move from morning till night. A close and mutually warm emotional relationship developed between Feroze and Kamala; during the four-year period, between 1931 and 1935, when Jawaharlal was out of prison for a total of six months and Kamala was seriously ill with tuberculosis, it was Feroze who travelled to the sanatorium in Bhowali to be with her and became a source of comfort and succour. Sick, lonely and in the midst of tense times, she began to look upon him as a son. In fact, Feroze had proposed to Indira three years before her mother passed away, when she was just sixteen. 'My mother was alive then,' Indira told Kamala's biographer, 'but she and I both felt that I was much too young. Of course, I said I was never going to get married at all, because even then I was deeply involved in what was happening.'[16]

Kamala's death left Indira devastated. At the Badminton School, a classmate, Iris Murdoch, remembered her as a grieving girl, 'very unhappy, very lonely, intensely worried about her father and her country'.[17] It might almost have been natural for her then, to turn to Feroze for solace while she was at Oxford; Feroze, who got an aunt to sponsor him for the London School of Economics in order to be near Indira, who became companion, confidant and emotional mainstay. Her father's – and her family's – reservations about the young man as a husband for her were in direct contrast to her mother's feelings for him, as well as, of course, her own.

Nehru's anxieties about his daughter were real and of long standing, compounded by his frequent absences and Kamala's increasingly fragile health. Indu's thinness (till the age of twenty, she weighed a mere 75 lbs) and general health were an abiding preoccupation, as were her interrupted education and repeated dislocation. Although he clearly doted on her, her own feelings for him may have been more enigmatic. As early as 1934, he wrote to Mrs Pandit to say that Indira wrote to him only once every three or four months, 'and then too, merely out of a sense of duty'.[18] For his part, Nehru wrote his famous *Letters to a Daughter* that began as his way of keeping in touch with her while in prison, but which became instructional in tone and content, albeit unusual and charming as lessons in history. It was with her mother that Indira spent long evenings reading from the Ramayana or Dostoevsky and other novelists, while Kamala lay on her sickbed. It was a bond forged in the knowledge of her mother's slow but sure death, of time snatched from an illness that shadowed all their lives. It was also a bond forged in the knowledge, on both Kamala's and Indira's part, of a woman who longed to be her husband's emotional and intellectual helpmeet, but who knew she might never be. 'I saw my mother being hurt,' Indira told Kalhan, 'and I was determined never to be hurt.'[19]

Years later, and after Nehru's death, Nayantara wrote to Bunchi to say that Indira 'could be very inhuman with her father on occasion, which her mother could, too, and was ...'

> The relationship between her and Mamu is one that would be fascinating to explore ... All his life I think he was burdened a little by the guilt of having neglected his marriage ... she took it out on him in whichever way she could. I don't think he even realised it ... but I think she succeeded in hurting and bruising him into an almost unnatural reticence, far beyond the reach of anyone to be able to hurt him again – and only Indi retained the power

> because he loved her dearly. I have heard her fling at him in temper, 'Look what you did to my mother!'[20]

One cannot know this with any degree of credibility, but although it is clear that Nehru was troubled by Indira's less-than-happy marriage, rather like his own, it is not at all evident that she confided in him about it. Despite her resolve 'never to be hurt', in Nayantara's opinion Indira neither got over her rift with Feroze, nor reconciled herself to his philandering. When he died in 1960, Nehru told Nayantara that 'Indu hasn't stopped crying, she bathed his body herself,' and Indira herself told Lord Chalfont of the BBC in an interview:

> I was actually physically ill. It upset my whole being for years, which is strange, because after all he was very, very ill and I should have expected that he would die. However, it was not just a mental shock, it was as though someone had cut me in two.[21]

And to Mohammad Yunus, an old family friend, she wrote:

> I don't know what to write. I am feeling so utterly desolate and miserable. You know more than anyone else how much Feroze and I disagreed and quarrelled over the years, yet instead of separating or slackening the bond of friendship, we were closer than ever before. We had a wonderful holiday together, nearly a month in a houseboat in Srinagar, and we made so many plans for the future ...[22]

At the time, she had been living with her father in Teen Murti House for close to ten years, with Feroze living in MPs' quarters just down the road from them; an irregular and, by all accounts, uncomfortable presence when he visited. Three years after he passed away, Indira Gandhi wrote about what it had meant for her, setting up home for her father after independence and 'coping with the social obligations of the Prime Minister's House', noting with regret that 'life does not always run according to our desires or expectations'.[23] Yet, as Feroze was equally involved in contemporary politics and an active parliamentarian, their shared interest in India's political future should have enabled her to do both – be a support to her father as well as live with her husband. 'It is a fact,' said Nayantara later,

> ... that Indi lived in the house with Mamu but with so little interest in its ordinary running or even ordering of food, that this man was not certain of getting a cup of hot tea when he came from office. There was no loving concern for him, no anxiety of the sort that one looks for in those one lives with and loves.[24]

With Edwina Mountbatten's death in February 1960 and Feroze's later that very year, both father and daughter were bereaved within a few months of each other. The poignancy of their situations could not have been lost on either.

Nehru referred to himself, only half in jest, as Vijaya Lakshmi's friend, philosopher, guide and brother all rolled into one; for her, Bhai 'was a knight sans peur et sans reproche' (without fear, without reproach). Eleven years separated Jawaharlal and Vijaya Lakshmi, but when he returned from England after his education and lawyer's training was complete, Vijaya Lakshmi said meeting him was like 'an awakening, a dream come true'.[25] He was in his early twenties, she was just twelve, but he read with her and rode and swam with her, discussed plays and poetry, made her write essays, introduced her to Buddhism – in short, treated her like an adult and sowed the seeds of a relationship that evolved into something more than normal sibling affection. Mrs Pandit's autobiography, published in 1979, was dedicated 'to the memory of two men I loved, my brother and my husband'.

When Nehru married Kamala Kaul in 1916, both she and Vijaya Lakshmi were sixteen years old to Nehru's twenty-six. Much has been written about the unkindness that Kamala experienced at the hands of her sister-in-law, implying even that Vijaya Lakshmi might have kept Nehru away from her (indeed, Indira Gandhi herself maintained that her aunt wanted to 'monopolise' her father). Whatever the truth or otherwise of these speculations, Nehru's qualms about his parents' search for a bride had been communicated to Motilal Nehru long before his wedding took place. 'There is not an atom of romance in the way you are searching out girls for me,' he wrote to his father, 'the very idea is extremely unromantic. And you constantly expect me to fall in love with a photograph. The days for that are gone by.'

And to Swaruprani, his mother, he said, 'There should be no marriage without mutual love. I consider it a crime and ruination of one's life if one has to marry merely for the sake of creating children.'[26]

It would not have been uncommon in 1916 for a Western-educated young man in India to marry a woman who had never left home or had a formal education, let alone been exposed to an anglicised lifestyle. So it might not have seemed to Jawaharlal that he was neglecting his young wife when he pursued interests and engaged in activities that excluded her but that he shared with his sister. After all, companionate marriages were the exception, not the rule. And yet Kamala's unhappiness is understandable. As Nehru's involvement in the freedom movement intensified, so his absences grew more frequent and his preoccupation with politics all-consuming. When her health began to fail within a few years of their marriage, the emotional vacuum she was in must have been even more difficult to deal with. The months they spent in Europe when she was being treated for tuberculosis were the only time they had together as a family, but even though Nehru was physically by her side, solicitous and concerned about her treatment, he was otherwise quite detached. His numerous letters to Mrs Pandit during this period indicate the lengths to which he went to keep abreast of events both in Europe and in India, and the extent to which he shared his concerns, personal as well as political, with her. Of the years immediately before and after Kamala's death in 1936 he wrote to his sister to say:

> So far as I was concerned, I was wrapped up in my work and lived in a state bordering on intoxication. With a single track mind I went along the paths of my choice, absorbed and contented in that deep and basic way which comes from an identification of thought and action. I almost forgot my family for a while.[27]

The one person he could not put out of his mind and whose welfare was an abiding concern, was Indu; and with

Vijaya Lakshmi he shared his worries about her and how he should deal with problems as they cropped up. The one routine he stuck to, he told his sister, was to write to Indu every fortnight wherever he might be, but he noted ruefully that it had been a one-sided business. A hasty note with apologies was what he often got back after two or three months' silence, while she was in school or at Santiniketan. 'I know that Indu is fond of me and of Kamala, yet she ignores us and others completely,' he wrote in a letter to Mrs Pandit in 1933. Of course, Indu was only sixteen at the time and, like most teenagers, casual about corresponding; but to a parent who was in jail often and for long periods, letter writing was the only contact possible. Its absence would have been more keenly felt for that.

Tensions at home among members of the extended household also troubled Jawaharlal, and the 'lack of harmony, a touch of non-cooperation' that he sensed in it caused him much sorrow. His letters to Mrs Pandit about this are not explicit, but he surely had in mind his wife and some of the problems she had confided in him about. He raised them with Vijaya Lakshmi, he said, because she was very dear to him, one of the very few persons who really counted in his life. 'I should like you therefore,' he wrote, 'to remove any discordant notes that might have unwittingly crept in – it is futile to consider how they came, whose fault or carelessness permitted them. It is everybody's fault.'[28]

Worries about Kamala's care and nursing at Anand Bhawan which seemed to suffer from either too much attention or hardly any, meant that little irritations on everyone's part assumed magnified proportions. This concern bloomed unexpectedly into an issue with graver implications the following year, when Kamala was convalescing in Bhowali for an extended period. At the time Feroze Gandhi was her main carer, but the fact that he was there with her, the fact moreover, that he was spending a great deal of time with a family whose politics were highly suspect in *his* family's opinion, led to extreme displeasure on their part. As far as they were concerned, Kamala's influence on his political activity was wholly undesirable – he should be completing his studies, not wasting his time with the rabble-rousing Nehrus. This had somehow been communicated to Nehru, probably by Feroze himself, and Vijaya Lakshmi was asked to mediate; would she, he asked, go and meet Feroze's mother and sister in Allahabad and reassure them that neither he nor Kamala, nor any other member of their family, wished to detain Feroze or exploit him and lead him astray? Apologise to them on his, Jawahar's, and Kamala's behalf for unwittingly coming between Feroze and his family? This was the last thing they wanted to do.

Feroze himself sought out Mrs Pandit in 1938 when she was in London, confiding in her his feelings for Indu. 'Perhaps you know that we love each other,' he wrote, 'it is now nearly four years since we have been attached to each other ... I think it is only fair that you know this, it is the first time I am mentioning it to anyone besides Jawaharlalji.'[29] He asked for her sympathy and friendship as one to whom he could open his heart and place his complete trust. 'I should like,' he said, 'to tell you anything in my mind.'

But it was not just family matters that Nehru discussed with his sister, although it was she who managed the household when she was in Anand Bhawan and to whom he entrusted many of his personal affairs. After Kamala's death in 1936 and then, some years later, Ranjit Pandit's passing away, the bond between them became stronger, reinforced now by their more or less total involvement in the nationalist struggle and in active party politics. The correspondence between them, extending over many years, covered an enormous range of subjects, events, personalities and issues; it indicates not only their shared interests but the implicit and unwavering trust they reposed in each other, and in each others' responses to what confronted them, either in their personal lives or politically. Or for that matter, as far as their children were concerned.

Post-independence, Vijaya Lakshmi became Nehru's trusted emissary abroad, and the fifteen years between 1947 and 1962 that she was India's representative to the three major Western capitals – Moscow, Washington and London – were marked by a more or less perfect synchronism between them on India's foreign policy. Nehru, as foreign minister, embarked on his formulation of non-alignment, enunciating a policy of equidistance from the US and the USSR that became a guiding principle for many newly independent nations and earned him considerable unpopularity among the superpowers.

On the eve of his very first visit to the US in 1949, he sought his sister's advice on how he should conduct himself while there. In what mood should he approach America? How deal with the government, businessmen and others? Which facet of himself should he present to them – Indian or European? His faith in her abilities was complete: when she was appointed high commissioner to London, he wrote to her to say:

> So far as you are concerned, you should know that apart from my deep affection for you, I have a very high opinion of your capacity and ability; to that of course we must add the great value of your personality. You have my complete confidence.[30]

For her part Mrs Pandit saw her task during all her assignments overseas as that of effectively communicating and upholding India's position as a sovereign, democratic country, speaking on behalf of many former colonies whether in the UN, at the Commonwealth Ministers' Conferences or in the White House or Whitehall. Over and above this, however, she was Nehru's representative. As she had said to him many years earlier,

> I don't want to be sentimental & silly, but my love for you is not only that of a sister – I love you with the devotion of a soldier for a beloved leader. There is nothing at all I would hesitate to do for you if I could help in the smallest way to share any of your burdens. So whatever you say becomes a law for me.[31]

For her aunt, Indira was like a fourth daughter, and even though Indu might not have returned the compliment, she was affectionate enough in an undemonstrative way while she was growing up. When her mother was alive and during the years she was at school and university in Switzerland and England, Indu's contact with Vijaya Lakshmi was sporadic; it was her other aunt, Betty, who was more often with them on extended sojourns in Lausanne where Kamala was being treated.

When Indu and Feroze decided to return to India by boat in 1940 at the height of the war, Vijaya Lakshmi wrote to Nehru (then in Dehradun) that she was in a state approaching near hysteria about Indu's safety. On 1 January 1941 she received a telegram from her sister, Betty, which she said she could not bring herself to open, convinced that it contained bad news about Indu. After her arrival in March 1941, in relatively poor health, it was agreed that Indu would go to Mussoorie for a couple of months to rest and recuperate. Vijaya Lakshmi arranged for everything to be sent up to Mussoorie from Allahabad for Indu's comfort, including attendants who would look after her and keep her company. Things didn't quite work out the way they were expected to, however, and Indu wrote to her aunt to say that after the Hutheesings left, she found she was alone for long stretches, and felt lonely and isolated in Mussoorie. In a letter to Nehru Mrs Pandit said she wished she had insisted that Indu go with them to Khali, but because Jawaharlal had made the Mussoorie plan she hadn't wanted to upset it.

> Indu is very dear to me (she wrote) and when I see things going wrong, it hurts. I am quite willing to live with Indu in any place that is considered good for her, for any period. To be quite frank, I consider Indu more important than India ...[32]

The country, she continued, had enough people fighting for her and looking after her affairs, but 'Indu needs a home very badly and if we do not wake up and realise this we shall all be sorry one day'.

Only a few months later, however, the situation had changed enough for Vijaya Lakshmi to write to her brother (still in jail) to say that she thought it was time for her and Ranjit to move out of Anand Bhawan:

> For many months now I have been feeling that my presence in Anand Bhawan is perhaps no longer desirable. Please do not imagine that anything has happened to create this impression. As far back as last year I mentioned the subject to Ranjit & told him that when Indu came home I considered it only fair that she should have a free hand and run her house in the way she considered best. We never developed the argument because Indu's return at that time was uncertain. Now that she is back in India I think it is up to us to give her every chance to establish her roots & feel that this is her home.
>
> Indu has had a difficult childhood & adolescence. She has returned to India with certain definite views & she probably has some ideas about her own future. It is only right that she should be able to live her life in her own way without feeling that she has to fit herself into a scheme with which she may or may not be in sympathy. Besides this I have been disturbed by various rumours which keep coming to me regarding Indu's proposed marriage. This is a subject which is painful to me & I do not wish to mention it except in so far as it concerns this letter.
>
> Whatever Indu's plans about marriage may be I feel very definitely that even this step will be hastened unless she feels she has a home of her own where she can live according to her own plan. At present she goes from one house to another with no definite aim and feels at home nowhere. She hesitates about asking her friends to Anand Bhawan because she does not know if I approve and meets them outside – & things like that. Now that she is grown

> up she should, I think, take over charge of her house & run it as she desires fully. After all, when Ranjit & I first came to Anand Bhawan it was a temporary visit which circumstances made more or less permanent. I think the time has come in everybody's interests to make a change. I can always look after such things as Indu does not want to be bothered with & living in Allahabad, I shall be at your disposal, but I have thought these things over & I feel we should leave.[33]

Vijaya Lakshmi had been prescient about Indu's intentions, for within six months she had both announced her decision to, and had married Feroze, on 26 March 1942.

Indu too had written to her father to say that there was little interaction between the first floor at Anand Bhawan where she stayed, and the ground floor where the Pandits were. Eating together was rather formal, she said, rather like a hotel, that 'the house without you is asleep and unresponsive'. News about her aunt's decision to move reached her indirectly, via the servants, and Mrs Hutheesing. 'I didn't know how to broach the subject with her,' she wrote to Nehru, 'so I wrote her a note.'

> It seems ridiculous to me that I should occupy this big house on my own while the four of them are crowded into some bungalow. Of course, having been kept completely in the dark so far it was difficult for me to say anything.[34]

Nehru was naturally upset at this turn of events, but being in prison, was hardly able to intervene on behalf of either his sister or his daughter. His mind had been 'wandering like a vagabond into all manner of dark lanes' as a consequence, but as he said to both of them, he had long given up trying to influence decisions that people, including his family, took. Nor did he think it desirable to interfere in the personal lives of others, 'however near and intimate they might be'.

When Vijaya Lakshmi had last visited Gandhi in Sevagram, she discussed her proposal with him and he had concurred. As far as she was concerned, she said, it made no difference to her where she stayed; her life was so closely linked to her brother's that a mere change of residence was hardly likely to come between them. But political events intervened soon after, with arrests in August and September 1942, including of Indira and Feroze; the Pandits finally moved to their new home at 2 Mukherjee Nagar only in October 1943, after Vijaya Lakshmi was released from jail. A month later, in November 1943, Nehru wrote to his sister to say:

> I am glad Indu is better and that both of you are being drawn to each other. It is not merely a question of relationship – I think both of you have something worthwhile about you and each can help the other in many ways. That comes only with true understanding.[35]

Indira's relationship with her other aunt, Betty, was evidently closer and warmer; she vacationed with the Hutheesings in Kashmir or Mussoorie and stayed with them in Bombay when she visited. When pregnant with Rajiv in 1944, she spent the entire period of her pregnancy and confinement with them; and when Sanjay was born three years later Indira wrote to her aunt to say:

> Darling Chitti (her affectionate address for her aunt)
>
> I always seem to be saying thank you to you. And it is such an inadequate way of expressing what I really want to say. I wish I could do something for you in return. I'm not a bit satisfied with your 'daughter' complex.
>
> However, it was really the greatest bit of luck for me that you were here when the baby arrived. I was quite dreading being all alone on the occasion. ... The wonderful thing about you is that you have always appeared whenever I have wanted somebody to stand by. Not once but so many times.[36]

After Ranjit's death in January 1944, Mrs Pandit was in Allahabad only intermittently, in Lucknow – where Indira and Feroze also lived while Feroze was with the *National Herald* – as education minister in the interim government and after independence, as ambassador and high commissioner of India to the major Western capitals. And Indira moved to Delhi to Teen Murti House to be with the prime minister, both as his official hostess as well as his daughter.

Only three members of the Nehru-Gandhi family were in active politics, post-independence: Jawaharlal, Indira and Feroze. By the time Mrs Pandit returned to India in 1962, she had been out of the country for fifteen years, and in December 1962 she was appointed governor of Maharashtra, thus continuing in official life. She re-entered politics only after her brother's death in 1964, contesting his seat in UP, and became a parliamentarian.

In the meantime, Indira had assumed a definite role in the Congress having been president of the party in 1959, held other party offices and been on sundry committees, including the one on the linguistic division of states. She had also made her presence felt internationally, following, in an almost unintended way, in Mrs Pandit's footsteps. By 1962, when her aunt returned, she was already on the Congress Working Committee and the Congress Parliamentary Board, and a member of the Congress Central Election Committee for the 1962 elections (of which the other two members were her father and UN Hebbar). After her father's death in 1964 she was made a minister in Lal Bahadur Shastri's cabinet; and after *his* death, elevated to prime ministership in 1966.

Vijaya Lakshmi tells a by now well-known story of a meeting with her niece soon after Mrs Gandhi became prime minister. She received a message from Indira asking her to see her, at which time she informed Mrs Pandit that there was a suggestion from people in the UK that she be reappointed high commissioner to that country. 'Well,' said Mrs Pandit after a few minutes, 'what do you think about it?' There followed a long silence, after which Indira replied softly, 'Well, Phupi, I don't really trust you.'[37] After the Emergency was lifted and elections announced in 1977, Mrs Pandit joined Jagjivan Ram's Congress for Democracy, against Mrs Gandhi; the mistrust now became total and the rift unbridgeable. As Nayantara said to me three decades later, 'The family that Indi was closer to and trusted completely was her mother's, because she felt they would be loyal to her through thick and thin.'[38]

It has become almost a truism to say that Mrs Gandhi followed in her father's political footsteps, that she inherited not only his mantle but his mission; yet it is almost as likely that she took on Kamala Nehru's passionate politics and was influenced deeply by her mother's ardent and unrelenting fight for the emancipation of women and the rights of subject peoples; had Kamala Nehru lived, and lived a healthier life, her political footprint might well have been stronger than we know. As Mrs Gandhi's own political personality evolved in the years following her father's death, it became clear that she would define herself in her own terms, being neither parent's political heir, or at least, not always in consonance with the political values that they had held dear.

As early as 1940, when still in her twenties, Indira spiritedly expressed a difference of opinion with her father on political developments in Europe. Writing from her hospital bed in Switzerland, she railed against Britain's policy with regard to the war and their support of Baron Mannerheim and the Germans against Russia. As if this were not enough, they rationalised arms and weapons purchased by Spain; was this, asked Indu witheringly, 'because, as Lady Ironside remarked at a certain house party I remember, "Franco is such a gentleman"'?

> This is the 'democracy' that world imperialism is aiding against the country [Finland] that was practically alone at the League of Nations in upholding the one method of banishing war from the world. And the Liberals and the Labourites go on glibly talking about the 'freedom of the press' and 'freedom of speech' even as, in their own countries and all around them, Communists and socialists are being hounded down into concentration camps.[39]

It is another matter that only a couple of decades later, she would be singing a different tune. In the debates around the linguistic division of states during the 1950s her position was at complete variance with Nehru's; he was reluctant, she was proactive, encouraging the formation of Gujarat and Maharashtra. In 1959, she (together with B.N. Mallick of the Intelligence Bureau) seemed to have been responsible for the dismissal of the communist government in Kerala. On the flight back from Kerala, where she had been sent as Congress president by Nehru, she wrote to her father to say that she didn't know what line he would take with the government in his discussions with them, but her impressions were as follows:

1. There is no point in calling the agitation communal. It is communal only in so far as everything is communal in Kerala, including the communists. The communists very cleverly played the Nairs against the Catholics and now are trying to play the Ezhavas against both.
2. If we are going to ask the local Congress to withdraw from the present movement, we must outline some other programme for them. They cannot just stand aloof.
3. If the Education Bill is to be discussed, the question of textbooks is important. Naturally, I have not checked them myself but the newspapers reported that they tell a lot about Stalin and Mao Tse-tung, nothing about modern India except our foreign policy. This matter was taken up with the Union Ministry of Education – Dr Shrimali is reported to have replied that education was a state subject. This is not good enough. We should not permit any anti-national bias in education.[40]

Although, as she had told Nayantara, she stepped down as Congress president after only one year because she couldn't do what she wanted, to her father she said that her decision was based on the realisation that the time had come for her to live her own life. She had worked hard for the past many years, driven by the thought that she could never do enough. Now she just wanted to be free, 'as a piece of flotsam waiting for the waves to wash me up on some shore, from where I shall arise and find my own direction'.[41]

However, shedding the office of president was one thing, distancing herself from active politics was quite another. Within a year of her resignation Feroze would pass away, followed by Nehru a couple of years later, and Indira was back in the fray.

The departure from a Nehruvian policy of equidistance from the big powers became evident in Indira Gandhi's first foreign tour after she became prime minister in 1969. Her visit to the US and Europe signalled the emergence of a style and strategy that provoked admiration and criticism in more or less equal measure. She impressed the then US president Lyndon Johnson hugely, was pragmatic with Alexei Kosygin of Moscow, and departed from the norm by visiting British prime minister Harold Wilson *after* her trip to the US rather than on her way there. To her critics in India who accused her of 'deviating' from her father's policies, she said quite plainly,

> If it is necessary to deviate ... I would not hesitate to do so. I must pursue policies that are in the best interest of the country as a whole. If you don't like these policies, you have every right to remove me.[42]

Chinks in the non-aligned armour had begun to appear as early as 1956, however, with the covert CIA Operation, S.T. Circus, which trained and equipped 300 Tibetans in sabotage against China. Nehru may or may not have known of the Indian Intelligence Bureau's involvement at this stage, but by the time of the China war in 1962 it had his explicit approval to create a Special Frontier Force of 5,000 Tibetans, with more or less the same objective. Obviously, the Americans were part of the plan.[43]

It could be argued that Indira Gandhi's interpretation of non-alignment was based on realpolitik, keeping both superpowers in the balance and tilting towards one or the other as circumstances – and 'national interest' – demanded.

Be that as it may, Mrs Gandhi systematically and with a clear-eyed strategy, set about distancing herself from her father's style of consensus-building politics and governance, moving towards a more centralised concentration of authority, and of isolating those who contradicted her policy prescriptions. One by one, she vitiated all the important institutions that might act as a brake to her power – trade unions, the press, the judiciary, the Opposition – all institutions that Nehru had nurtured as being critical for democracy. The further Indira moved away from what Nayantara saw as her uncle's legacy and political wisdom, the more stridently critical she became in her columns and consequently, the greater the rift between the cousins.

The Congress split, Nayantara wrote, had transformed the political atmosphere in the country. Nehru and Shastri, inheritors of Gandhi's principled approach to politics, had 'personally practised and upheld a meticulous standard of political behaviour'; Mrs Gandhi, on the other hand, had perfected the politics of manipulation and intrigue.

> She represented something ruthless and new. She had astonished people with her flair for cold assessment, shrewd timing and the telling theatrical gesture; above all with her capacity for a fight to the finish, even to bringing the eighty-four-year-old party of liberation to rupture.[44]

In Mrs Gandhi's assessment, the fact that it was Nayantara who wrote against her might well have seemed an equivalent betrayal, a breach of family loyalty that was both unwelcome and inexcusable. Easier, after all, to comment from the outside than to effect change from within and from an embattled space.

As Mrs Gandhi's displeasure grew, Nayantara found she was either being treated with kid gloves, socially, or being warned off by well-wishers. At a dinner party one evening she was accosted by a Supreme Court lawyer who said to her, 'I wish to let you know that you are very much out of line with the kind of articles you are writing, and it would be better for you if you modified your view.' Nayantara rounded on him, told him she came from lawyers on both sides of the family, and informed him that 'the regime today has no respect for the law and I have no intention of kow-towing to it'.[45] Her sustained and detailed assessment of her cousin's political style would be the subject of her next book, written while she was at Radcliffe in 1976. Writing it had symbolic and poignant importance for her; she saw it at the time as 'a duty to the voices the Emergency had silenced, and as an act of commitment to the values of the free society Jawaharlal Nehru had built during his seventeen years in power'.[46]

With Mrs Gandhi's electoral defeat in 1977 and the lifting of censorship, a slew of post-Emergency books were published, intended for a readership that had been deprived of news and analysis for two years. Among them was the first edition of Nayantara's *Indira Gandhi's Emergence and Style,* published in 1979 by Vikas (which had earlier declined to take it up as being too risky). It was subsequently updated and revised and reissued in 1983 by Macdonald & Co. in the UK with the title *Indira Gandhi: Her Road to Power*, and was dedicated to John Kenneth Galbraith. By this time, Mrs Gandhi was back in power.

As account and analysis the book takes its cue from Nayantara's columns and, as such, shares their outrage as well as their conclusions – which, as she herself acknowledged in retrospect, might have been unduly judgemental. Commentators before and since have noted how little the erstwhile Congress did to break the hold of industrialists and the rural elite on the economy; how reluctant Nehru was to dislodge vested interests and how corruption and power politics grew under his watch; how unfree large sections of the population actually were. But with Indira, the difference was qualitative; when Sanjay Gandhi came into politics crony capitalism, according to Nayantara, blossomed and prospered. 'Indi was fed up with Rajiv and Sonia who were most disinterested. Sanjay brought dynamism into the system – he soothed the capitalists and she soothed the communists. This was her brilliant politics.'[47]

Re-reading her articles for *Everyman's* in 2013, she wrote to me to say she had often wondered since whether she should have been so blunt and outspoken, made herself so vulnerable. But, 'Once again I realised I could have reacted no other way to what I saw as the destruction of the idea of India.'[48]

Nehru's idea of India, that is.

For although Nayantara's book is about Indira Gandhi and the India she sought to create in *her* image; and about the challenge to her realpolitik by the principled and moral force of JP's satyagraha, the hidden referent – the towering absent presence in it – is her uncle. Mrs Gandhi's tryst with power is counterposed to Nehru's tryst with destiny; in dismantling her cousin's house, built on weak and unsound foundations, Nayantara is at the same time writing a requiem for everything her uncle stood for – and strove towards. Her book is at once a cry from the heart and an elegy; with it, her explicitly political writing came to an end. 'I made a deliberate decision not to do so any more,' she said, 'I wanted to withdraw from that scene of combat. I would have to get to the bone and marrow of politics and I didn't want that degree of involvement any longer.'[49]

Their political estrangement completely destroyed her relationship with Mrs Gandhi. 'Indi was an either/or person,' Nayantara told me:

> ... no grey areas. She wasn't like her father who had a lot of the tentative in him – his personality was full of nuance. She just felt her kith and kin should support her – so it was a great loss for me because we had been very close. She had been fond of me ... and, politically inside, I saw where I could have been different.[50]

But she didn't try to seek out her cousin, to talk about their differences, for by now the rupture was too deep. To Bunchi she said that unhappy as she was about the break, she saw no real possibility of reconciliation; 'Indi shuts herself in,' she wrote, 'and then she starts from a desert, a coldness and aridness, whereas in Mamu one felt a human warmth, a loving response.'[51] For Nehru the family was a 'living, growing thing towards which he felt both interest and obligation, but for Indi, cultivating relationships – except in a formal way – or conserving values is not a priority.' Reminiscing about that time Nayantara said,

> There is no way Indi would not have entered politics, but if her marriage had succeeded, if there were no divided loyalties pulling her apart, if she had had the loving support of her husband, that would have made a huge difference.[52]

Endnotes

1 Chandralekha Mehta, *Freedom's Child: Growing Up During Satyagraha* (New Delhi: Puffin Books, 2008), pp. 57–62.

2 Quoted in Zareer Masani, *Indira Gandhi: A Biography*, p. 33.

3 Quoted in Nayantara Sahgal (ed.), *Before Freedom: Nehru's Letters to His Sister 1909–1947* (New Delhi: Roli Books, 2004).

4 Krishna Nehru Hutheesing, *Dear to Behold: An Intimate Portrait of Indira Gandhi* (London: The Macmillan Company, 1969) p. 98.

5 Chandralekha Mehta, *Freedom's Child*, p. 157.

6 Nayantara Sahgal to Vijaya Lakshmi Pandit and Chandralekha Pandit, 1 February 1948.

7 Nayantara Sahgal, *Indira Gandhi: Tryst With Power*, p. 8.

8 Nayantara Sahgal to E.N. Mangat Rai, letter dated 1 November 1967 (unpublished).

9 Promilla Kalhan, *Kamala Nehru: An Intimate Biography* (New Delhi: Vikas Publishing House, 1973), p. 143.

10 Krishna Nehru Hutheesing, *Dear to Behold*, p. 91.

11 Quoted in ibid., p. 92.

12 Zareer Masani, *Indira Gandhi: A Biography*, p. 7.

13 Promilla Kalhan, *Kamala Nehru*, p. 142.

14 Ibid., p. 28.

15 Zareer Masani, *Indira Gandhi: A Biography*, pp. 11–12.

16 Promilla Kalhan, *Kamala Nehru*, p. 141.

17 Nayantara Sahgal, *Indira Gandhi: Tryst With Power*, p. 373.

18 Nayantara Sahgal (ed.), *Before Freedom*, letter dated March 6, 1933 from Dehradun Jail, p. 96.

19 Promilla Kalhan, *Kamala Nehru*, p. 139.

20 Nayantara Sahgal to E.N. Mangat Rai, letter dated 14 March 1966 (unpublished).

21 Zareer Masani, *Indira Gandhi: A Biography*, p. 117.

22 Tariq Ali, *The Nehrus and the Gandhis: An Indian Dynasty*, p. 270.

23 Zareer Masani, *Indira Gandhi: A Biography*, p. 97.

24 Nayantara Sahgal to E.N. Mangat Rai, letter dated 14 March 1966 (unpublished).

25 Vijaya Lakshmi Pandit, *The Scope of Happiness: A Personal Memoir*, p. 55.

26 Tariq Ali, *The Nehrus and the Gandhis*, p. 17.

27 Nayantara Sahgal (ed.), *Before Freedom*, p. 286; letter dated 9 November 1943.

28 Ibid., p. 103.

29 Ibid., p. 200; letter dated 8 November 1938, from Feroze Gandhi to Vijaya Lakshmi Pandit.

30 Vijaya Lakshmi Pandit, *The Scope of Happiness*, p. 287.

31 Vijaya Lakshmi Pandit to Jawaharlal Nehru, letter dated 24 September 1941, Nehru Memorial Museum and Library (Private papers, reserve collection).

32 Vijaya Lakshmi Pandit to Jawaharlal Nehru, ibid., letter dated 1 January 1941.

33 Vijaya Lakshmi Pandit to Jawaharlal Nehru, ibid., letter dated 24 September 1941.

34 Sonia Gandhi (ed.), *Two Alone, Two Together: Letters Between Indira Gandhi & Jawaharlal Nehru, 1922–1964* (London: Hodder & Stoughton, 1992), p. 281.

35 Nayantara Sahgal (ed.), *Before Freedom*, p. 200; letter dated 30 November 1943.

36 Krishna Nehru Hutheesing, *Dear to Behold*, p. 114.

37 Vijaya Lakshmi Pandit, *The Scope of Happiness*, p. 5.

38 Personal interview, Dehradun, October 2008.

39 Sonia Gandhi (ed.), *Two Alone, Two Together*, p. 32.

40 Ibid., p. 626.

41 Ibid., p. 628.

42 Inder Malhotra, 'Rearview', *Indian Express*, 13 May 2013.

43 I am grateful to Praful Bidwai for drawing my attention to this fact.

44 Nayantara Sahgal, *Indira Gandhi: Tryst With Power*, p. 82.

45 Personal interview, Dehradun, October 2008.

46 Nayantara Sahgal, *Indira Gandhi: Tryst With Power*, p. xi.

47 Personal interview, Delhi, February 2011.

48 Letter dated 17 March 2013 to the author.

49 Personal interview, Delhi, February 2011.

50 Personal interview, Dehradun, August 2010.

51 Nayantara Sahgal to E.N. Mangat Rai, letter dated 14 March 1966 (unpublished).

52 Personal interview, Delhi, February 2011.

7

AWAY FROM HOME

A Situation in New Delhi

Rich Like Us

Plans for Departure

Mistaken Identity

Before Freedom: Nehru's Letters to His Sister

A *SITUATION IN NEW DELHI*, DEDICATED TO RONALD SAMPSON, was a novel interrupted. Begun in Texas in 1974, it was stalled by Nayantara's return to India and her involvement in the JP movement. By the time she managed to complete it the Emergency was in full swing, and 'nobody would touch it with a barge-pole – it went into limbo'. Finally, in 1976–77, it was serialised in *London Magazine* and subsequently published by them as a book.

The opening words of the novel 'Shivraj is dead' announce its real hero – Shivraj/Nehru. He is mourned not only by his sister, Devi (read Vijaya Lakshmi Pandit) but by his biographer, the Englishman Michael Calvert and his erstwhile comrade-in-arms, Usman Ali. Devi is education minister (as Vijaya Lakshmi Pandit had been in the interim government of the 1930s, in Lucknow); Usman is vice chancellor of Delhi University, which is seething with student discontent. Michael, Devi's former lover, returns to India when he reads about Shivraj's death in London, impelled by the force of his emotional response to mourn in the very city where he had come under his spell. And Devi's.

Shivraj and Devi; Nehru and Vijaya Lakshmi.

> What I had in mind was the extraordinary relationship between Mrs Pandit and Nehru, a relationship between a brother and a sister, and into that relationship I brought

> the English lover as part of a threesome or foursome because there was this Muslim ... I wanted to convey that Shivraj had that effect on people, created that kind of love and loyalty, that these three people were devoted to him in this extraordinary way. I wanted to bring out Mamu's personality ... that was really my main focus.[1]

Only the threesome is left now, Usman hopelessly in love with Devi, but married; and Devi, widowed (at forty-four, like Vijaya Lakshmi Pandit) but heavily reliant on Usman, especially now, with Shivraj gone. All three are in an emotional limbo. Michael, long reconciled to the fact that Devi's primary attachment was to Shivraj, finds himself wondering and hoping; Usman, friendly with Michael and fond of him, but only too aware of the fact that unlike him, he himself is not a free agent; and Devi – how would she rearrange her life now?

If Shivraj and Devi are statedly modelled on Nehru and Vijaya Lakshmi Pandit, is Usman a putative Syed Hossain? And could Michael be a displaced Edwina Mountbatten, all part of a foursome-that-never-was? It is tantalising to think of how subconsciously, even subliminally, apprehended relationships find a fictional articulation that simultaneously suggests and subverts what might have been.

Yet, despite the novel being what the *Financial Times* called a 'provocative piece of fact-based fiction', this is about as far as the autobiographical element in it can be stretched. The point of departure is Devi's son, Rishad, sharply counterpointed to her brother Shivraj. If the latter is the novel's absent hero, Rishad is its all-too-real and present anti-hero; a living, pulsating repudiation of all that Shivraj represented. The means that Rishad adopts to realise *his* vision – an India liberated from deprivation and injustice – would have been anathema to Shivraj. A vision as idealistic as his uncle's, no doubt, but Rishad has no patience with namby-pamby non-violence. His objective is revolution, and as a revolutionary he will kill if he has to, to eliminate the hideous fact of poverty and inequality. But

> ... This cult of violence had to be clean, cold and disciplined, unaided by motive, by drugs or mental aberration. This was the violence of the sane with a passion for justice. To build a new world the old one had to be razed to the ground ... Only then could the new social order arise. Not Utopia. Just food in the stomach and a decent wage.[2]

Rishad is nineteen years old, a student at Delhi University in the late 1960s, in the grip of Naxal activity. Its best and its brightest are on the warpath, and Rishad is one of the revolution's most promising recruits. This is the same seething unrest that Usman has to confront as VC. Where Rishad and his contemporaries are bent on revolution, Usman looks to reform. The universities, the educational system, the whole edifice will have to be overhauled, he tells his minister, Devi, but if Rishad were to discuss 'the system' with his mother, he would tell her it had to be jettisoned. Destroyed. Neither Usman nor Devi suspects that Rishad is among the university radicals.

The story proceeds on two more or less parallel tracks: Usman's attempts at pushing educational reform, Rishad and his cohorts' at dismantling the very structures of power. Both endeavours are almost certainly doomed to failure

– but with an unexpected twist. Rishad dies a futile and tragic death, killed in an explosion he is trying desperately to forestall; Usman, in a dramatic turn, resigns as VC and morphs into a JP-like icon. He spearheads a student movement, drawing all those who were discontented but not yet Naxalite to himself and his call to resist. Although the fate of his movement is not spelt out, one message is clear – reform is to be preferred over revolution.

And yet, Nayantara says the Naxal phenomenon interested her greatly because it involved the most intelligent, sensitive and idealistic young people of the time. A likely inspiration for Rishad could have been Dilip Simeon, a St Stephens College student, whose parents she had known in Allahabad and who, like Rishad, had been radicalised in the university. But there were many Rishads and Dilips in cities in the late 1960s and '70s, all from roughly the same sort of social and economic class, generally privileged, who were mesmerised by the Naxal ideologue, Charu Majumdar. *Situation* captures the tumult of those years during which Indira Gandhi was driving a wedge in the old Congress; the Communist Party of India split into its Soviet and Maoist avatars; and later, the CPI (M) government in West Bengal came down brutally on the Naxalites. Of the Naxalites and the party that now openly supported them, the CPI (Marxist–Leninist), Mrs Gandhi had said: 'These Naxalites or Guevarists or anarchists have much misdirected idealism but no basic framework to effect social transformation. However heroic their individual acts might appear to them, they cannot succeed.'[3] Many years later Dilip Simeon would write his own novel, *Revolution Highway,* about that experience and the fervour with which a large number of men and women of his generation left their studies and struck out on a revolutionary road. Oddly enough, he came to much the same conclusion as Nayantara in *Situation*: resistance was necessary, but killings could not be the means by which to eliminate injustice or effect social change.

The tension in the novel between older and younger generations, old values and new compulsions is muted. Till he dies, Devi does not even know that Rishad is immersed in the violence that she reads about and is reported to her, and Rishad's pangs of conscience and ambivalence regarding means-and-ends trouble him, despite his rationalisation of violence. It is the turmoil on campus and the open discord in parliament that are mirror images of each other, both indicating inevitable ruptures. The irresolution at the end, the lack of closure, are deliberate: something has ended, but nothing has yet replaced it. This is as true of personal relationships as it is of the political situation; the tension, such as it is, is the tension of suspended animation.

With *A Situation in New Delhi* Nayantara reached a point of departure in her fiction: it was the last of her novels in which an autobiographical element is clearly recognisable, either as personal experience or by way of her protagonists. After her divorce and after *A Situation in New Delhi*, she withdrew herself from the text, is no longer in it. 'Writing is engagement,' she has said, 'a writer is not separate from what she writes;'[4] but where in the earlier novels this bonding, this overlay of fiction on first person is evident, in *A Situation in New Delhi* it is really only Devi and Shivraj who are so intimately drawn from the author's family. It is as well that Rishad and the student uprising are offered as a foil to this duo who might otherwise have risked being overwhelmed by cloying sentimentalism.

The passive woman too is absent from its pages. Devi, of course, is the active, assertive female subject, but even the minor characters – Rishad's accidental girlfriend, Suvarnapriya, and Usman's wife, Nadira – are women to be reckoned with. Devi's high, and highly visible, public office does not come in the way of her resuming her affair with Michael – or indeed, in her taking Usman as her lover in her widowhood – just as Suvarnapriya's conventional, even conservative upbringing does not prevent her from giving herself to Rishad. Their choices and decisions are autonomous, made in full awareness of any consequences that might have to be borne. This trajectory is developed more fully in Nayantara's next novel, *Rich Like Us*, where her main character, Sonali, a civil servant, refuses to follow orders she believes are inimical to her office. She will not be a stooge. Like Devi, she is a woman alone; neither of them needed either a man or the institution of marriage as reinforcement. Devi, though widowed, doesn't bury herself in widowhood; in fact, it is her Muslim lover who brings her back to life. She lives, she chooses the men in her life, becomes successful in her own right.

The juxtaposition of violence and non-violence as two opposing strategies for resistance, and the desirability of one over the other as the means by which to achieve the desired end, is introduced here as a moral choice. Thus, Usman, recognising the power of a crowd, the leashed force of passion that seethes just below its surface, 'knew at once how he must begin his speech' to the thousands of students he was addressing:

> In a ringing voice that carried clearly over the microphone he gave a grim warning. Here and now, those who were with him must pledge themselves to peaceful action. A roar of voices rose in agreement as he raised both his hands for their response.[5]

In Nayantara's view, the equation of non-violence with passivity is a complete misunderstanding of the concept, it is in fact quite the opposite. 'It has to do with active will-power,' she said to me.

> In passivity you stand by, hold back, you wait. In non-violence you put your mind and body on the line, you are in the battle, part of it.[6]

This is why it was, and had to be, the civilised choice, not the last or only resort of the helpless. It needed solid preparation, needed discipline, for being the only approach that 'employed the whole human being constructively' in the resistance to wrongdoing or evil. What could be more exciting, she asked, than the idea that a human being needed no other resource but himself, 'nothing but his own invincible spirit' to confront tyranny or oppression?[7]

In 1979, Bunchi and Nayantara finally got married, although by that time it seemed a mere formality. What occasioned it was the decision of the Janata government to send her as India's ambassador to Italy. Morarji Desai, then prime minister, told her quite clearly that an unmarried couple at the embassy was undesirable. If she accepted the offer, she would have to marry Bunchi.

In July 1979 a magistrate was called to their flat in Massey Hall, but he couldn't distract them for long enough to sign on the dotted line because they were glued to the news – the government was falling. Noni and her then boyfriend had brought a bottle of champagne to celebrate, but it was flat. Nobody was in the least bit concerned about the marriage, there was so much other excitement around. In the event, the government did fall, Indira Gandhi swept back into power, and Nayantara's chance at an ambassadorship vanished into thin air. She was more than a little disappointed; with her appointment, she believed she had been recognised for her uncompromising opposition to the Emergency and her support to the JP movement. Representing India abroad at this juncture would have been a welcome opportunity and she was ready to shift gears, which such a move would entail, in their personal lives. That it didn't materialise remained a matter of regret. A different, perhaps more relevant, acknowledgement came her way in the early 1980s. The eminent lawyer, V.M. Tarkunde, invited her to join the newly formed Peoples' Union for Civil Liberties; she did, and was appointed its vice-president, a position she held through the 1980s.

Marriage might not have been on Nayantara's mind any more for herself, but it was certainly a preoccupation as far as Noni and Gita were concerned. Gita, now back from England and her studies, had joined Action India, an organisation working with working-class men and women in Delhi, and was active with brick kiln workers and migrant labour in the Mehrauli–Chattarpur area, where various members of the extended Sahgal clan had their farms, along with Mrs Gandhi. This was all very well and Nayantara supported her politics and her activism, but the work wasn't bringing in an income. As she said quite frankly to her daughter, 'All the other women you're working with have husbands. You need a job.'

Noni, who did have a job – had worked ever since she graduated from college in 1970, in a variety of places from Air India and the Ashoka Hotel to the beauty and garment businesses and the World Wildlife Fund – had walked out of her first marriage (in 1976) and was single again. Although not living with her mother and Bunchi, she was in Delhi and within easy reach.

But then, in 1983, Gita married Colin Partridge, a junior diplomat in the British high commission, at least temporarily putting her mother's mind at rest on this score. Mrs Pandit was delighted, pleased that her grandson-in-law was English, and hosted a party at which she invited all the ambassadors she knew in town. The architect, Piloo Mody, then a member of parliament, demanded to know why he hadn't been invited, and turned up anyway. Gita sent an invitation to her father through her aunt Premilla (Baby) Menon, Gautam's younger sister, but he ignored it. Not being a chiffon-and-pearls kind of person at all, Gita told her mother she wanted to get married in one of *her* old saris. Nayantara flatly refused. Said she had been unlucky in her marriage, so it was out of the question. No amount of reasoning had any effect – she simply wouldn't budge.

Gita and Colin moved to London, where Gita would continue to live and work for the next thirty years. Between 1986 and 1991 she worked on one of the most exciting programmes on British television, Channel 4's *Bandung File*. A Black current affairs programme, it was commissioned by the writer Farrukh Dhondy and produced by the Pakistani commentator, Tariq Ali, at one time a member of the Trotskyist International Marxist Group. Gita was initially a presenter, but moved on to researching and directing documentaries. The India programmes included films on dowry deaths and sati; on the Film and Television Institute of India (FTII) in Poona; and on the writer Nirmal Verma. In the UK Gita produced several programmes on racism, community relations and women's rights. Salman Rushdie's last interview before he disappeared underground went out on the night Khomeini issued his fatwa against him in 1989. After Gita left in 1991, she plunged fully into activism through Women Against Fundamentalism and Southall Black Sisters, followed by an extended period of working on human and women's rights with Amnesty International.

But her marriage with Colin was short-lived, and they separated amicably in 1988.

Reviewing *The Day in Shadow* in *The Sunday Times* in 1972, Maurice Higgins had remarked:

> Mrs Sahgal is not only an able novelist but a likeable writer with a certain grace of spirit, a stubborn core of honour and goodness. Unlike some of our rootless intellectuals, she is not guilty of that *trahison des clercs* which has betrayed western civilisation ... she is a moral writer, though not a moralist. She sees art as an

instrument for discerning and affirming the difference between right and wrong.

It was only a matter of time, then, before Nayantara wrote *Rich Like Us,* her Emergency novel, which was published by Heinemann in the UK in 1985, about six months after Indira Gandhi's assassination in October 1984. It was dedicated to the 'Indo-British experience and what its sharers have learned from each other', and was written while she was a Fellow at the Woodrow Wilson International Center for Scholars in Washington DC, in 1980–81.

These were comparatively carefree years for her. She was back in Washington for the first time since the 1950s when her mother was ambassador, and the Center and DC were a wonderfully stimulating environment. She and Bunchi lived in an apartment building, with other Woodrow Wilson scholars, that was within walking distance of the Smithsonian, where the Center was located. That daily trip to her office and workspace became a rare pleasure and she luxuriated in the freedom to do nothing but write. No anxieties about housekeeping, about earning an income, even about the children. It had taken her a long time to get off the ground, but now that she had, it was as if her writing had taken wing. *Rich Like Us* was completed in record time, six months – the novel just flowed from her pen, practically wrote itself – and it was shipped off to her agent, A.M. Heath in London, before she left the US for India. Especially convivial were the sherry evenings with the other fellows (among them Ariel Dorfmann), sampling the widest selection of sherries she had ever tasted. When, after completing her final draft, she had taken it to one of the secretaries to type up, she was told, 'You're the only one of the fellas who ever finished anything here.' All the others, she implied, were busy imbibing!

Before *Rich Like Us* Nayantara had, unknowingly perhaps, been following a stage by stage sequence of where the country was going politically. The idealism and hope in democracy that had imbued her earlier novels and the early years of India's independence came to 'a dead end' with the Emergency. 'I think that provoked me to break free in my modes of expression as well,' she said to me. Two facts coincided here: the political fact of the Emergency, and the personal fact of having the time and mental space to write unencumbered. It made a great and qualitative difference to her writing, to be free of deadlines and interruptions. Certain depths within her could now be plumbed because she had left her stresses behind – familial, post-divorce, financial, even political because, as she said, 'I wasn't writing *about* politics, I was writing it.'[8]

The Emergency was the trigger for, as well as the subject of, *Rich Like Us* and, in a quietly despairing way, it is an epitaph for the idea of India. A ruthless and authoritarian prime minister and her son have brought the country to its knees, browbeaten officialdom into craven sycophancy, and unleashed hoodlums and exploiters onto the economy and society. Two women, (English) Rose and (Indian) Sonali resist the rot and the horrors of misrule, and both pay the price. Sonali is a civil servant who refuses to obey ruinous orders and so is shown the door; Rose, second wife of Ram – whose son Dev, from his first wife, is thick as thieves with the real thieves – meets a violent and horrific end. Both represent the best that their particular upbringing and background offer: Rose's is practical good sense and unfailing honesty and warmth; Sonali's, an unwavering sense of right and wrong and commitment to principle. Dev and Ravi Kachru, Sonali's former lover, now a senior bureaucrat, are the PM's hatchet men, with Dev serving as a conduit for slush funds and motor parts for her son's automobile factory. Ram is the conventional male, charming and fickle and, in the end, comatose, literally and metaphorically. His relationships with Mona, his first wife, with Rose and then Marcella, his upper-class English infatuation, are paradigmatic, with each woman signifying one kind of encounter with Western modernity by the colonised Indian male. Resistance to colonisation entails the kind of marginalisation experienced by Ram's father, Lalaji, and Dev's father-in-law, Kishori Lal; yet they, together with Rose and Sonali, stand firm in the face of wayward brutality and exploitation – whether by the coloniser or his successor. Hired hoodlums conspire with unscrupulous 'enter-prenuers' (Rose's word) while rulers look away, turning the country into a moral wasteland.

Rich Like Us won the Sinclair Prize for fiction in 1985, awarded to an 'unpublished novel of political or social significance'. It was one among 329 entries that year, and the award carried a cash prize of £5,000. The runner up was Tim Parks, and both novels were published by Heinemann, who offered Nayantara an advance of £2,000 for hers. David Caute, chairman of the jury, which included Terry Eagleton, Hugh Stephenson, Fay Weldon and Marina Warner, said of *Rich Like Us* that:

> The author is above all a writer of acute political intelligence – the servile attitude of the middle class towards Mrs Gandhi's rule, the opportunism and snobbery and place-seeking, are recounted with wonderful acerbic humour.

Praise came pouring in from a slew of reviews in *The Listener*, *New Statesman*, *London Magazine*, *The Observer* and others, all commending the author for her subtly subversive style, for 'the intensity of her beliefs and her passion for truth and freedom' (*London Magazine*). The historian E.P. Thompson wrote to Nayantara to say how much he had enjoyed reading it, called it 'a superb, beautifully crafted, searching and compassionate book ... one of the very few books of our time which will last'. In particular, he congratulated her for her constructive feminism, which he said she shared with Nadine Gordimer and which, he believed, was 'so much more effective than trendy western stridencies'.[9] At the award ceremony which took place at the French restaurant, L'Escargot, in London, Nayantara said that in her next life she 'wanted to live in a small country which is very prosperous and has very few people. In the meantime I'm stuck with India.'

Rich Like Us was published by W.W. Norton, Nayantara's publisher in the US, in paperback by Sceptre in the UK and by New Directions in the US, as well as in Germany and The Netherlands. Nayantara had hoped that Patricia Mountbatten's husband, John Brabourne, a well-known film producer, would consider adapting it for a film but, as with Satyajit Ray and *A Situation in New Delhi* earlier, this proposal did not materialise.

Seven thousand pounds may not, by today's standards, seem like a huge amount of money, but it liberated Nayantara temporarily from pressing financial preoccupation – and success was very sweet. The Sinclair Prize, followed by the Sahitya Akademi Award, also for *Rich Like Us* in 1985, more or less made for a done deal on the two novels that followed in quick succession: *Plans for Departure* and *Mistaken Identity*. The experience of untramelled writing time had been so exhilarating that Nayantara's head was buzzing with ideas for her new novel even before the ink had dried on *Rich Like Us*.

But family matters intervened in 1982, which made for an interruption, and a second relocation, this time to Dehradun. In 1967 Nayantara's mother decided to retire to Dehradun. Delhi would have been a more practical choice, but given Indira Gandhi's hostility Vijaya Lakshmi wisely chose a town in another state. Her daughters made several trips to Dehradun looking for land or a house that she could buy, and finally located a lovely spot on the upper reaches of Rajpur Road, framed by a sheer cliff and forested slopes. Here she built her house, surrounded by mango and litchi trees and an enormous ficus tree on a three-quarter acre of land. Dehradun was not quite Khali, but it was close to the mountains, in the Himalayan foothills, unhurried and quiet. It was where both Nehru and Ranjit Pandit had served prison sentences in the 1930s and '40s, and Mussoorie, twenty-one miles further up, was where her daughters had gone to school at Woodstock. Mussoorie was also the summer holiday resort of her girlhood and, after Allahabad, the two places that were more 'home' than any other. A host of memories and associations, happy and sad, suffused both towns.

Vijaya Lakshmi set about establishing a home with characteristic vigour, beginning with a grand housewarming held on her seventieth birthday, 18 August 1970. Close friends, her daughters with their families, grandchildren and well-wishers joined in, and the children gave her a book of tributes from colleagues and friends called *Sunlight Surrounds You*. Two years earlier, in 1968, her eldest daughter, Chandralekha, had bought a piece of land just down the road from her mother's and built a kind of weekend cottage there, to which she and her husband retired in 1979. And a few years later, in 1985–86, Nayantara and Bunchi moved to Dehradun as well, after Bunchi retired as chairman from the Faridabad Institute of Engineering in 1982.

The question of where they would live after Bunchi's working life ended had been a preoccupation, but no immediate decision was necessary because of their sojourn in the US. Vijaya Lakshmi Pandit suggested Dehradun as a possibility, suggesting also that she would welcome their company and offer them her home. Although she had built the house for her youngest daughter (whose marriage by then was virtually over), Rita didn't think she wanted to leave Delhi or her job for Dehradun, and as Lekha already had two houses, one in Delhi and another in Dehradun, Vijaya Lakshmi asked Nayantara and Bunchi if they would agree to live there and take over the house.

A house in the hills had always been an attractive idea, and for a long time Bunchi's sister, Sheila's estate in Kulu–Manali had seemed to be just the thing. It was a beautiful apple orchard, filled with flowering trees, and almost as easily accessible as Dehradun or Nainital. But then, in 1980, Sheila was murdered in a ghastly incident – three intruders, hoping to make off with cash from the harvest, bludgeoned her to death, but found only a paltry Rs 1,500 for their effort. No one was ever arrested, and the family decided to sell the house and gardens and divide the proceeds. The decision about where to live, whether to rent a house in Delhi or not, was sort of made for them – the house in Dehradun was there, Lekha and her mother were there, all three living together in the same place for the first time since Allahabad – it seemed a good decision.

At the time. For Dehradun entailed a major adjustment and it was a difficult period for Nayantara. Bunchi had no relationship with UP; he was very much a Punjab person and would have preferred to retire in Chandigarh, but with both Champa and Gautam there, that choice didn't really exist. While Nayantara had her family as neighbours and companions, Bunchi had few friends in the city and never really found a community in which he was at home, socially or intellectually. Naturally gregarious, unlike Nayantara who was a homebody, content to remain within the family circle, there were times when Bunchi felt that Dehradun was distinctly stifling. Meanwhile, Nayantara's writing career was blossoming, she was in demand, travelling and savouring her success, with which Bunchi was wholly delighted and in which he participated happily. But this was not his milieu. Nor was it always easy to remember that he was living in his mother-in-law's house, even though he brought his considerable management skills to the job of looking after her affairs and her household.

For Nayantara, this living together, separately, worked rather well, as it freed her from the distraction of daily housekeeping. Vijaya Lakshmi had always been an inspired homemaker, enjoying hugely the opportunity to extend her warm hospitality to friends, family and grandchildren, all of whom revelled in her affection. Her relationship with her daughter was close, even though Nayantara knew that Vijaya Lakshmi's strongest emotional bond was with her eldest daughter, Lekha. 'All children are not loved equally,' Nayantara said to me, 'why should they be?'[10] Her mother being close to Lekha didn't bother Nayantara, but Rita minded terribly. Mrs Pandit told Nayantara that she knew 'there would be no trouble between you and Lekha after I'm gone' but that there might be between Rita and Lekha. In a curious reversal, Nayantara and her mother were mutually protective of each other, each thinking the other was peculiarly vulnerable on account of the choices they made. In an oddly uncanny mirroring, Vijaya Lakshmi's anxieties about her daughters anticipated Nayantara's own worries regarding Noni and Gita, and for much the same reason – incompatible marriages and financial insecurity.

For Vijaya Lakshmi, Tara had always been trouble-prone, always leaving herself open to injury, either emotional or political. This had been so from the time she was a teenager, with her normal teenage escapades threatening to spiral out of control. Her affair with Noguchi, for instance, might have been known to Dorothy Norman, whose apartment was a convenient meeting place when Nayantara visited from Wellesley, but her mother knew nothing about it. The romance with Nicky she did know about, and she had made her feelings on the subject very clear – there was no way she would allow Tara to encourage Nicky while being engaged to Gautam. With Gautam too, although she was relieved that Tara was settling down, she worried that she was too young for marriage. Her daughter's impulsiveness was something she would continue to be anxious about, but couldn't forestall.

Marry in haste, repent at leisure might well have been coined for Nayantara, but she was careful to keep the full extent of her marital troubles from her mother. In 1955, she and her two older children, Nonika and Ranjit, had spent six months with Mrs Pandit in England while she was high commissioner there, without her realising just how fragile her daughter's marriage was; and in 1959, it was her uncle whom Nayantara confided in, rather than her mother. She knew not only that Mrs Pandit would worry, but that she was conventional enough to want the marriage to continue, as far as possible. She was relieved when Tara returned to Gautam in 1959, but her concern resurfaced with the appearance of Bunchi on the scene.

Nevertheless, once Nayantara decided that divorcing Gautam was the only option, she had her mother's unwavering support, moral, emotional, financial and practical. Although she felt it as a huge blow, Mrs Pandit fielded questions in parliament, deflected jibes and innuendo, mediated on her daughter's behalf with Morarji Desai, and of course sought an array of legal opinion regarding maintenance and custody of the children. What might actually have been the most onerous of her tasks though, was dealing with the fallout of Gautam's raging unhappiness. She managed then to keep him from going off at the deep end, but had she been alive when *Relationship* was published, she would have been appalled and heartbroken at the violence that Nayantara experienced at Gautam's hands. She had no inkling that this had been the case.

Politically, of course, Nayantara and her mother had always been on the same page, beginning with their total commitment to the Nehru-Gandhi creed, and to the pluralism of Indian democracy. Post and pre-independence, Tara had rejoiced in her mother's political and diplomatic successes as proof not only of Mrs Pandit's ability to make a mark in public life, but as affirmation and endorsement of the confidence reposed in her by Nehru. After her uncle's death, when Mrs Gandhi began the slow but sure process of politically marginalising her aunt, Nayantara felt the slight almost as keenly as her mother. For her, the move was not merely political chess, it was a repudiation of that close emotional and political bond that had existed between brother and sister; a repudiation, in effect, of Nehru's political trust in Mrs Pandit. When she resigned from parliament in 1968, it upset Nayantara greatly and she was deeply concerned about how her mother would adapt to a life bereft of political activity, in a cul-de-sac like Dehradun. Temperamentally, she belonged in Delhi and in the hurly-burly of a political life; she needed that stimulation. Nayantara's decision, thirty years after her mother resigned from active politics, to publish the letters from Nehru to Mrs Pandit before independence was an attempt not only to restore her to the political record, but to stake her claim to the Nehru legacy. At a personal, familial level too, Mrs Pandit could have been the natural successor to Nehru after 1964, but that role was denied her by Mrs Gandhi.

After Nayantara began living in Delhi in 1968, she became her mother's link with political developments in the capital. When she started writing her political columns Mrs Pandit took a keen interest in what she wrote but cautioned her against going 'too far' in her criticism of Indira Gandhi. There would be repercussions, she warned, worried once again that Nayantara's tendency to breach the norms would rebound on her, as well as on the rest of the family. She, like Nayantara, was against the Emergency, but Lekha's husband was vociferous in his support of it, and Rita's, though unhappy about it, was also extremely apprehensive. Rita and Lekha were wary of Mrs Pandit's decision to join Jagjivan Ram's Congress for Democracy, seeing little hope of a political comeback for her. And they were right. When the Janata Party came to power in 1977 and was considering whose name to put forward as president, Vijaya Lakshmi Pandit was a strong contender, but the party was divided. Of all the unlikely choices, Morarji Desai wanted Rukmini Devi Arundale, and eventually Sanjiva Reddy became the compromise candidate. The party might have been hoist with its own petard, but for Mrs Pandit it was a particularly painful let-down. 'For the last twenty years of her life,' Nayantara said, 'my mother felt isolated and unhappy, a political outcaste. Not that she wanted any assignment, just a feeling of belonging and being part of the Congress she had served all her life.'[11]

While still at the Woodrow Wilson Center in Washington, Nayantara had two sets of dialogues going on in her head about a new book, which were confusing her utterly until she realised they were two separate books! So she set about concentrating on one, took up the Center director, Prosser Gifford's suggestion that she apply for a National Humanities Center grant, and left for Chapel Hill, North Carolina in 1983. That book in her head became *Plans for Departure*, written and completed while she was at Chapel Hill, just as *Rich Like Us* had been at the Smithsonian. Everything was thoroughly congenial, as at the Woodrow Wilson Center, but this time in an environment that was also naturally beautiful, wooded and lush with greenery; she, like all the other fellows, lived in a cottage surrounded by trees and birdsong. Daytime was spent at the Center, the evening went by in long walks with Bunchi and social get-togethers with the others, all similarly inclined. Those nine months at Chapel Hill were a calm, reflective, fruitfully engaged time for Nayantara, repeating the kind of serene writing experience she had known in Washington. In between were trips to meet Bunchi's brother, Raj and his family in New Jersey, and Ranjit and Franca, then in New York.

Rich Like Us might have ended the post-independence chronology of the earlier novels, but not the political intent; in *Plans for Departure* Nayantara decided to go farther back in time, to Bal Gangadhar Tilak, before Gandhi and non-violence took hold. Published in 1986 by Heinemann in the UK, issued as a paperback by Penguin in 1987 (with an advance of £5,000), and by W.W. Norton in the US in the same year, it was dedicated to Gautam Sahgal's younger sister, Premilla Menon, whom Nayantara referred to as her 'companion in laughter'.

Plans is deft and light and witty, so assured and confident that her pen just skimmed along the pages. Freed of the compulsions and demands of the contemporary, it soared and circled above ground, providing a bird's-eye view of the last days of the Raj in a small hill town in north India, and of the gathering momentum of the nationalist movement, albeit only through the disembodied voice of Lokmanya Tilak. At the centre of the novel are an unlikely pair: a Danish woman, Anna Hansen, amanuensis to an eccentric scientist, Sir Nitin Basu; and Henry Brewster, district collector, an Englishman who 'had had malaria five times, suffered from philosophy and had chronic attacks of ruling-class conscience'.

Anna finds in Henry's pangs of conscience an echo of her own unease with Empire (although Denmark had long been divested of her colonial ambition), and a counterpoint to her English fiancé, Nicholas's service to it. Henry has recently been deserted by his Raj-loving wife, Anna has temporarily left Nicholas for India; so, inevitably, they are drawn to each other. Their slow, sweet falling in love seems as natural as the day. An unexpected turn of events, stunning and inexplicable, intervenes and the war, looming over the Empire and its custodians, becomes the arbiter of their destinies. In the end Anna, in a moment of sudden and blinding clarity, acknowledges the 'ineffable mystery of why one loved or stopped loving', and the realisation has the 'grazing edge of a butterfly's wing'. Departure then, of many kinds, becomes the informing metaphor of the novel.

Plans is probably Nayantara's most lyrical work, and ironically a swansong for the Raj. In it are found her most lovingly and delicately delineated characters, each one a foil to the others. It was awarded the Commonwealth Prize for Literature from the Eurasian region in 1987, the same year that Margaret Atwood won it for Canada with *The Handmaid's Tale*, and Ben Okri for Africa with *Incidents at the Shrine*. The prize carried a cash award of £1,000, and the award-giving ceremony was held at Overseas House (headquarters of the Royal Overseas League, a cosponsor of the prize) on St James's Street, London. Tickets for attending the event were £1.50 and included a glass of wine! *TIME* magazine commended Nayantara, who

> ... with a chilly wit and metaphysical calm, mastered the difficult task of dealing with revolution and religion ... *Plans* is a witty and fleshy dialogue, both practical and metaphysical, about revolution and transcendence.

Back in Dehradun, the second set of dialogues was still buzzing in Nayantara's head and she got down to writing almost as soon as she returned. *Mistaken Identity*, which she thought was the easiest of her novels to write, is a tour de force – light-footed, wry, a triumph of understatement. And very funny. It was dedicated to the historian E.P. Thompson and his wife Dorothy, and Thompson wrote to Nayantara to say that they were both proud of the dedication. He thought the book was

> ... amazingly successful in its tangential address to heroic themes, which have become weary and clichéd from their bombastic, rhetorical reiteration. To use Bhushan Singh as a kind of Candide or Idiot or Holy Fool is a marvellous foil ...[12]

The heroic themes of sedition, treason and empire; of resistance and revolutions, religion and politics, and of individual destiny caught in their interstices. The year is 1929. Nine – or rather eight plus one – men are thrown into prison on charges of conspiring to overthrow the King Emperor. Eight are declared resisters, Congressmen, communists and student revolutionaries. The ninth is a case of mistaken identity – Bhushan Singh, son of a minor Rajput raja, who has no interest in politics or revolution or the Empire. He is indolent and comfort-loving, dabbles in poetry (most of it mediocre) and is filled with longing for a lost love. He has no idea why he has been cast into the same cell as the other firebrands, resents being charged as a co-conspirator and has little patience with his cellmates' declamatory politics.

The Meerut Conspiracy case of 1929 and the execution of Bhagat Singh in Lahore in 1931 propel the narrative, but in creating Bhushan Singh as a counterfoil to the other eight, and also as the unwitting interrogator of all the isms being upheld by the Crown and its subject citizens, the author pulls off a hilarious romp through jailhouse and courthouse, palace and zenana. Along the way, she demolishes all the cherished prejudices regarding Hindu and Muslim, caste and community, as the novel rushes to its completely unexpected, but poetically perfectly just ending.

Harold Pinter, whom Nayantara had met in 1989 at the PEN International Congress in Toronto, wrote to her to say that he was crazy about the book, thought it was 'absolutely brilliant'. Her prose sparkled and glinted, rippled along the rocky and the smooth, letting fall such priceless gems as calling Gandhi '... a comma in the middle of a sentence which would read a hell of a lot faster without it'; or offering up Bhushan's mother's theory that the British 'needed a Hindu-Muslim riot now and then; no riot, no raj'. Your mother sounds like a shrewd and clear-headed lady, his lawyer says. 'Yes,' replies Bhushan, 'she is. She doesn't read or write, you see.'

The key concern in the novel is the question of India's identity and what it means. Indian secularism is both an intellectual and an emotional truth for Nayantara, a condition to be cherished and staunchly defended at a time of what she called 'exploding Hindu fundamentalism'. In Bhushan Singh the Hindu and Muslim traditions are combined as an inseparable joint inheritance – what her other contemporary, Qurratulain Hyder, called the Ganga-Jumni culture. (Nayantara says that she considers herself 'born a Hindu but half Muslim by culture'.)[13] When Bhushan is asked in court what his religion is, he replies, Hindu-Muslim. Or, put another way, Muslim-Hindu. Mother tongue? asks the judge. Poetry, he replies. And continues:

> But if you're going to finick about it, my mother tongue is Hindi and my father tongue is Urdu, she – illiterate though she is – hailing from the Sanskrit script and paraphernalia, and he from everything that hit us when Islam rode in. Let me assure you, Father wouldn't know Hindi letters from a crab's crawl. His tongue doesn't rise to the higher pillars of Hindi pronunciation. The glories of Sanskrit are Greek to him. The capital of his culture is Persia. For Mother it's all tongue and no script. She's forgotten how to read and can't write. The Ganges valley has other plans for its women.[14]

And after all, Bhushan falls for Razia, his elusive long-lost love, because she has Hindu eyes and Muslim cheekbones. Bhushan, says the author, is a lover not only of women but of the hybrid culture that has bred him; Hinduism and Islam meet in him in ways that are both practical and mysterious.

The novel was uncommonly prescient in its apprehensions regarding the rise of right-wing Hinduism and its claim that India is a Hindu society. Within a very few years of its publication, Bharatiya Janata Party cadre had demolished the Babri Masjid in Faizabad and dealt a body blow to secularism, imperfect though it might be. The fragile, often elusive, nature of this secularism in practice is symbolised by Bhushan Singh's forbidden love for Razia – all he ever wants is a reunion with his beloved, and all that their fleeting love manages to accomplish is a Hindu–Muslim riot.

Mistaken Identity was published by Heinemann in the UK in 1987, and by New Directions in the US in 1988. Heinemann paid the author an advance of £5,000, New Directions $4,000 and Coronet £7,000 for paperback rights. Financially and critically, it was Nayantara's most successful novel, receiving abundant, glowing praise from the most influential periodicals of the day for her prose, her plotting and her impressive command over history and politics. It was submitted for a slew of prizes, among them the Booker, the James Tait Memorial Prize, the Royal Society of Literature Award and the Commonwealth Writers' Prize, but was not selected for any of them. Perhaps it was a case of the Empire striking back too hard, for as *The Independent* noted, 'British colonialism has never been treated so disparagingly, yet so humorously.'

After the success of *Mistaken Identity*, there followed a sixteen-year hiatus in Nayantara's fiction writing, her next novel appearing only in 2003. In 1988 her sister, Rita, was diagnosed with cancer, a harrowing and stressful time for the whole family, and in the same year, Vijaya Lakshmi Pandit suffered a massive stroke which entailed a long recovery and convalescence. They had been dining, en famille, at General Rummy Bakshi's house in Dehradun when she collapsed suddenly. Military doctors who saw her advised immediate transfer to a hospital, and Rajiv Gandhi, then prime minister, helicoptered her to Delhi and the All India Institute of Medical Sciences. It was an inordinately long hospitalisation, so long that her eighty-ninth birthday in August 1989 was celebrated at AIIMS! During her convalescence the Dalai Lama sent his doctor to treat her as well, and Nayantara was convinced that it was his treatment that enabled her mother to walk again. It was a short respite, however, for the following year – but only after she had thrown a huge party for family and friends on her ninetieth birthday – she had a second stroke, and this time she didn't recover. Once again, Rajiv and Sonia (who had maintained a relationship with Mrs Pandit despite Mrs Gandhi's distancing herself from the Pandits), rallied round and took over; Rajiv himself flew the family to Allahabad to scatter her ashes, and dealt with everything down to the last detail. 'He was like the son she never had,' said Nayantara of that time, 'devoted to her.' Mrs Pandit's death left a void almost as large as her presence had been. Life – or at least, home life – had to be rearranged around her absence now, but fortunately for the sisters, Lekha was just a stone's throw away in Dehradun, a comfort to both of them.

Rita's illness, however, was traumatic. She roamed the world in search of a cure, hoping some new remedy might work a miracle. Both Nayantara and Lekha urged her to come to Dehradun to be looked after by them, but she declined. She passed away in 1992, followed soon after by her husband. The previous year Rajiv Gandhi had been assassinated, and Nayantara was emotionally so drained that it wasn't easy to put all that aside and write.

In a sense, those sixteen years without a novel were wilderness years. Had Nayantara been what she called a 'real writer, if I had been hell-bent on writing,' she said, 'I would have shut the door, sat down and written – no real writer would have let this time go by.' She maintained always that she wasn't a writer, just someone who wrote; when asked by Nadine Gordimer, at an event in South Africa, what the difference was, she replied, 'It's the difference between being a bachelor and an unmarried man, a very different kettle of fish.' This was also why she never became more confident as a writer; with each new novel, she said, it was like 'trying to get onto a bicycle with your hands and feet tied'.[15]

These fallow years, however, were rich in awards and recognition, and in travel. Nayantara went abroad every year during most of that decade, participating in conferences, renewing acquaintances and meeting writers and academics. She visited E.P. and Dorothy Thompson in their country home at Wick Episcopi in Worcester, on two occasions, spending the days in reminiscence and discovery.

Thompson's father was an India hand, had been a friend of Tagore's, and E.P. himself had written a monograph on his father's relationship with the poet. This he gave to Nayantara, together with a heap of his father's papers excavated from their attic, to take to India.

Then there was Harold Pinter and his wife, Antonia Fraser, with whom she would lunch, once together with Stephen Spender, his wife and Marianne Wiggins, who had just left Salman Rushdie. Marjorie and Randolph Boxall, old friends from the 1950s, who had been introduced to her by Surendra Ali Rajpur, were her home away from home. Both were friends of, and had numerous friends in, India; Randolph was a barrister, Queen's Counsel, politically conservative but warm and generous, and their flat in north-west London was always available to Nayantara. And there was the Pakistani writer, Aamer Hussein, with whom she discovered many links – Lekha and her husband had lived down the road from his parents in Karachi, when posted to Pakistan; Aamer's sister, Yasmin, was a friend of Noni's in Delhi; he himself had got to know Gita in London, and then, of course, there was their shared interest in literature.

For the rest, Nayantara was at universities in the UK, at Kent and Sussex, Oxford and Warwick and Leeds, lecturing and delivering addresses. She was elected fellow of the American Academy of Arts and Sciences in 1990 and awarded an honorary doctorate in literature by the University of Leeds in 1997. And then, in 2002, she received the kind of recognition of her work from her alma mater, Wellesley College, that had a special significance for her – she was conferred the Alumna Achievement Award for 'bravely confronting authority in defence of the world's largest democracy', and praised for being 'an ardent and eloquent writer whose bravery and passion have inspired all of us as we seek freedom through just democratic governance'.

In 1990, a young writer and film-maker from Calcutta, Ruchir Joshi, walked into the house on Rajpur Road in Dehradun and, in a manner of speaking, walked into their lives as well. He and Gita had met in Delhi the previous year and had what Gita called 'an intense fling'. Short and sweet. But when Ruchir demanded to see photographs of Gita as a child and young woman – which a surprised but polite Nayantara showed him – it marked the beginning of a relationship that was unusual even then. Gita and Ruchir never married but they had two sons, even though they lived in two different countries, thousands of miles apart, and practically speaking, led separate lives. Ruchir belonged to a nationalist Calcutta family, Gujaratis settled in Bengal, and his father was a highly regarded writer. But Ruchir was a nomad, emotionally as well as otherwise, and an itinerant life seemed to be his preferred mode. This might have worked for him and Gita, but it was highly unsatisfactory in Nayantara's opinion and did little to assuage her worries about her daughter.

In 1996, her misgivings were borne out, suddenly and dramatically. Gita, by then in advanced pregnancy with her second son Zum (Ayan), was told by Ruchir that he was in love with someone else and that he was no longer available to fill in as a father when required. Nayantara, never judgemental when it came to romantic and sexual liaisons, was nevertheless stunned by Ruchir's irresponsibility. Unable to work while Zum was still an infant, with no financial stability and a second child to feed and care for, how, she worried, would Gita manage? 'I have felt so anxious about you for so long,' she wrote to her in October 1996, 'that anxiety is not new. But it is very "wearing and tearing", and I feel rather worn out with it.'

Without Gita's consent, she wrote to Ruchir to communicate both her disappointment in him, as well as her displeasure at his cavalier disregard for basic decency. At a deeper, more personally felt level, however, Gita's prospective single parenting in England, assuming near-total responsibility for the children, seemed to her an unwelcome repetition of her own circumstances after her divorce from Gautam.

Of her three children, it was with Gita that Nayantara shared her closest relationship, finding in her a kindred spirit, a child who lived her political convictions and stood by her choices, no matter how hard the consequences might be for her. With her she shared too the political developments of the day, in England or India, discussing issues that preoccupied her and developing an emotional and intellectual bond that became mutually sustaining. This closeness notwithstanding her preoccupation with Gita's precarious circumstances would never quite leave her; it didn't look like there would be a respite from uncertainty and anxiety on the family front, at least for the next few years.

During that time Nayantara revived herself by going back into the past, re-reading, selecting and putting together two volumes of letters between herself and Bunchi during 1964–67; and between her mother and Jawaharlal Nehru between 1909 and 1946. *Relationship: Extracts from a Correspondence* (1994) and *Before Freedom: Nehru's Letters to His Sister 1909–1947* (2004) were Nayantara's testament to the sustaining power of those bonds between individuals forged on the basis of a shared sense of values, of political purpose, of principled personal and public conduct – and of moral and emotional certitude.

As a family the Nehrus wrote letters almost as naturally as they breathed. The frequency with which they communicated with each other in this way is astonishing, making for the kind of rich and intimate archive that is much more than a family history. Letters from prison are now considered a genre by themselves, but at the time the correspondence between Jawaharlal Nehru and his sisters and between him and Indira, especially their letters from jail – and in Indira's case, from Oxford, from hospital in Switzerland and from home in Allahabad – became daily diaries of sorts, sometimes bulletins, encompassing national and international developments as well. At the same time, the letters allow us to enter their worlds and their lives, to see their personalities evolve in response to momentous events and upheavals, positive or otherwise.

As it happened, Bunchi Mangat Rai was more than a match for the Nehrus as a letter writer, as a writer, moreover, for whom the letter was a serious mode of communication that demanded equally serious time and attention.

Relationship is made up of one such exchange. It was published by the feminist press, Kali for Women, in India, in 1994, a deliberate choice on Nayantara's part in order to avoid the kind of sensationalism that the volume might have been vulnerable to with a more mainstream publisher. Her purpose, she said at the time, was to put the record straight on her marriage to, and divorce from, Gautam, as well as to place on that same record, and celebrate, the relationship that the letters literally brought into being. Letters that she had wanted to destroy even as they were being written, but was now glad that they hadn't been. A third, underlying impulse was to communicate, through personal experience, what it was like even for a woman like her to live in and negotiate a man's world, a world in which the onus of keeping things going to everyone's satisfaction is still on a woman.

The book received mixed reviews, more or less equally divided between those who called its publication an act of courage on the author's part, and those who wondered what all the fuss was about. Why air a correspondence that was thirty years old and served no social or political purpose? Why this narcissistic outpouring? As far as Nayantara's own family and the Sahgals were concerned, however, it opened the floodgates. Her sister Lekha was aghast at the level and extent of violence experienced by her in her marriage, and she regretted bitterly that neither she nor their mother nor Rita had imagined such abuse possible. Gautam Sahgal's older brother, Narottam, and his younger sister, Baby (Premilla) Menon disapproved thoroughly, with the former telling Nayantara that the book should *never* have been published, 'no matter what happened'. But it was Noni who was frankly disapproving of her mother's decision to make public their marital discord, to rake up what was long past. As the disclosures involved more than the two correspondents, she felt the others in the family should have been consulted; had her mother asked her, for instance, she would have said, 'Don't do it.' Why relive the trauma? Why not let bygones be bygones? And although she was never able to 'square her accounts', as she said, with her father, she thought her mother owed it to the children to have sought their opinion on going public.[16]

It was left to Ranjit to bear the brunt of Gautam's rage. He went ballistic. His nephew, Lakshman Menon, gave him a copy, he read it, then stormed over to Ranjit's house in Switzerland and gave him a complete battering. 'It took four years of me being put through the washing machine,' Ranjit said,

> ... and at the end of four years I had to tell him, look, this has to stop. It's not my book, not my story, it's your story ... I'm not involved. You can't confront me with it.

He told his father that he thought his mother shouldn't have published it, told his mother that he wished she hadn't, but he accepted the fact that she had her reasons for doing so. He wouldn't sit in judgement on her over it, but he agreed with Gautam. For four years he was the butt of his father's fury and pain, for Gautam had never got over Tara.[17]

On 25 July 1994, Gautam sent a letter to Noni and Ranjit from his home in Ruvigliana, regretting that he was unable to come and meet Noni, then holidaying with Ranjit in Basel.

> Since I do not want to talk to you both about the shame, humiliation and disgrace my association with your mother has brought upon me and which would be inevitable if we met, I am writing this letter.

He had always known, he said, that Nayantara found it easy to distance herself from the truth 'when her interests seemed to demand this'; but he hadn't realised how far she would go to distort the truth as far as he was concerned.

> The letters which she has now marketed reflect the evil and degraded character of the two correspondents ... and their deceitful behaviour and planned hypocrisy point to two sick minds.

Two more letters followed, detailing Nayantara's lapses, calling the publication of *Relationship* her 'confessions' – minus the regret that confessing entailed. He then insisted that Noni and Ranjit decide whose 'side' they were on – either his or their mother's. If they 'applauded' what she had done, then his relationship with them would come to an end.

Gita alone supported her mother's choice, believed she needed no one's consent or permission to make decisions regarding either her life or her writing. This might explain why she was not included in Gautam's 'notes' to Ranjit and Noni; as he said, she had 'clearly charted her course' by choosing to live with a man without marrying him, and then having two children by him.

A Situation in New Delhi might well have been Nayantara's last novel to draw on identifiable figures from her life, but she was not yet done with Nehru and Vijaya Lakshmi Pandit. *Before Freedom: Nehru's Letters to His Sister 1909–1947* appeared twenty years after *A Situation in New Delhi* was published and, she noted, constituted 'domestic history in a political setting substantially different from our own'.[18]

But the letters are not merely a record of family matters and relationships; they were arranged to reflect a political context, especially of the 1930s and 1940s.

Long absences, either while in Switzerland with Kamala, or in prison when in India, made for a more or less continuous correspondence between Nehru and Vijaya Lakshmi Pandit during this time. While in jail, Nehru was allowed to write three letters a week to close family, and receive the same number back. Indira, Betty (Krishna Hutheesing) and Nan (Vijaya Lakshmi) were the three he wrote to regularly; but it was with Nan that he shared his views on, and responses to, events, people and the family, most openly and in detail. For, in addition to being the two elders in the family after Motilal Nehru's death, Bhai (Nehru) and Nan were political siblings as well. The letters, while deeply personal, are simultaneously political, communicating in an idiom that is intimate yet transparent. After freedom, when both were engaged in nation building and forging relationships internationally, the personal and political bonds were reinforced in such a manner that they became indivisible. This undoubtedly made for tensions within the party as well as in government, but they never became serious enough to make for a rupture between them.

And they shared friends. The Naidus, Sarojini and Padmaja; the Mountbattens, whom they visited and stayed with together, in England; the Paul Robesons in America; the E. P. Thompsons; the Chiang Kai-sheks; the Henry Walshes and John Kenneth Galbraiths in the US; and many others with whom too the distinction between social, personal and official was difficult to maintain. They overlapped, flowed into each other, coalesced and separated, with brother and sister complementing each other and on occasion, standing in for each other.

After Motilal Nehru's death, Jawaharlal stepped into his father's shoes, willingly assuming the responsibility of head of household. When Kamala passed away in 1936, he informed Nan of his decision to sell Anand Bhawan – the house was too large and he was too lonely in it. It was only when she and Ranjit agreed to return with their daughters and live there again that Nehru was persuaded to reconsider. Although close to Betty, her family didn't form a unit with Nehru in quite the same way as the Pandits – Raja and she lived in Bombay and couldn't conceive of leaving that city, and their involvement in politics ceased after independence.

Eighteen years separated Nehru and Betty, and he and Nan shared concerns about her too – about her marriage, her sometimes irresponsible actions and opinions expressed in public, her willingness to trade on the family name and make things difficult for them. Nan and Nehru, by common consent, became the buffer in an attempt to neutralise Betty's tendency to 'take sides' when tensions arose in the family, especially between Kamala and Vijaya Lakshmi.

With Nehru's death in 1964, that intense emotional and political relationship came to an end. As Nayantara remarked many years later,

> She was not a person who would have functioned well on her own, so much, as being very good at implementing a brief. Her greatest desire had been to return to India after Washington, she'd had enough, she wanted to get back to politics in India, to UP, but Mamu was very keen that she go to Britain, so she took that up.[19]

A much fuller treatment of how well Vijaya Lakshmi had implemented her brief on foreign policy matters would follow in Nayantara's 2010 publication, *Jawaharlal Nehru: Civilising a Savage World*. Her assessment of Nehru's enunciation of non-alignment in a polarised world is based, in large part, on official communications between Nehru and his sister when she represented India at key capitals of the world – Moscow, Washington, London and, as importantly, the United Nations. In a sense, the publication of the two volumes of personal correspondence, followed a few years later by Nayantara's last novel, marked a kind of closure to a particular chapter in family relations, and with the abandonment of non-alignment as a principle of foreign policy, in national affairs as well.

Endnotes

1 Personal Interview, Delhi, March 2009.

2 Nayantara Sahgal, *A Situation in New Delhi (*New Delhi: Penguin Books, reprint, 2008), p. 64.

3 Zareer Masani, *Indira Gandhi: A Biography,* p. 286.

4 Personal interview, Delhi, March 2009.

5 Nayantara Sahgal, *A Situation in New Delhi,* p. 183.

6 Personal interview, Dehradun, August 2008.

7 Nayantara Sahgal to E.N. Mangat Rai, letter dated 13 February 1965 (unpublished).

8 Personal interview, Dehradun, October 2008.

9 E.P. Thompson to Nayantara Sahgal, letter dated 1 July 1986.

10 Personal interview, Delhi, June 2013.

11 Ibid.

12 E.P. Thompson to Nayantara Sehgal, letter dated 27 August 1988.

13 Nayantara Sahgal, *Mistaken Identity* (New Delhi: Harper Perennial, 2007), P.S., p. 13.

14 Nayantara Sahgal, *Mistaken Identity,* p. 177.

15 Personal interview, Dehradun, October 2008.

16 Noni Sahgal, personal interview, Delhi, 2009.

17 Personal interview, Chandigarh, November 2008.

18 Nayantara Sahgal, *Before Freedom: Nehru's Letters to His Sister 1909–1947*, p. 5.

19 Personal interview, Delhi, June 2013.

8

WRITING A LIFE

Lesser Breeds

THE SCHIZOPHRENIC IMAGINATION, NAYANTARA HAS SAID, is rooted in a particular subsoil but doesn't belong to any particular context, has no single home. What it has is a multiple tradition that it can never disown, which usually means that an individual with such an imagination ends up being a misfit.[1]

The divided self is divided by both history and circumstance. History had shaped or at least impinged upon Indian culture and society repeatedly, most obviously on account of recurring invasions into north India. In the immediate recent past, of course, there was the experience of colonialism but before that there had been a long history of Muslim rule and a mingling of ways of life that made for an inseparable joint inheritance. The city in which she was born and grew up was the ancient Prayag of the Ramayana, and is now Allahabad; these were two parallel traditions. In a country 'where cultures have criss-crossed and bloodstreams have mingled', she says, 'there is no such thing as racial purity or an exclusive identity.'[2] For a westernised Indian, she maintained, being heir to a plural tradition entailed a 'daily reckoning ... a balancing act, where the priorities are never in doubt' but other horizons remain in view. This balancing act is what provides the creative tension necessary for any literary endeavour.

Speaking for herself, she said that in all the years she was growing up, she and her sisters were told that 'history was ourselves and we were making it', a concept so far from what she was taught in school that she soon put school history in the same category as Kipling's *Gunga Din*, 'a rousing, frollicking white man's fable that had nothing to do with the reality and dignity of India'.[3]

It was this sense of India's history as being simultaneously ancient and contemporary, continuous yet unsettled, that informed her fiction. To this was added the fact that she was both novelist and political journalist, a combination not amenable to promoting either sanity or peace of mind: as a journalist she was obliged to keep in touch with the world of facts and data; as a novelist she must needs lose touch with it in order to create a fictional world. Fiction was her abiding love, journalism was her conscience, a troublesome thing. How to avoid being ambushed by both? A quote from Sartre enabled her to reconcile the contradiction: 'For a long time I took my pen for a sword; I now know we're powerless. No matter, I write.' And so, although she has said that she cannot see how any writer can avoid being 'political' in the sense of reflecting the anxieties of his or her society, its hopes and fears, she would never see fiction as a form of political intervention. For that she had journalism.[4]

And yet she was certainly among those writers, like Doris Lessing and Nadine Gordimer, who wrote their country from an experience of colonialism. To write one's country without affectation, without being patronising, writing with what Nayantara called 'a certain tenderness' is perhaps a woman's way of writing it. Essential too, as ingredients in this endeavour, are the ideas of non-violence, secularism, freedom – both personal and political – and democracy; not merely as political goals for a country that had cast off the colonial yoke, but for creating a society in which women and the disadvantaged would find their rightful place.

A feminist project then. A writing life in which the personal, the political and the literary were so intertwined as to be like three-ply yarn.

A writer is not separate from what she writes. In Nayantara's case, her individual story and family history became the means by which she could tell two stories at the same time: a fictional one that drew its material from her personal and political selves, and a 'national' one, about the making of modern India. Carrying politics – which was an emotional engagement for her – into fiction came naturally, that's what she had to do because the material compelled her to. In the early novels, up until *Rich Like Us*, the resemblance between characters and situations, the resolutions in them and those in her own life are immediately recognisable. So too specific political developments and conjunctures in the life of the country. In this regard, there is no attempt on her part to present herself as dispassionate, to see the personal as 'subjective' and the political as 'objective'. This twinning is what resonates in all her writing, fictional and journalistic, it is transparent and unambiguous.

Yet she herself does not claim to be a feminist.

> 'It's not just a matter of believing,' she says, 'but of doing, and I haven't been an activist. A certain kind of politics has been in my blood which hinges on Gandhi's statement, "My life is my message, not my text is my message." I have never put myself on the line for any feminist issue.'[5]

But was there, in fact, such a difference between her text and her life, a divergence that rendered one inconsistent with the other and made them irreconcilable?

In choosing to begin her writing life with an autobiography Nayantara was not doing anything very unusual; by now this was a well-established convention. In a crucial sense, writing her autobiography is a woman's way of narrating her own story, of knowing deep down and in a fundamental way, that 'to be storyless' – as Carolyn Heilbrun, Nayantara's classmate at Wellesley has said – is her ultimate anonymity, and that narrating her story might even allow her to reinvent a life and so possess it more fully.

Prison and Chocolate Cake and *From Fear Set Free* departed from such an impulse in two important respects: they offered up none of the common features of the 'feminine' – the confessional, the lament, the cloistered or the domesticated; and they located the author squarely in the middle of a glorious, public, political juncture in the nation's life. Nayantara's story is set against the backdrop of a far larger, more momentous story unfolding; as she said in *Prison*, 'Our growing up was India's growing up into political maturity.' It is true that *From Fear Set Free* represented something of a retreat into the 'domestic', but by then she had already written her first novel and found her medium: fiction as relational autobiography.

Nayantara's detractors might complain that the greater part of her writing, fiction and non-fiction, simply extends and mythifies the cult of the Nehrus as the National Family, and the Nehruvian project for the country as *the* ideal to be attained. She is unapologetic about the latter; and regarding the former, one might say that even if one were to evacuate the 'familial' and the familiar from her novels, the foundation and superstructure would remain inviolate, for her main 'character' is India. Placing the country at the centre of her novels enabled her to break free of both exoticism and Orientalism, to present a contemporary reality without either romanticising its past or pandering to received notions of what India was all about. In this sense she pioneered a kind of English writing in India that simply bypassed the nomenclature of Indo-Anglian and became confidently and matter-of-factly Indian. She was also among the earliest writers in English to set her novels in an urban locale, among the professional middle class living in and negotiating a culture that is modernising. Where many of her contemporaries were valorising the 'village' or romancing the 'rural', Nayantara articulated preoccupations that had to do with how a country and a people were defining themselves, with all the contradictions and ambivalences that this entailed.

Another aspect of the divided self now surfaced, that of language. Which tongue was best suited to represent the reality that a 'schizophrenic imagination' was trying to communicate? Mother-tongue or father-tongue? This is a question that has long troubled writers in this multilingual country of ours, with a rich and old literary tradition in each of its languages, but it would be fair to say that it did not become a primary concern for Nayantara. She drew her influences and her literary genealogy as much from Iris Murdoch, Graham Greene and *Jane Eyre* as she did from contemporary Hindi writers and poets. They were profoundly important for her in finding her literary voice, in 'removing certain barriers between me and my surroundings'. They showed her that she was part of the province she lived in, like the writers themselves.[6]

But the choice of language had other implications; the coloniser might have left but the metropolis was still in the erstwhile ruler's country, and India was very much on the periphery, literarily speaking. The capital of English-language publishing was London, and influential arbiters of literary taste, however liberal, still tended to think of Indians writing in English as colonial subjects. For a young writer to break the mould and break into that charmed circle was a challenge, and so it is interesting that Nayantara's first few books were published originally in the US and only later in the UK, a reverse flow for a former colony. New York in the 1950s and '60s was beginning to emerge as an important publishing centre, and publishers like Victor Gollancz and Allen Lane, picking up the scent, added those non-Western writers published by imprints like Knopf, Farrar, Straus, and Crown to their lists. Nayantara's was a fresh young voice with a difference, and she was in the vanguard of a kind of fiction writing in English by Indian women that Anita Desai, Shashi Deshpande and Nisha da Cunha later continued with such assurance – but none with her sense of humour or irony.

There was yet another important sense in which Nayantara claimed her rootedness in the society of which she was a part. Some writers, she said, having decided they were 'modern', solved the problem of how to come to terms with their Hinduism (or Islam or Christianity) by dumping it, calling themselves atheists, agnostics or secular. But this was not a solution for her. Could she, she asked, quick-change her bones, her myths, her grandparents? Forget that her great-grandmother became a sati? As a writer, she found it was more useful to figure out what exactly Hinduism meant to her, and fiction was part of the process of finding out.

> I used to try to feel at ease with an overpowering heritage, but I've discovered that I'm not supposed to feel at ease. It is not only inevitable, it is also quite natural to feel fragmented. And I have learned to treat my own particular muddle as a priceless asset. It is for my Third Eye to reconcile the fragments through fiction, and through my sense of a plural self to produce a fiction other than that which a less ancient, more homogeneous, more settled society would produce.[7]

As an oeuvre comprising fiction, non-fiction political columns, monographs, correspondence and autobiography, Nayantara's writing is remarkable for the consistency of her vision, no matter which genre she is writing in. Very clearly, and with careful consideration, she was putting forward a point of view – her point of view – on national affairs, via novel, column and essay, and that perspective retained its political edge even though she might not have thought of her fiction, at least, as being interventionist.

Some might call this a vicarious politics, conducted from the safety of the sidelines, yet in stepping out of line, consistently and constantly, whether in her personal life or in her political choices, she managed to combine personal and political, political and literary, and literary and personal in a uniquely individual idiom.

Lesser Breeds, Nayantara's ninth and last novel, was a kind of epitaph to non-violence, a tribute, 'my wind-up book on all those people who had the tremendous courage to be non-violent when the other side used terrible violence'.[8] In an unintended way perhaps, it also became her own wind-up novel, bringing together autobiography and fiction, recalling what began in *Prison and Chocolate Cake* as an attempt to recount a personal–political childhood and adolescence that coincided with India's emergence into independence.

The novel is dedicated to her four grandsons, Gautam and Giorgio Sahgal, and Kabir and Ayan Joshi, and was published by HarperCollins India in 2003. It started out as two different stories, two novellas, one based in India, the other in the US, beginning in 1943. But as the idea grew and the notion of 'lesser breeds' took hold, Nayantara wove the two together to write what she said was her 'angriest' novel yet. The re-emergence of the West as an imperialising, globalising power in its new incarnation as world ruler, marginalising every other history and civilisation, challenged her earlier optimism in the power of non-violent resistance to overcome exploitation. In the novel, the poor peasant under the Raj and the foot soldiers recruited to fight England's wars exemplify colonial exploitation; the lesser breeds are the non-European subjects of the British Empire.

The India story is set in Akbarabad/Allahabad, and Nurullah, its young hero, is attached to Nikhil/Nehru and lives in his house, a Swaraj Bhawan lookalike. This is the scene of Nayantara's own childhood, familiar to readers from her very first book. The narrative follows in fiction what she related in her memoir, retrospectively as it were.

Switch to America and the novel's heroine, Shan/Nayantara is a student, observing and commenting on a culture and society as remote from the one she has known as north is from south. The link between the two is an American student, Pete Ryder, in India in the 1980s, researching 'non-violence and its use of soul force'. He, naturally enough, meets Nurullah, and who better than him to reflect on the relevance today of this once-powerful weapon.

By far the most interesting character in the novel is the heroine, Shan, a curiously composite creation; her rebellious girlhood is reminiscent of the young Indira Nehru, but by the time she goes to college in the US she has morphed into Nayantara-at-Wellesley. She subjects American society and culture to a reverse gaze, the non-West studying the West, and (like Mahatma Gandhi) concludes that Western 'civilisation' would be a good idea. In a fleeting, feather-light brush against the Second World War, then drawing to a close, Shan notes how the US treated its own 'lesser breeds' by interning its migrant Japanese population, post Japan's attack on Pearl Harbor.

Unfortunately, the notion of lesser breeds is not robust enough to sustain the strategy of equating the 'Island of America' with the subcontinent of India. Shan realises that there are subject peoples in rich and free societies as well, with Blacks and the Japanese in the US ('negroes' and 'Japs') experiencing entrenched prejudice, discrimination and injustice; but beyond this tenuous link, and the characters of Shan and Pete Ryder as present in both narratives, there is little to hold them together. The reflection on non-violence proceeds more or less independently of the US connection, even though it is counterpointed with the war in Vietnam and recalls the horrific violence of Hiroshima and Nagasaki.

What does work, and admirably, is the author's excoriating denunciation of the hypocrisy of empire, masquerading as benign while bleeding its colonies dry. Today, it's the empire of commerce, as rapacious as the erstwhile one, that she deplores.

The idea of lesser breeds remained with her, however. Writing to Aamer Hussein after its publication and apropos her comments on his stories, she said:

> ... a fragmented or splintered identity is attributed to expatriates like yourself who are uprooted and living transplanted lives. But isn't this only one aspect of the situation? Doesn't this whole phenomenon apply, on a much larger scale and a wider canvas, to all us lesser breeds who inhabit a world not of our own making or choosing, one that does not reflect the current of *our* history, or allow us any space of our own? In *Lesser Breeds* Nurullah compares life under foreign rule to 'a box whose candle is the sun' (Khayyam), a life where only stunted growth is possible. And because the world continues west-centred and west-dominated, we, to this day, suffer a condition of permanent alienness. We 'belong' to the extent that we adjust, accept, embrace this outer world, its terms, its laws, and to that extent we wipe out our essential selves.[9]

Bunchi Mangat Rai passed away in January 2003, one month before *Lesser Breeds* was published. He had been in an on-and-off state of dementia for some years, often disoriented, sometimes not even able to recognise Nayantara, or their home. On the morning of 10 January Nayantara called her daughter Gita in London to say that Bunchi had slipped into a coma, but that she had decided against taking him to a hospital or intervening medically in any way. Scarcely had she put the phone down than he woke up, and she asked him if he would like a cup of tea. Yes, he said. She brought it to him, he sat up and drank it, then looked straight at her and said, quite clearly, 'Thank you.' And he lay down and died. She said afterwards that she felt he was saying thank you for life.

Nayantara, stunned and in shock, nevertheless dismissed suggestions to the contrary and fulfilled all the engagements organised for the launch of the book in Delhi on 3 March. She gave interviews, attended book signings, met whoever wished to meet her. Answered endless questions patiently. For, as she had said to Bunchi more than once, she had no patience with people who couldn't buckle under and get on with whatever had to be done.

The grieving came later. Although she had told Bunchi many times that she was 'geared emotionally more to death than life', didn't feel strongly attached to it, the loss of a soulmate was almost unbearable. She might have steeled herself, after Bunchi's cremation, to complete commitments made, but her heart was in pain. That old habit of deep unhappiness rose to the surface again, clouding her days and threatening to engulf her. Evenings, when the light dimmed and shadows crept in from the garden where they had whiled away so many hours under a starlit sky, now hung heavy. Living, always an effort for her, now became more so. Hadn't she herself written about that 'haunting twilit prelude to night when anguish closes in on the spirit'? The sadness that had been implanted in her childhood, the desperate loneliness of being without her parents for long stretches had never quite left her, even as an adult. Looking back, she acknowledged that she had no buoyant optimism about anything, had struggled to keep pessimism at bay, to grasp every hope. Upheaval, rather than equanimity, seemed to have been her constant companion.

She read, went for long walks, dropped in to see her sister, Lekha, but it was hard now to summon up the energy to write. The refuge she had earlier found in it remained elusive. Never having been the kind of person who shared confidences or talked about her problems with anyone except Bunchi, she was once again solitary in her sorrow. In Bunchi she had realised that ideal of companionship, love and intellectual compatibility which renewed her faith in marriage – a relationship built on equality and mutual respect. It was what she meant when she said that with him she had 'come home'. But now, a darkness of the heart. Bunchi's death had released him from life, but in no way did it release her from her mourning. She was devastated.

What, she wondered, is the meaning of the meaning of life? Which religion or belief system could she hope to find an answer in? What, anyway, did it mean to believe? Hers was a family of agnostics in which not a day's religious instruction had been forthcoming. Everyone was determinedly rational and disbelieving in conventional gods and goddesses, or even in the broadest, most eclectic form of Hinduism. How was it to be defined, anyway? Nayantara's old interest in its philosophy and its 'civilisational' attributes endured, but this couldn't be called believing. As a young woman in college she had a very definite belief – based, she said, somewhat on Spinoza and Pluto – in God as the idea of goodness and the universe existing because of the preponderance of good in it. To be was to be good. Goodness was related to order, chaos to evil. There was no such thing as perfection, only perfect ability, and living itself was a daily struggle of good against evil.[10]

That might have served as a working definition, but how different was it from being an agnostic? Yet she couldn't help herself from believing in *something*. She struggled hard to become an atheist but the day she realised she wasn't one, everything fell into place. Somewhere, at some subliminal level, the memory and experience of her great-aunt, Bibima, who had lived with them as a young widow in Anand Bhawan, bestirred itself. In that largely irreligious household, Bibima was deeply religious, giving herself up to a life of denial and self-abnegation, as was customary for widows. Nayantara loved her dearly and was profoundly affected by the aura of love and serenity that surrounded her. A kind of inner yearning began to grow within her.

In the mid-1980s, after she and Bunchi returned from the US, Nayantara had begun to seriously practise meditation to satisfy a need, 'to find a path for myself. I wanted something personal', something that would respond to that inner yearning. At more or less the same time, she encountered Swami Yogananda's *Autobiography of a Yogi* and was greatly impressed by it. He had passed away in the 1950s but there was a hatha yoga ashram in Bihar, one that taught his brand of yoga, and she procured a course of study and instruction from them. She followed it diligently, taught herself, and found to her surprise and delight that it was working. 'Whatever they said would happen was happening; inside me, I could feel the change. It was a fascinating journey.'[11] The meaning of religion for her was 'search yourself'; with yoga and meditation, she began to acquire a kind of clarity about situations and events that had been confusing and distressing. Always highly vulnerable emotionally, she slowly developed an inner strength which helped to prevent her from being buffeted about.

This healing healed others too, through a form of prayer that had little to do with conventional praying, and she believed it had worked on more than one occasion with her children, her sister and herself. 'There are forces all around us,' she said to me, 'we have to learn how to use them, direct them, and I've been doing that.'[12] Belief, she maintains, is a matter of figuring out when and how abstract conjectures become personal. Having been able to do so, she is 'now a believer to the marrow of my bones, and much has become clear to me after I faced the fact'.[13] In the days when Bunchi's dementia had seemed to deteriorate, Nayantara had had a special puja performed for him, for the resting of his soul. His passing away as he did, in peaceful completion of his life, she attributed to the power of the puja.

A funeral – and a wedding. In July 2003, Noni married Rajan Bhatia, son of Dr Dipak and Pushpa Bhatia, friends of the family, then working with the firm of Dunn & Bradstreet in Delhi. His mother, Pushpa, née Bery, had been at Woodstock with Nayantara and her sisters, and his grandparents knew hers, the senior Sahgals, from Simla.

Rajan, like Noni, had been married earlier, and the two of them now set up home in Jor Bagh, Delhi. Nayantara was happy and relieved, for although her concern about Noni was of a different order from that regarding Gita, she had been meditating on Noni's situation for some time, praying for a breakthrough soon. Now it seemed that Noni had obtained what she always wanted – someone who admired and cared for her, and who could provide the emotional and material security that she needed.

In 2005 Gautam Sahgal died of a stroke in Chandigarh, at home in his beloved Anokha. Of his immediate family, only Rosemarie and Franca, his daughter-in-law, were with him when he went. Ranjit was in Switzerland, Nayantara and the girls, Noni and Gita, would not have been told, and indeed, it was only an accidental phone call to Anokha by Gautam's favourite younger sister, Baby, that alerted them to the seriousness of his condition. The stroke had left Gautam with severe disorientation, living a lot in the past and liable to extreme agitation when people dropped in. Despite the doctor's 'No Visitors' order, Baby visited Chandigarh to see Gautam – the only other member of his family to do so – to say a final goodbye. He died in bed, 'as he wanted', said Ranjit, 'no hospitals, no doctors, no rituals, no epitaphs, no obituaries'. In the last days of his delirium he kept calling out for Tara: 'Where is she? Has she gone out?'[14] But neither Nayantara nor his daughters were with him when he passed away. Noni and Gita did attend Gautam's funeral along with their uncle, Narottam and his son, Arjun; and Baby's daughter, Nalini, published an obituary in the *Hindustan Times* in Delhi, where she was working. But there were no epitaphs, no rituals and no memorials, except for a *chautha* held in Baby's house in Delhi, for the family. Gautam's ashes were scattered in the river Ghaggar and Ranjit read out a poem to mark the occasion. As Gita remarked many years later, 'My father died an angry, incomplete man. Nothing could have presented a greater contrast to Nirmal's (Bunchi's) passing, than Pa's death.'[15] And for Noni, not having been able to see him before he died meant that a sense of closure eluded her for a very long time.

His father's death almost killed Ranjit. He couldn't forgive himself for being away when his father died, and took to drinking heavily. Two bottles of whisky a day till he began bleeding internally and had to be hospitalised. The doctors had almost given up.

> I didn't want to carry on, I couldn't bear the thought of him not being there ... there were so many things we had left unsaid. When I was confronted with his death I just gave up. It took me one year to get back on my feet. The doctor said it was a miracle I had survived.[16]

Perhaps it was his mother's prayers too that saw him through. Nayantara had never forgiven herself for having caused the estrangement between Gautam and the girls, or for their being disinherited by him. She regretted bitterly the effect of their divorce on all three children, on their having to live with the consequences of choices *she* had made. Noni and Gita, especially, were denied the opportunities that would have been theirs had she remained with Gautam. 'They never had it easy,' Nayantara said later, 'and I blame myself for it.'

As far back as 1966 she had written to Bunchi to say:

> Without being in the least maudlin about it, I can say that I do not think much of myself as a person, never have. I have, on the whole, a rather poor rating in my own mind ... I have no firm, vigorous hold on life. I don't love life for itself ... I have never been able to bestir myself to any kind of belief in myself. I just don't possess it.

An unduly harsh verdict, for what could be said of her – as it could not of many others – was that she had tried to live up to her upbringing, to the need for upright thinking and action, to upholding a principle, and to believing in non-violence as an active, positive force; and as an ideal, personal as well as political.

Endnotes

1 Nayantara Sahgal, 'The Schizophrenic Imagination', Address delivered at Kent University, August 1989.

2 Nayantara Sahgal, *Mistaken Identity*, P.S., p. 7.

3 Nayantara Sahgal, 'The Schizophrenic Imagination'.

4 Nayantara Sahgal, 'A Brief Statement', n.d.

5 Personal interview, Delhi, November 2009.

6 Nayantara Sahgal, conversation with Shirley Chew, Leeds University, 2005.

7 Nayantara Sahgal, 'The Schizophrenic Imagination'.

8 Personal interview, Dehradun, August 2008.

9 Nayantara Sahgal to Aamer Hussein, undated letter.

10 Personal interview, Dehradun, October 2008.

11 Personal interview, Dehradun, August 2008.

12 Ibid.

13 Interview with Nergis Dalal, *The Sunday Review* (*Times of India*), 30 June 1985.

14 Ranjit Sahgal, personal interview, Chandigarh, November 2008.

15 Gita Sahgal to Ritu Menon, Delhi, July–August 2013.

16 Ranjit Sahgal, personal interview, Chandigarh, November 2008.

Afterword

'Writers have, through the cloistered act of writing, stepped into controversies, taken sides, made it clear that this is right and that is wrong, not as polemics or propaganda but by fashioning the truth as they see it, into the stuff of people's lives.'

—Talk delivered by Nayantara Sahgal at Churchill College, Cambridge, on 28 May 2011

In May 2014, the Bharatiya Janata Party (BJP) swept to power in India after a stunning electoral victory, winning a remarkable 282 seats to gain an absolute majority in the Lok Sabha. For the first time in the history of the party, it was able to form the government without having to enter into an alliance with any other political party, should it choose not to. As unprecedented as the BJP's tally was the Congress party's total of 44 seats, its poorest showing ever in its history.

Neither result came as a surprise to Nayantara. The Congress-led UPA had been in power for two terms and was beset with scams and charges of corruption in high places. The BJP's coffers had been handsomely replenished by corporate India, waiting in the wings for a regime change that would work openly in its favour. Narendra Modi had campaigned and canvassed and electrified the electorate in order to wipe out the Opposition, to replicate Gujarat in Delhi. He projected 'a muscular, macho leadership', Nayantara said, 'there was high drama in all this, and it had an attraction for young and first-time voters'.[1] His message was aspirational, announcing an India that was technologically savvy, economically resurgent, unbound by politics-as-usual, ready to take her place on the world stage. A New India, Modi said, implying the end of the old Nehruvian India – secular, democratic, plural, culturally and ethnically diverse.

To Nayantara that idea of India had signified a 'glittering aspiration', a pledge made at Independence by all those who had fought for it, to forge a nation that stood for an alternative definition of politics, and a society that welcomed the promises of modernity while remaining culturally confident. What she apprehended now was an un-making of that idea of India by those who had played no part in its creation, were, in fact, driven by an ideology that was avowedly majoritarian, that deplored the very notion of non-violence, valorized an aggressive, masculinized, cultural nationalism, abhorred diversity and had no time for a consensual, participatory democracy. 'The hundred-year-old RSS had waited a hundred years for power,' she said, 'and now its opportunity had come. It was obvious to me that they would take their dangerous and divisive agenda to the limit, though it was hidden behind the election theme of development.'[2]

In Nayantara's view, it was no longer possible to separate the RSS as a cultural organization from the BJP as a political party, because 'there is no such distinction any more. The RSS is what is ruling us,'[3] they are the 'front-room boys'.[4] She recalled that it had learnt its lessons from Hitler and Mussolini, that its leader, B.N. Moonje, had sought an audience with Mussolini and met him in the Palazzo Venezia in 1934. Moonje had taken Mussolini's words to heart: 'From the age of six a child's mind must be ready for war ... peace has to be based on millions of steel bayonets.'[5] The RSS shakhas were a direct outcome of envisioning and forming the ideal Hindu male: disciplined, regimented, battle-ready in the service of the motherland.

A half-century and more of rehearsing for power, later, the RSS was ready to bring a Hindu Rashtra into being. Within the government, ministerial and senior appointments required clearance from Nagpur, the RSS' headquarters; key positions were held by those who had been trained by them; key institutions, particularly educational and research, saw rapid change as men (and sometimes women) of little or unknown academic worth were placed in charge. Research priorities were reoriented, with a dubious focus on obscurantist, and sometimes outright laughable, ideas and propositions. A great deal was made of Vedic science and Vedic mathematics; history textbooks were being rewritten, history itself, it seemed, was recast, not in the light of new evidence or research, but to conform to the RSS version of events. The media, print and broadcast, yes, but as importantly, social media, were a critical element in this remaking, this trumpeting of a New India; it acquired a powerful charge via the prime minister himself, an avid consumer and producer of content.

Other members of the extended Sangh family were flexing their muscles in ways intended to demonstrate the primacy of Hindus, to openly and violently show Muslims and Dalits, especially, who was in control. Who could, and would, enforce a way of life, of livelihood, of dress and food. And, of course, of inter-dining and inter-marriage. No mixing of the pure and impure here. The Sanatan Sanstha, the Hindu Yuva Vahini, the Hindu Gau Raksha Samiti, the Hindu Ekta Manch, and assorted senas and ragtag outfits took to the streets and barged into homes, engaging in the kind of moral policing that was violent at its core.

Twenty-eighth September 2015 would be remembered as the day the country woke up to the full horror of what could be perpetrated in the name of cow 'protection', by a lumpen crowd, proudly claiming to be cow vigilantes. Mohammad Akhlaq, a poor villager in Dadri (western UP) was lynched on suspicion of storing 'beef' in his house, an unforgiveable 'crime'. No evidence was ever found, and the provenance of the meat in Akhlaq's house was never proved. Unsurprisingly, no one was ever brought to justice for his murder.

Akhlaq may have been the first to be slaughtered for the cow, but he wouldn't be the last. Cattle traders and transporters, cattle fairs where animals had been bought and sold for hundreds of years; eateries serving meat that the ignorant might decide was beef – across north India self-styled protectors of the cow attacked and assaulted, terrorizing those who were legitimately plying their trade. It so happened that the majority of those whose livelihoods were linked to cattle were Muslims and Dalits.

Before Akhlaq's lynching, however, three other killings had taken place that demonstrated the murderous intent of their perpetrators. In August 2013, the rationalist writer, Narendra Dabholkar, was shot dead by two gunmen, outside the Omkareshwar Temple in Pune. They fired at point-blank range, then fled on a waiting motorcycle. Dabholkar was founder-president of the Maharashtra Andhashraddha

Nirmoolan Samiti (Maharashtra Committee for Eradication of Blind Faith, 1989). He had campaigned vigorously against superstition, dubious tantriks, miracle cures and godmen, urging the government of Maharashtra to promulgate a law against superstition and black magic. He was anathema to those who traded in both. Two years later, in February 2015, the labour lawyer, Govind Pansare, was shot dead in eerily similar circumstances. Like Dabholkar, he was out on his morning walk with his wife, in Pune, when motorcycle-borne gunmen shot him five times; he died four days later. Pansare was a staunch opponent of the Putrakameshti yagna, a ritual to ensure male progeny, and a strong advocate of inter-caste marriage. In September 2015, roughly six months after his assassination, the Kannada writer M.M. Kalburgi was killed in his home in Mysore, by a man claiming to be his student. He knocked on his door, had a brief conversation with him, shot him dead, then escaped on a waiting motorbike. Kalburgi, like Dabholkar and Pansare, was accused of being anti-Hindu because of his denunciation of certain Hindu beliefs and practices. No one was ever apprehended, arrested or convicted for these crimes.

On 6 October 2015 Nayantara Sahgal returned the award she had been given by the Sahitya Akademi in 1986 for her novel *Rich Like Us* in protest against the murders of Dabholkar, Pansare and, especially, Kalburgi, also a recipient of a Sahitya Akademi award. In her letter to the Sahitya Akademi she said,

> It is a matter of sorrow that the Sahitya Akademi remains silent. The Akademis were set up as guardians of creative imagination and promoters of its finest products in art and literature, music and theatre ...

> ... In memory of the Indians who have been murdered,
> in support of all Indians who uphold the right to dissent,
> and of all dissenters who now live in fear and uncertainty,
> I am returning my Sahitya Akademi Award.

Sahgal had been preceded by Uday Prakash, the Hindi writer, but within a few days of Sahgal returning her award, Shashi Deshpande resigned from the Advisory Board of the Karnataka Sahitya Akademi, in a similar gesture of protest. In a very short span of time other well-known writers – Ashok Vajpeyi, Keki Daruwalla, Sarah Joseph, Krishna Sobti, among them – followed suit, creating a wave of what the media called, 'award wapsi', a wave that very quickly became a flood. Each writer's letter to the Akademi echoed the disquiet and unhappiness expressed by Sahgal at the continued silence of this national academy of letters, as well as at what they apprehended was the growing intolerance of points of view, opinions and beliefs, that did not conform to dominant ideologies. Nonagenarian Krishna Sobti said: 'I protested because the country cannot afford Babri and Dadri,' referring to the lynching of Mohammad Akhlaq. Uday Prakash said he protested because, 'Authors stand with ordinary citizens and the disadvantaged last man. Now, no one is safe against offenders.' Sarah Joseph protested because, 'Writers are murdered and the right to eat what one wants is denied. Plurality of society is at stake.' Ghulam Nabi Khayal said he protested because, '...returning the award is the only way to express my resentment. I want to live in a country that is secular, not a place where freedom of speech and religious identities are facing threats from communal forces.'

By the end of October, more than forty writers had returned their awards, and their protest was joined by 400 artists, twelve film-makers, 53 historians and more than 100 scientists. Resolutions in support of the writers came from all quarters, including the international PEN, which noted the vitiated environment in which books were no longer burned, and writers no longer censored – they were simply killed for their views or for what they wrote.

The world had never seen anything like this spontaneous, collective protest ever before.

The hundred scientists who joined the writers, artists and film-makers in their protest, responded to what they saw as an alarming erosion of rationality, and the threat that this posed to any scientific enquiry. In an extraordinary and unequivocal declaration, the scientists acknowledged that they had been influenced by the writers:

> The writers have shown the way ... we scientists now join our voices to theirs, to assert that people will not accept such attacks on reason, science and our plural culture. We reject the destructive narrow view of India that seeks to dictate what people will wear, think, eat and who they will love.

A spate of rallies, marches, protests and petitions followed, an indication of the outrage that thousands of citizens had felt compelled to express.

Alarmed by the fact that a symbolic protest by two writers had snowballed into a nationwide declaration of solidarity, as well as a repudiation of crude attempts at silencing dissent, the BJP swung into action. The protests were 'manufactured' they said, you could see the Congress hand at work. If the writers' protest had been genuine, they would return not only their awards but the cash component that went with them, as well. This was the hypocrisy of pseudo intellectuals and pseudo secularists, their disconnect with Asli Bharat was evident.

Speaking at Panjab University in Chandigarh, in March 2016, Nayantara said:

> What the authorities have said was 'manufactured' was nothing of the kind. It was neither planned nor organized. We writers live in different far-flung parts of this country. We don't speak each others' languages. We haven't read each other. We haven't met each other. We made individual decisions about returning or not returning our awards. That is the most remarkable fact about this protest. It has been a spontaneous upsurge and a matter of individual conscience. Nothing like it has happened in any other country.

But she went further:

> Our battle, as Indian writers, began as a demand for freedom of expression, but it became a much larger battle when the blacksmith Mohammed Akhlaq was dragged out of his house in Dadri village and brutally lynched on the excuse that he was a beef eater. The whole country was shocked and repelled by this incident. It raised the question of the very meaning of India, and of the rights guaranteed to us by our Constitution, which gives Indians

the right to live as equals, to worship as they choose, and to eat what they like. Indian citizenship means a celebration of our diversity and differences, and its very meaning was undone by that hideous lynching of a poor man who had done no one any harm. By that time our premier institutions, starting with the Nehru Memorial Museum and Library, which attracts scholars from all over India and abroad, had already been under assault when their qualified heads were dismissed, one by one, and replaced by obedient servants of the RSS, making it clear that disagreement with the ruling ideology or any questioning of it would not be tolerated. Going further, we see that dissent is now being treated as 'anti-national'.

When the Moon Shines by Day, dedicated to the writer, Kiran Nagarkar, is Nayantara's most explicitly political novel, set against the growing spectre of Hindutva and what she referred to as 'its crimes and its fantasies'.[6] Rejecting totally the view that the crimes the country had witnessed were the work of a 'lunatic fringe', she said they were 'part and parcel of the outlook known as Hindutva, whose objective is to establish a Hindu Rashtra which will divide Indians into Hindus and others'.[7] As early as December 2014, she had hinted that her new novel would be about 'the great leaps' taken by Hindutva in contemporary India:

> One was when Nathuram Godse killed Gandhi, second was when L.K. Advani did a rath yatra which led to the demolition of the Babri Masjid, and the third was Gujarat

in 2002 ... I think there is a great sequential connection there.[8]

In the novel, Rehana is a recently widowed woman living in a large unnamed city, where she and her four women friends are part of a book club that meets to discuss a book that one of them proposes. Among the cast of characters are Kamlesh, former diplomat and now a writer of historical non-fiction; his old German friend, Franz Rohner, in India to launch the Indian edition of his book on revolutions; and Zamir, whose novel *Unholy Love* was written pseudonymously. Hovering over them is the spirit of Rehana's father, a historian, whose books have been disappeared from libraries and bookshops.

Early in the novel, Rehana recalls what her father had told her about the power of art and literature. The world, he said, would never forget the horror of the Spanish Civil War because Picasso had painted the *Guernica*, and because so many novels had been written about it. 'That is why novels have to be written and paintings have to be painted. Without art and literature we would never know the truth.'

The written word as witness, as testament, as document, and as historical record thus assumes a central role in the novel. Writers, as keepers of the word, become the tellers of truth and cannot remain silent, especially when concerted attempts are made to silence them, even to the point of death. Nor can they remain silent when cherished societal values are being rubbished and cultural norms 'transformed' to reflect a majoritarian, supremacist bias; when all criticism is violently suppressed.

All stories proceed from reality, Nayantara has said, and the material for her novels has always been the social and political situation in the country prevailing at the time of writing. No particular event triggered *When the Moon Shines ...*, she said, but 'the signs ever since the (2014) election had been so disturbing' that they became the backdrop for it. 'Much of what I wrote actually started happening and events started mirroring what I had already written, not the other way around.'[9]

And so Rehana's servant, Abdul, prefers to call himself Morari Lal in order to avoid being victimized; Cyrus Batlivala's gallery, which is exhibiting the painter Nikhil's work, is attacked with knives, rocks and shears because the artist was suspected of being a 'Communist'; Kamlesh, who is writing a book on the Taj is warned by his publisher to avoid being controversial, and told that all references to the Non-Aligned Movement in his previous book would be expunged; Rehana, who works with Asians Against Torture, is gently reminded by the concerned minister that atrocities against Dalits are unfortunate, but they happen; while the Director of Cultural Transformation sings paeans to what he thinks is 'the crowning glory' of caste: 'fine-tuning each inherited skill (read caste occupation) which is why he (the Director) can tell one flower's scent from another with his eyes closed, even one rose from another, a yellow from a pink or a white'.[10]

Meanwhile, Abdul's friend, Suraj, is set upon by a faceless mob and flayed till his shredded skin is separated from his bones, because he cannot explain where he got the leather suitcase he was carrying, from. The same suitcase in which Rehana had kept her precious personal copies of her father's books.

In such murderous ways is the glittering aspiration that was India unmade, its rich multiculture reduced to a repressive monoculture by an insecure majoritarianism seeking to establish a nation peopled by a Hindu master race. Yet the novel offers up the possibility of redemption by none other than those who have experienced Hindutva's – and it must be said, Hinduism's – most blatant and brutal practice, that of untouchability. At a lavish celebration organized for the opening of the Directorate of Cultural Transformation's Culture Week, its assembled guests are treated to a shocking display of collective resistance. As they gather under the shamiana to partake of the evening's delights, the women bejewelled and resplendent in silks, the men immaculate in bandh-galas, they are assaulted by dozens of cow carcasses flung into their midst. Fore and hind legs splayed on a rose creeper, another dead animal thrown on the flower beds; many others in various stages of putrefaction, their stench and fumes choking lungs and making eyes water. Here they are, the Dalits were saying, those who had been skinned and sliced and butchered by the cow maniacs, take them, they are all yours.

'There are times in history,' Nayantara said at the Idea Exchange with journalists in December 2014, 'when you have to stand up and be counted, and this is one of them.' There was a bomb in the basement which would rock the very foundations of India, and the time had come to defend with every fibre of one's being its foundational values of secularism, pluralism and democracy.

When the Moon Shines by Day, like all Nayantara's novels, constitutes her political activism as much as it defines her literary endeavour. Her novels are to be read as not only telling a story about a particular moment in the life of a country, but as a record of that moment, and as a document that is both literary and passionately political.

Endnotes

1 Personal communication, 5 April 2018.
2 Personal communication, 5 April 2018.
3 *Indian Express Idea Exchange*, December 2014.
4 Indian Culture Forum, interview.
5 *WMSBD*, p. 44.
6 'The New India', *The Tribune*, 13 December 2017.
7 'Reject Hindutva, Embrace Insaniyat'; speech at Hyderabad Literature Festival, 8 January 2016.
8 *Indian Express Idea Exchange*, op.cit.
9 Personal communication, 6 April 2018.
10 *WMSBD*, p. 65.

The Families

Nehrus – Pandits – Gandhis – Sahgals – Mangat Rais

Motilal Nehru: father of Jawaharlal Nehru, Vijaya Lakshmi Pandit and Krishna Hutheesing.

Swarup Rani Nehru: mother of Jawaharlal Nehru.

Jawaharlal Nehru: first-born and only son of Motilal and Swarup Rani Nehru. Known to his sisters's children as Mamu, to the country as Panditji. Was India's first prime minister till his death in 1964.

Kamala Nehru, née Kaul: married Jawaharlal Nehru in 1916. Died 1936.

Indira Gandhi, née Nehru: only daughter of Jawaharlal and Kamala Nehru, called Indu or Indi by the family. Married Feroze Gandhi in 1942. Assassinated in 1984.

Bibi Amma: widowed sister of Swarup Rani Nehru who lived with the Nehrus in Anand Bhawan. Known to Nayantara and her sisters as Bibima.

Feroze Gandhi: Political activist from Allahabad. Studied at the London School of Economics. Married Indira in 1942. Died in 1960 at the age of forty eight.

Braj Kumar Nehru: referred to as Bijju, son of Brijlal and Rameshwari Nehru.

Shobha Nehru, also called Fori: Hungarian-born wife of Braj Kumar Nehru.

Vijaya Lakshmi Pandit, née Sarup Nehru: sister of Jawaharlal Nehru. Called Nan, shortened form of Nanni or young girl. Married Ranjit S. Pandit. Was minister in the United Provinces. After independence, represented India in London, Moscow and Washington. President of the United Nations General Assembly. Governor of Maharashtra, 1962-4. Member of Parliament, 1964-8. Died in 1990.

Ranjit Sitaram Pandit: husband of Vijaya Lakshmi Pandit. Participated in the freedom movement. Imprisoned along with Jawaharlal Nehru. Died in 1944.

Chandralekha Mehta, née Pandit: eldest of Ranjit and Vijaya Lakshmi Pandit's three daughters. Referred to as Chand or Lekha. Married Ashok Mehta.

Nayantara Sahgal, née Pandit: second daughter of Ranjit and Vijaya Lakshmi Pandit. Referred to as Tara. Married Gautam Sahgal in 1949. Divorced him in 1967. Married E.N. Mangat Rai in 1979.

Rita Dar, née Pandit: youngest daughter of Ranjit and Vijaya Lakshmi Pandit. Married to Avtar Krishna Dar. Died in1992.

Krishna Hutheesing, née Nehru: sister of Jawaharlal Nehru. Called Betty, the Anglicised form of beti or daughter. Died in 1967.

G.P. Hutheesing: husband of Krishna Hutheesing and known in the family as Raja. A member of the Socialist Party.

Rajiv Gandhi: Eldest son of Indira and Feroze Gandhi. Married Sonia Maino in 1968. Assassinated in 1991.

Sonia Gandhi, née Maino, daughter of Stefano and Paola Maino. Married Rajiv Gandhi in 1968.

Anand Bhawan: Motilal Nehru bought a large house which stood in groves measuring more than ten acres in 1900. In the late 1920s, Motilal built a smaller house on the same grounds, which he also named Anand Bhawan, gifting away the original house to the nation. The 'old' house, which was renamed Swaraj Bhawan (or Freedom House) was the headquarters of the Congress until India attained independence.

Gautam Sahgal: younger son of Bashiram and Roop Kaur Sahgal, from erstwhile West Punjab. Married Nayantara Pandit in 1949. Died in 2005.

Narottam Sahgal: Gautam Sahgal's elder brother, known to the family as Gogu.

Premilla (Baby) Menon: Gautam Sahgal's younger sister.

Bimla Thapar: Gautam Sahgal's older sister.

Nonika Sahgal (Noni): Nayantara and Gautam's Sahgal's first-born daughter. Married Rajan Bhatia in 2003.

Ranjit Sahgal: Nayantara and Gautam's son born after Nonika. Married Franca Dal Banco in 1975. Died in 2014.

Gita Sahgal: Nayantara and Gautam's youngest daughter. Married Colin Partridge in 1983, divorced in 1988.

Ruchir Joshi: father of Kabir and Ayan Joshi.

Edward Nirmal Mangat Rai, known as Bunchi: second son of Rai Bahadur and Dora Mangat Rai. Married Champa Singha in 1944, divorced her in 1972. Married Nayantara Sahgal in 1979. Died in 2003.

Priobala Nina Mangat Rai: elder sister of E.N. Mangat Rai.

Charles Rajinder Mangat Rai: older brother of E.N. Mangat Rai.

Lena Susheila Mangat Rai: younger sister of E.N. Mangat Rai, married to Arthur Lall.

Publications

Novels

A Time to be Happy, 1958, Alfred Knopf, New York; Victor Gollancz, London.

This Time of Morning, 1965, W.W. Norton, New York; Victor Gollancz, London.

Storm in Chandigarh, 1969, W.W. Norton, New York; Chatto & Windus, London.

The Day in Shadow, 1972, W.W. Norton, New York; London Magazine editions, London; Einaudi, Torino (1995).

A Situation in New Delhi, 1977, London Magazine editions, London.

Rich Like Us, 1985, William Heinemann, London; W.W. Norton, New York (1986); Diana Verlag AG, Zurich; De Geus, Breda (1993). Paperbacks: Sceptre (British); New Directions (American); Knaur (German).

Plans for Departure, 1986, William Heinemann, London; W.W. Norton, New York (1986); Paperback: Penguin (British).

Mistaken Identity, 1988, William Heinemann, London; New Directions, New York; De Geus, Breda, (1992). Paperback: Sceptre (British).

Lesser Breeds, 2003, HarperCollins Publishers, New Delhi.

History

The Freedom Movement in India, 1970, Commissioned and published by the National Council of Education, Research and Training, New Delhi as a supplementary textbook for schools.

Politics

A Voice for Freedom, 1977, Hindi Pocket Books, New Delhi, a collection of speeches and writings during the Emergency 1975–77.

Indira Gandhi: Her Road to Power, 1982, Frederick Ungar Publishing Co., New York; Macdonald, London.

Point of View: Personal Response to Life, Literature and Politics, 1997, Prestige Books, New Delhi.

Jawaharlal Nehru: Civilising a Savage World, 2010, Penguin Books India, New Delhi.

Autobiography

Prison and Chocolate Cake, 1954, Alfred Knopf, New York; Victor Gollancz, London; Chuo-Koron-She Ltd., Japan; Editions Mondiales, Paris (1957).

From Fear Set Free, 1962, W.W. Norton, New York; Victor Gollancz, London.

Relationship, 1994, Kali for Women, New Delhi.

Edited

Before Freedom: Nehru's Letters to His Sister 1909–1947, 2000, HarperCollins, New Delhi; Roli Books (2004), New Delhi.

Other writing

Short stories in *London Magazine*, *Vogue*, *Cosmopolitan*, *Hemisphere*, and various magazines in India.

Political commentary in *London Magazine*, *The New Republic*, *Atlantic Monthly*, *Christian Science Monitor*, *The Times (London)*, *Dallas Times-Herald*, *The Far Eastern Economic Review*, *Indo-Asia*, *Hemisphere*, and various newspapers and magazines in India.

Awards and Honours

1976	Fellow, Radcliffe Institute, Cambridge, Mass., USA.
1981–82	Fellow, Woodrow Wilson International Center for Scholars, Washington D.C., USA.
1983–84	Fellow, National Humanities Center, North Carolina, USA.
1985	Sinclair Prize for Fiction (Britain) for *Rich Like Us*.
1986	Sahitya Akademi Award (India) for *Rich Like Us*.
1987	Commonwealth Writers' Prize (Eurasia) for *Plans for Departure*.
1988	Diploma of Honour, International Order of Volunteers for Peace, Salsomaggiore, Italy.
1990	Elected Foreign Honorary Member, American Academy of Arts and Sciences, Cambridge, Mass., USA.
1999	Hon. Doctorate (Doctor of Letters) conferred by University of Leeds, UK.
2002	Alumnae Achievement Award conferred by Wellesley College, Mass., USA.
2003	Distinguished Alumnae Award conferred by Woodstock School, Mussoorie.

Professional Appointments

1971–75	Member, Advisory Board for English, Sahitya Akademi (resigned during the Emergency).
1978	Member, Indian delegation to the UN General Assembly.
1978–79	Member, Committee on Autonomy for Radio and Television, set up by the Janata Government.
1979	Appointed ambassador to Italy (cancelled by Indira Gandhi, 1980).
1980s	Vice President, PUCL.
1990–91	Chair, Eurasia Jury for Commonwealth Writers' Prize.
2000	Guest of Honour, Commonwealth Writers' Prize, New Delhi.

Keynote addresses and readings at festivals and conferences: Toronto, Melbourne, Hong Kong, Sri Lanka, Norway, Kuala Lumpur, Banaras Hindu University, University of Rajasthan, Universities of Leeds, Kent, Warwick and Oxford.

Index